CW01642570

The insightful innovator

HOW TO LEVEL UP YOUR EMPLOYEE EXPERIENCE

DANNY SEALS

The Insightful Innovator

Copyright © Danny Seals 2023

All rights reserved.

Printed in the United Kingdom. No part of this book may be used or reproduced in any manner whatsoever without written permission from the author. Brief passages may be quoted for the purposes of interviews, reviews, or press with permission and must be credited.

Every effort has been made to ensure this book is free from errors or omissions. However, the publisher, the author, the editor or their respective employees or agents, shall not accept responsibility for injury, loss, or damage occasioned to any person acting or refraining from action as a result of material in this book whether or not such injury, loss or damage in any way due to any negligent act or omission, breach of duty or default on the part of the publisher, the author, the editor or their respective employees or agents.

Paperback ISBN: 978-1-7393465-0-8

Publisher: Knot Publishing
Foreword: Mohammad Saqib
Editor: Kirsten Rees
Illustrator: Dave Officer
Design and production: Catherine Williams

Connect with the author:
Twitter: @thedannyseals
Website: www.weareknot.co.uk
Email: hello@weareknot.co.uk
Newsletter: www.weareknot.co.uk/subscribe
Podcast: Mindchimp Podcast

For Helen – thank you for being the brightest of stars in the darkest of skies x.

WHAT'S IN THE ~~BOX~~ BOOK (AKA CONTENT)?

FOREWORD

When Lorenz (a hygienist) in 1910 decided to experiment with learners who were making far too many mistakes in their afternoon sessions, he came up with a plan to boost learning and reduce their errors. His idea was simple, to spray the classroom with a nerve gas called antikenotoxin (a word that would score you 24 points in Scrabble). The results were astounding, mental processing skills increased by 50% and overall mistakes were far less.

The above-mentioned piece of educational research has got nothing to do with Danny's first book, *The Insightful Innovator*. In fact, the only similarity you'll find is Danny's ability and willingness to experiment to enhance any experience.

HR, learning and development, and employee experience professionals usually adhere to a set of guidelines which brings them success. These guidelines are rooted in well-established theories that form the very basis of our new and innovative ideas today.

Now you're probably thinking, this is not the traditional way or cultural norm to start a foreword of any book. This is, in fact, the very essence of *The Insightful Innovator* which breaks from tradition by making learning adventurous and immersive. And it's these two attributes of adventurous and immersive that I would choose to describe Danny, having known him since 2008.

As far as forewords go, they are usually written by people who are more well-known than the author. In this case, it's quite the opposite. My name is Mohammad Saqib and I would describe myself as having a passion for learning. I've not authored any books or written any research papers and outside my own circle of friends, I'm relatively unknown. My claim to fame is having met Jan Needle, the author of *My Mate Shofiq*, a book I would totally recommend along with Philippa Pearce's, *The Way to Sattin Shore*; I also had the honour and privilege of training Danny as part of a three-week induction in 2008. It was from there on in, that myself and Danny became friends and later on we were on the same team designing visceral experiences for learning and the employee experience.

Whilst I worked alongside Danny, he was always looking at making marginal improvements to existing solutions. In some cases, completely tearing it up and starting again with only one thing in mind, creating impactful experiences using human-centred design. For Danny, it was always about the experience. He embraced failure openly when some of his wacky and crazy ideas didn't come to fruition. As far as Danny was concerned, as long as you learnt from that failure and made the changes, then it was all part of the process.

Nowadays, we label people who go against the status quo as rebels, mavericks, or even crazy innovators. If it wasn't for all the red tape, these rebels, mavericks, and crazy innovators would have huge followings and may even be considered as reformers. Danny fits into all of these categories and has really grasped the very essence of this in his first book.

By his own admission, the mad scientist within Danny is still ever-present. I remember tag-teaming with Danny at a large conference in 2018 where we delivered this ridiculous 30-minute session on how to design an emotive experience. On paper, it looked very impractical and very difficult to execute, but Danny was adamant and persistent on delivering this immersive experience to a crowd of people we didn't know.

No doubt it worked in his head but for me, it was a logistical nightmare. How could anyone learn in this chaotic manner? How could a non-confirmative session which goes against traditional learning work? I was glad I was proved wrong as I witnessed first-hand the learners following a carefully designed pathway which appealed to their emotions. There was something for everyone.

According to the online Cambridge Dictionary (March 2023), learning is knowledge or a piece of information obtained by study or experience. Organisations seldom focus on the experience element of learning. Looking at learning from an etymological point, its origins can be traced back to the Latin word 'lira' which means track or pathway. *The Insightful Innovator* is a book which speaks to the heart and mind about the various pathways that should be considered when designing any experience as there is no one right strategy for every session, course, or group.

Before you become engrossed in Danny's first book, *The Insightful Innovator,* I leave you with a quote from Booker Washington, who said, "Success is to be measured not so much by the position that one has reached in life as by the obstacles ... overcome while trying to succeed." Happy reading.

—Mohammad Saqib

PREFACE

The mad scientist is what they used to call me. Well, if you ask my grandad that is. For as long as I can remember, I've always had a really active imagination and an even more curious mind as I am sure most children do – that is until they grow up and forget they were children in the first place.

I've always been a little bit weird with my ideas, thoughts, and ways of trying to understand the world around me. I used to have an imaginary friend called Thor. I rocked an eye patch for a good few years of my life. I was always a keen artist, drawing pictures all the time. One of my other quirks, when I was around ten, was that I used to go to various family members – my gran, grandad, uncles, etc. – and hound them to see if they had any junk they didn't want. They would always humour me and find something for me to use in some experiment or another. It could be anything from a piece of 1m x 1m clear plastic, to a bit of drainpipe, or some broken clocks.

As they handed over their cast-offs, I was already in semi-wonderment at the world of possibilities that lay ahead and of what might be, or what I could make with these items. I would then follow up with a few pertinent questions:

- Why don't you want this?
- How did you break it?
- What were you doing for that to happen?
- Lastly, but most importantly, is it worth anything and can I sell it for sweets?

Then I'd take this so-called junk and rush off somewhere quiet so I could dissect, break, play with, and fix these random items.

I never thought of this as destructive behaviour. If anything, I was turning these items into something unique, better, more valuable, or more useful. Sometimes, I would just sit and think about the stories behind these various items, imagining all the hidden stories they could tell, and the things they had seen but could never reveal. I imagined tales of their production belts; maybe these items fell in love with other mass-produced items but then they got separated, never to be reunited again!

Even now as a fully-functioning adult, with years of business experience, I still find myself entering this daydream state and letting my imagination run wild. Sometimes, when I am in the passenger seat sitting in traffic on the motorway, I cannot help but look at the most obscure things on the hard shoulder: the blown out tyres, the random lonely traffic cones. Before I know it, these pieces of debris have a personality and a backstory of how they got there. I'm imagining all the experiences they might have had before this point where our paths now cross on the side of the M1.

I find myself wanting these objects to have a voice so I can hear about all their great experiences and stories, hear about the problems they have faced and what happened for them to find themselves on the hard shoulder.

Unfortunately, a mere beep of a horn and I am brought back to reality. And this reality is a bit like objects on the M1. We as humans all have stories, memories, and experiences we want to share with the world. We all have challenges, processes, and systems that drive our frustrations but also make us smile. Maybe it is an organisational challenge, a community challenge, maybe even a government-level challenge – the list goes on – but the good news is that great design can fix these things.

That young lad's curiosity and creativity is still ultimately what drives me and I try never to lose sight of it. He helps me not to take anything for granted. My inner mad scientist reigns to this day.

I will help you on this journey of understanding what Human-Centred Design is and point you in the right direction for alternative designs and solutions to your employee–experience products, services, and experiences because that is what that kid still does for me to this day.

My goal is that throughout this book your curiosity, creativity, and the way you look at things will change and grow. By the end, you have a better understanding of what being 'human-centric' means and how to get there. I expect that you use or find the imagination you need to look at things and see them, not just as what they are, but as what they can be.

Thanks,
Danny

JARGON BUSTER

EX – Employee Experience

HCD – Human-Centred Design

XD – Experience Design

SD – Service Design

ST – System Thinking

DARE – Design A Relationship Experience

HMW – How Might We

MOO – Moment Of Opportunity

L&D – Learning & Development

HR – Human Resources

WHY THIS BOOK, WHY IS MORE THAN ONE NEEDED?

It all started in 2018, having sent over a suggested chapter breakdown and synopsis to a publisher. I walked them through how my design approach is based on understanding the problem through sense-making, coming up with potential new solutions through incubation, then moving to experimentation and three levels of experience design macro, micro, and nano. Many people have asked for help on my approach and after giving so much of it away through talks, podcasts, blogs, etc., I decided to just write a book about it.

After many emails back and forth, and the publisher putting a contract forward, I decided not to go with them. This was for a handful of reasons, however, they were lovely and I would recommend them.

For me, it came down to the reader of the book and the adventure you will go on. To do this in one book, and in a very fixed publisher-like way, just felt like it might be short-changing the potential of the book. So, I decided to go down the self-publishing route and after seeing people reuse my approach, then call it something different (you know who you are, insert devil emoji), I finally decided 2023 will be the year that book one comes out.

I believe that the books need to be done in a very specific way, let me explain:

Throughout my career, I have been on a constant search for the silver bullets of design. That one magical way of doing things, the method that is effective and valuable to the business and its people.

However, this journey has brought me to the conclusion that 'one ultimate design method' does not exist, and in fact, all methods can simultaneously work and not work.

With that in mind, I decided to create my own flow that's based on four key principles:

- Human-centred
- Experience and experiment led
- Bias to action
- Informed and enabled data and technology

Throughout this book, I will share checklists, callouts, and some tools I've picked up or designed along the way. It's important to note this isn't a toolbox type of book though. If, by the end of this book, you are inspired to go and look into design more, then again my job is done, but the tools I share here are the 80/20 type i.e. the 20% of tools that you use to provide 80% of the impact. Hopefully, you will find them useful.

I want to call this out from the start – having a good list of tools is wonderful, but without the application of testing, applying, and failing, they will always be *just* a list. This is why a future book will be focused on a more expansive set of Tools and Behaviours, in the hope that by the time you get to it, not only will you know which tools to use, you will also know what works and what doesn't and more importantly when to pivot to another approach or tool. This ability will come from the knowledge gained in books 1 and 2. However, you will also then need to actually apply it all in the real world.

What we are building has to be desired by the user, it ultimately has to meet the needs of the customer/employee and often this involves us fixing a tension they are facing.

Social media is full of posts spouting about Human-centred Design (HCD or you'll likely have seen it spelled the US way Human-centered Design), Experimentation, Experience Design (XD) but from people who have actually never done it in the real world. Please don't be that person and instead be open to failure and learning – enjoy the journey.

In order to create a book that is valuable, I had to condense down the type of people who may read it. In the end, I came up with two key groups of people who I have written this book for:

The Explorers – this is someone who is aiming to create innovative employees, giving them the skills and awareness to help the business create new internal products, services, and experiences. Usually, it's a group of people designing these for the rest of the business.

The Scientist – this could be someone who, in functions such as HR, Learning, Talent, etc., invests a large amount of their time in sense-making what's going well in the current world, while wanting to iterate and maybe stretch current initiatives and internal solutions that can propel the employee experience up a level.

By identifying these two groups, I can tailor the message and give you the biggest bang for your book. Maybe you will be someone who moves across these two groups (which I encourage) then you will surely get a good bit of usage out of the upcoming pages.

WHY MORE THAN ONE GODDAMN BOOK?

I decided to turn this into a smaller, more focused book for many reasons.

1. I get to delve deeper in each subject, sharing foundations and stories, with the hope that by book three you will have solid foundations. That you will not only be able to pick up the tools and methods but you will also be able to adapt them to the situation.
2. We need understanding before methods, one of the things I've noticed is that we are not short on tools, playbooks, etc., but often the knowledge of when and how to adapt them is lacking.
3. By breaking this down into three books, you get to choose your own adventure, you can go on the full end-to-end journey with me (which I hope you do) or you can pick the bits you're interested in and save them precious pounds.

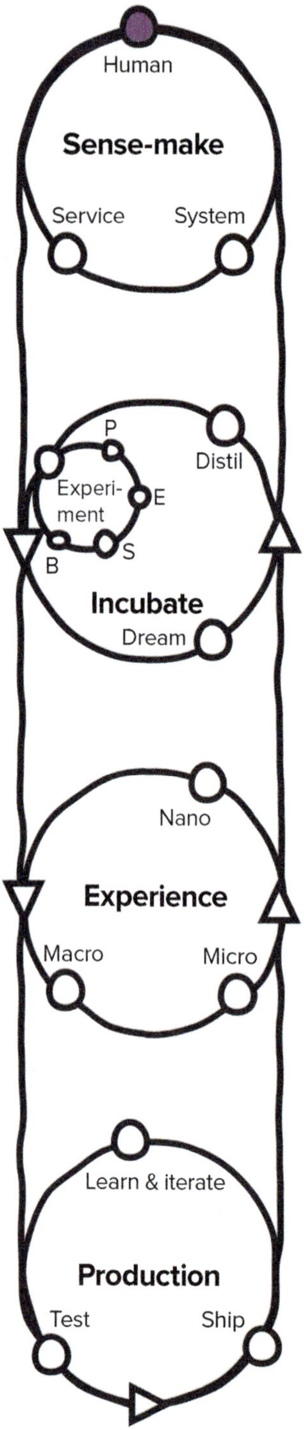

4. I make more money! Joking, I actually make less money as it's now triple the expenses for three books, covers, editing, etc. But for a dyslexic, writing these books and cutting them down into three chunks feels easier to do.

Now, perhaps you won't go on this three-book adventure with me but instead just want to see what the design flow looks like ... here you go:

Without colour (excluding the start point i.e. the purple dot), it looks a little underwhelming right? Good, the flow you're looking at doesn't need to look sexy. It's what is inside that matters. The key point is where you start, the purple touch-point i.e. the human. [P=Product; E=Experience; S=Service; B=Behaviour]

Let's add some colour now so you can see what is covered in each book.

BOOK 1: HUMAN-CENTRED (SEEN IN BLUE)

Sense-making is all about making sense of the current state. This is broken down into three touch points – the human, the service, and the system. Using this data-rich stage will allow you to move from data into insight that will help us identify new opportunities ripe for change.

Incubate – this stage is where we hit two touch points: dream and distil. Here, we will look at the rich internal and external narratives and bring them to life. We shape the skeletons of big, bold, courageous ideas and move them from fleeting thoughts to potential concepts ready for testing in the real world. Moving through typical superficial ideas into ones that could truly drive impact and change.

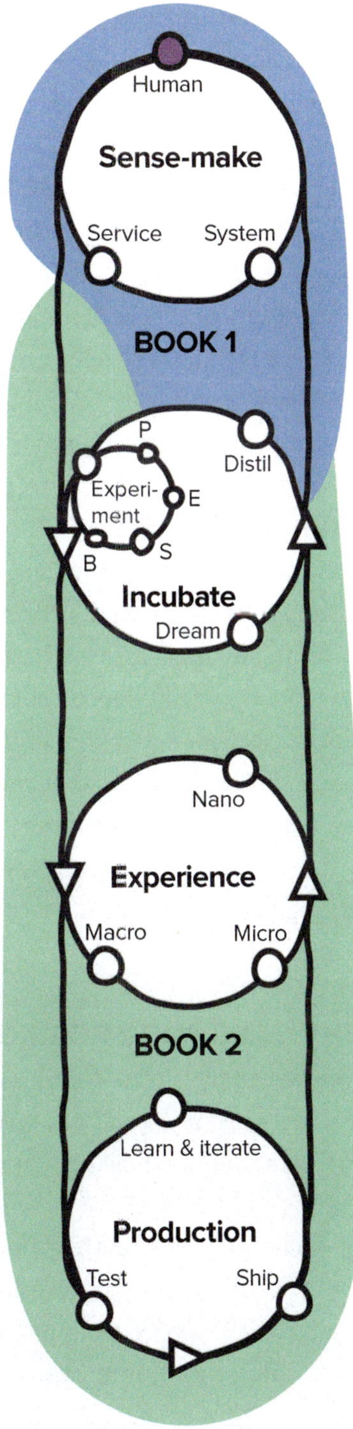

BOOK 2: EXPERIMENTS AND EXPERIENCES (SEEN IN GREEN)

This takes us into the world of experimentation and visceral experiences, here is where we look to pressure test these ideas against Desirability, Viability, and Feasibility.

Experimentation – allows us to identify and create experiments based on our hypothesis. These experiments will test Desirability, Viability, and Feasibility. Here we will also look at what experiments can be applied in the service, the experience, or the behaviour.

Experience – this is where we get to bring the new experience to life, making them more visceral than was mapped out in the Incubate phase. We get to design the experience from the customer/employees' point of view, walking in three levels of experience design Macro, Micro, and Nano.

Production – the final stage focus is around testing and measuring on the experiments we ran, identifying our learning, and deciding if we want to run another cycle of iteration or move into shipping.

FUTURE: MINDSETS, METHODS & BEHAVIOURS (THINK OF THIS AS THE BLUE AND GREEN NOW IT'S THERE)

We will look deeper at the core behaviours and methods that are needed to scale this out to wider teams. It also dives deep into a collection of behaviours that every team and person in the Employee Experience (EX) needs to design greater products, services, and experiences, which are all required to keep driving and testing the art of the possible.

You may be asking at this point, why does Behaviours come last? It is a great question and the answer to me is clear. It ultimately stops you having all the gear and no idea and being exposed for not being able to demonstrate what you are trying to scale.

A quick note, for ease of use, I will use the term 'EX products' when referencing the Employee/People Experience which to me is a collection of Services, Products, Interactions and Experiences. (SPIE) The goal is to create such great SPIEs that the employee i.e. the customer makes the daily, weekly, monthly and yearly choice to continue subscribing to the business... i.e. coming into work and cancelling the 'subscription' and leaving to go elsewhere. 99.9% of the time everything can be linked back to one of those.

WHY CARE ABOUT DESIGN?

I've learned over time that just because you see the value and impact of something, it doesn't necessarily mean that others have. When you realise this, you will be left with what feels like three choices:

1. Shake your head at them, look down on them, and feel disappointed in their lack of understanding.
2. Force-feed everything to them, then get frustrated when they do nothing with this information (because they don't get it or even care).

3. Demonstrate the value of design using everyday examples and use layman's language (I opt for this approach).

However, design is tricky! Just the word itself is always up for interpretation. When I was planning this section of the book I asked twenty people, 'What is design?'. Nearly all of them proceeded to talk about graphics, drawings, posters, colour, etc.

To me, this is confusing. That's not what design is at all to me – or certainly isn't limited to those things. But it seems that I am not the only one confused. In a recent study by the consulting company McKinsey, the leadership teams in 1,700 companies were asked the same question. What became clear was that most CEOs across all different types of industries had no idea either.

The study involved interviewing 200 senior design leaders and 100 top executives. One of the most interesting insights is that "only 1 in 10 CEOs say their senior designer plays a meaningful role in strategy development". This begs two questions. Firstly, if the business doesn't understand the value or role of design leadership, what's the point of it? And secondly, is the design leadership confused with its place within the organisation?

In an interview with *Fast Company*, Benedict Sheppard who co-authored the study and is a partner at the firm stated:

> "Design is like a strategy that seems to mean 100 things to 100 people. Many CEOs we interviewed are still using the 1980s definition of colour, material, and finish. The metrics are damning. Only one-third of CEOs could detail what their Chief Design Officer oversaw at the company. In other words, 66% of CEOs couldn't say what they actually did."

All of this can start to paint a bleak picture of design but it may go some way in helping to explain why design (not to be confused with colours, etc.) is not valued or understood by the business. It may help our emotions when we have to explain the value and impact of it to our people.

For this reason, I always recommend choosing option three from the above list of reactions. Here it is again:

Demonstrate the value of design using everyday examples and language. Be patient and have empathy.

After all, at some point in your life, someone taught you how to use a spoon for crying out loud. In another report by McKinsey in 2018, they found that companies who invest in their design processes had a higher revenue over a five-year period.

The good news when it comes to design is that you really don't need to look far at all. Everything from the train you may be sitting on while reading this or the phone you are using to message your friend (to tell them how good this book is, of course), or maybe even the toothbrush your little human uses to brush their teeth at night, have all been designed. Once we sit back and look at the world around us, we see great design everywhere, fixing the problems that we no longer see, good design is important and EX products are no exception.

Throughout this book, I will drop in random pieces of information, called Insightful Ingredients, these are not related to what you are reading but will make sense once you get to the incubate phase. As you read them try to just enjoy them for what they are and try to capture any fleeting thoughts that may come to mind for you as you read them.

The goal of these Insightful Ingredient moments is to inspire you, challenge you or, being completely honest, may not even make sense to you ... that's cool, just stick with it and underneath each Insightful Ingredient is a few lines to capture any fleeting thought. A quick way to do this is start the fleeting thought with: 'There is something about ...' or 'This makes me think about ...'

I have also sprinkled a few of my favourite case studies and where possible I have brought in real-life experience as well. Unfortunately not everybody has given me permission to mention the org names, often most of my work is done under strict NDA, but where possible I have used names.

INSIGHTFUL INGREDIENT

Github, the US-based software company, took a progressive approach in 2007 when it came to autonomy. Rather than having a top-down approach, Github were one of the first businesses to allow people to self-allocate the projects and work they wanted to be part of moving to a boss-free organisation.

#DANNYDISCUSSIONS

What comes to mind when reading about this?

....

....

....

....

....

....

....

....

....

....

....

....

....

....

....

A QUICK STORY — YOUR LITTLE HUMAN'S TOOTHBRUSH

In the early 1990s, all toothbrushes were the same apart from the ones for children, which were smaller in length. Other than the length, everything was equal.

On paper everything was fine, however, at the same time tooth decay in children was on the rise and showed no signs of stopping.

Toothpaste and toothbrush brand Oral-B wanted to understand why this was the case. So they worked with the design firm IDEO to try and understand what was going on.

One of the first things the designers at IDEO asked was how they could get access to the customers and how they could set up some observation sessions. This initially seemed like a crazy request. IDEO understood how children were supposed to brush teeth, but they wanted to see it in a live, safe environment.

What the designers found was that children were struggling with brushing their teeth. Although they eventually figured out how to overcome this challenge, the result was a poor clean.

What IDEO came to realise was that children didn't have the necessary level of dexterity in their hands to manipulate the toothbrush. Their approach was to grab the toothbrush in the centre of their hand and make a fist to control it.

With the help of some bright funky designs to make the toothbrush more appealing, Oral-B designed a new grip on the brush handle to enable better control for the children. As a result, they were clearly on to a winner and later became the leading brand for children's toothbrushes.

I imagine you are at the end of this section screaming 'show me the money', well at least I hope so, all I ask is that over the next pages you are open to having your ideas challenged and remove the doubt of "that approach would never work at our place".

SAID AND SEALED (AKA THE SUMMARY)

- There is no one best design method. The one I have created is based on four principles: human-centric; experience and experiment-led; informed by insight; and enabled by mindsets, behaviours, and tools.
- The book is intended for two groups: explorers, who are looking to create new internal Services, Products, Interactions, and Experiences (SPIEs); and scientists, who work in functions such as HR, learning, or talent and focus on sense-making and iterating on current initiatives and internal solutions.
- The huge amount of knowledge has been divided into three books in order to go deeper into each subject, provide solid foundations, and allow readers to choose their own adventure.
- The first book focuses on human-centred design and includes sense-making and incubation.
- The second book covers experimentation and experience design.
- The third book focuses on tools and behaviours and covers the importance of understanding before implementing methods, adapting tools to fit different situations, and the role of failure in the design process.

THE MANY DIFFERENT SHADES OF ~~GREY~~ DESIGN

You have probably heard the term human-centred design (HCD) a few times, often it is surrounded by other aspects of design. You often can't hear it mentioned without hearing the likes of design thinking, service design, experience design, and system thinking, all of which are vital in creating EX products. It makes sense to give a brief history of where it came from:

A BRIEF HISTORY OF HCD

The origins of human-centred design can be traced back to the early 20th century and the work of pioneers like Frank Lloyd Wright and Le Corbusier. However, it was only in the 1970s that the concept began to gain traction in the design community, with the publication of influential books like *Design for the Real World* by Victor Papanek. In the 1990s, the rise of internet connectivity and the global Web brought human-centred design to the forefront of the design world, as designers began to focus on creating user-friendly interfaces for new digital technologies.

The origins of human-centred design can be traced back to the work of early 20th-century psychologist Frederick Winslow Taylor. His work focused on increasing efficiency in industrial settings by studying and optimising workflows. Taylor's work laid the foundation for the scientific management movement, which sought to apply scientific principles to the management of organisations.

In the 1950s and 1960s, industrial designers like Raymond Loewy and Dieter Rams began applying sound design principles to consumer

DESIGN THINKING PROCESS TIMELINE

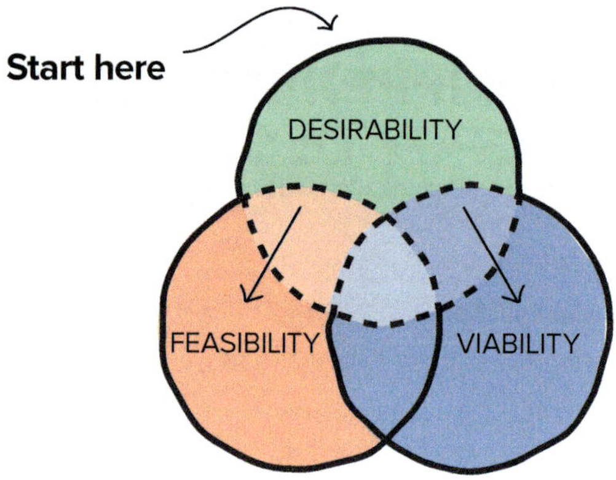

1960s
Attempts were made to make design scientific and the term "Wicked Problems" is coined

1970s
The principles of Design Thinking started to emerge

1980s
Solution-focused problem solving was observed

1987
Design Thinking was compared to architecture

1990s
IDEO brings Design Thinking into mainstream

1992
Richard Buchanan published his article *Wicked Problems* in Design Thinking

2000s

2004
David Kelly founded the Stanford University's Hasso Plattner Institute of Design known as the d.school

products. Their work helped to popularise the idea that products should be designed with the user in mind rather than simply for aesthetics or functionality. The main challenge was that the design process was designer-centred, not user-centred. In the 1970s and 80s, several researchers began to explore the concept of user-centred design, which put the user at the centre of the design process (Nigel, 1982). One of the most influential early works in this field was Don Norman's The Design of Everyday Things, which argued that good design should be intuitive and easy to use.

In the 1990s, the rise of internet connectivity and the global Web led to a renewed interest in human-centred design. The internet was initially intended for scholars and researchers, but it rapidly became evident that it required a more widely accessible audience. The main challenge was that the design product could not consider all aspects of the user experience from the initial contact with the product.

The design thinking movement is now gaining traction, with pioneers such as IDEO leading the way in the 1990s. This was followed closely by the Hasso Plattner Institute of Design at Stanford University (also known as d.school) in 2004 which offers a range of world-class programmes, courses, and workshops all focused on design thinking, human-centred design, and problem-solving. Other famous institutions, business schools, and forward-thinking organisations have widely embraced design thinking and even re-interpreted it to fit their unique environment or brand values.

If you took five minutes to jump on to LinkedIn Learning you would see a handful of courses (I will leave it up to you to decide if they are experts or not).

As you can see, HCD has gone through its own evolution. What this means is, over time, people use it, call it, and define it differently, for example:

IDEO says: "Human-centered design is a creative approach to problem-solving and the backbone of our work. It's a process that starts with the people you're designing for and ends with new solutions that are tailor-made to suit their needs."

Don Norman says: "HCD is an approach that puts the human needs, capabilities and behaviours first, then designs to accommodate those needs, capabilities, and ways of behaving. Good design starts with an understanding of psychology and technology."

Danny Seals says: "Human-centred design is a problem-solving approach that seeks to understand the wants, needs, and tasks of a human in a given circumstance, and co-creates with the participant a set of ideas and suggestions that could be designed and put into practice after experimentation and validation.

No matter where you fall on this, throughout its evolution, the one thing that seems to have stayed is its focus on the human at the centre. Because HCD is such an important aspect and is so broad and fundamental that it is nearly always mentioned in every design approach, not talking about it is like talking about making bread without mentioning flour. It is doable but just doesn't feel or taste right."

HCD AT ITS CORE

This is often broken down into a sweet Venn (see p.22) consisting of desirability, viability, and feasibility. Some now drop sustainability in there too, but let's keep it OG (original gangster) for now and let me give a bit of a brief on what each of these areas mean:

Desirability

This is the most important aspect of HCD and ultimately the first thing you need to do is sense-making. It is pointless having a solution that is feasible and viable (coming next) but lacks any form of demand from a customer who may want or need it. You will, of course, test feasibility and viability later on. However, doing this too soon, in the early stages of sense-making and incubation, can force us to limit our thinking and dare I say it 'cause the group to play it safe'.

So we must ask the following questions:

- Is this product even wanted by the customer?
- Is this needed by the customer?
- Does it fix a customer's pain point?

Viability

We are trying to drill down here: is this going to cost us more to make than it brings back in?

Questions:

- Is this going to be profitable for us?
- Is this solution going in the same direction as the business strategy?
- Can this be sustainable for the business?

Feasibility

Okay, our people want it, we know it's viable for us to do, and we can make some form of profit from it. The last question is should WE do it? You might have two green ticks with Desirability and Viability but it doesn't mean that your business is right to do it.

Questions:

- Should we do it?
- Are we the right people for it?
- Do we have the right capability for it?
- Can we officially actually do it?

It's important to keep these three lenses in mind while going through any form of design, constantly asking:

- Do they want it?
- Can we do it?
- Should we do it?

Along with Desirability, Feasibility, and Viability, you will hear other terms mentioned throughout the books. Let me give you a simple overview of all of them and later we will get into a little more detail.

Systems thinking (ST)

An approach looking at a large complex system, by looking at how various parts of the system work with each other, taking into account the whole system as well as its elements and parts – the eco-system is a great example of a complex system.

Service design (SD)

This is an approach used to understand and map out the whole end-to-end of service, this tends to look at the touch points of a journey between the customer and the service they are using. It looks at the people, the process, the props in the service as well as the channels the customer goes through.

Experience design (XD)

It is built from an employee/customer point of view, it looks at the interactions the person goes through on their journey. This involves looking at and designing the experience from three advantage points: Macro, Micro, and Nano.

The approach, mindsets, tools, and processes to build the house would be Design Thinking, System Thinking, and Agile/Lean UX

While there is debate around design and the hierarchy of it, the best way I like to see it is in the form of a house. The foundation and framework of the house, what everything is built on is human-centred. Wrapped around that house are the bricks and slates, you have various options when picking which slate and brick you want to go with. Each have their pros and cons, that's why a multi-design discipline is vital (you get the best of all worlds).

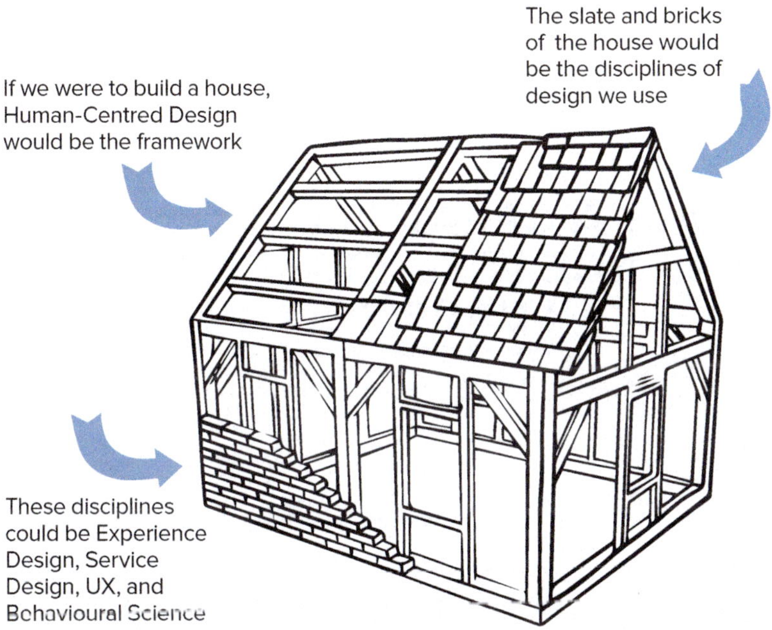

SAID AND SEALED

- Human-centred design (HCD) is a problem-solving approach that puts the needs and capabilities of people first.
- It has its roots in the work of early 20th-century psychologists and has evolved over time through the contributions of designers and researchers.
- HCD has been embraced by organisations like IDEO and the d.school and is often used in the design of products, services, and experiences.
- HCD involves understanding the needs and behaviours of the people using a product or service and using this knowledge to design solutions that meet those needs.

CREATE A GREAT RELATIONSHIP EXPERIENCE WITH STAKEHOLDERS, I DARE YOU

A quick Google search on what traits make a great relationship will present you with around 1,210,000,000 results in an impressive 0.59 seconds. If only building relationships was that quick. The reality is that it's a slower process, often built on affective trust, each relationship is unique and requires special attention. Overlook this aspect and you will be lucky to get any EX product off the ground.

Although, rather than investing the time at the start to turn these early moments into something more than a transactional relationship, we immediately rush into solution mode, leaving us dancing an awkward conga dance of working together while trying to not piss each other off.

So here's a question for you: if I was to ask you what traits you would want in a relationship or partnership, what five things would you pick?

After asking this same question on LinkedIn, here are the responses I received:

- Professional, courteous, breadth (thinking and curiosity)
- Honest, curiosity, extraversion, assertiveness, straightforwardness, sense of humour
- Generous, curious, honest, supportive, fun
- Communication, empathy, self-awareness, integrity, and honesty
- Trust, communication, integrity, humour, generosity

- Empathy, humour, great listening, ability to make connections, curiosity
- Integrity, trust, loyalty, respect, good manners

(I do wonder what response I would have got if I asked the same question on Tinder.)

A lot of those noted above are also words used when discussing Human-centred Design ... the big clue is in the word human. It is also fascinating to see phrases such as 'sense of humour' come up as many consultants get this drummed out of them and instead are told to be overly professional and dull and bland. Or as I like to summarise, they get told to be boiled rice (not all consultants).

Our working relationships, how we see challenges, and how we work together have to be human. How we show up has to be with authenticity and curiosity, without it, we lack the special ingredient of making something special.

What became clear after speaking to the hive mind of LinkedIn is that we all want different things. So why, in our professional relationships, do we never really take the time to understand what our business partners, stakeholders, or teams want?

If we could understand this before we even start working, we could shift from that 'conga dance' to something that is more personalised, highly impactful, and special. Something where we move together, perhaps it would be a bit like the Lindy Hop (which by far is the best dance ever).

I believe that to get this relationship off to a great start, we need to remove our ego and strip back the lies we tell ourselves that we are the smartest person in the room and just be human. Over my time in leadership and design, I've created a canvas called DARE (Design A Relationship Experience) which I think is perfect (of course I do) and will bring us all together and dancing in unison.

First, the DARE is for the very core of the people around the project; it's not for any group wider than that. I have found that before we go anywhere near the project the DARE allows us to warm up to each other and open up before we get into the nitty-gritty of the project. It allows us to ask some questions that could be tricky to ask later on in the relationship. Through the initial stage, we also want to pull out the names of core stakeholders, by asking who's missing and who has input on this project that can influence it. Doing this early will allow us to create a stakeholder map later when we get into specifics. A simple question to find these is asking who has skin in the game.

INSIGHTFUL INGREDIENT

Zapier, the web workflow product company, operates remotely first. However, they understand the value of face-to-face onboarding. Every month, they rent out an Airbnb for a week and all spend time together along with their soon-to-be managers. This builds up affective trust. From day one, the onboarding is named you guessed it AirbnbOnboarding.

#DANNYDISCUSSIONS

What does this get you thinking about?

....

....

....

....

....

....

....

....

....

THE CANVAS AND HOW TO USE IT

The DARE is all about investing time at the start to get a better understanding of your project, team, and stakeholders. Below is a primer of what's needed:

When to use: Start of a project
Who is involved: Only use this with the core project team and stakeholders of the project
How long: 90 minutes to half a day
Materials: Sticky notepads, flip chart, Sharpies, giant canvas print out (ideally)
Level of facilitation needed: high

Firstly, we would get together in a room and set this scene. The goal here is to make this as informal as possible. In the past, I've asked people to rock up in whatever they would wear behind the PC screen; if that's hoodies and joggers, great. If it's jeans and a tee, fantastic. Honestly, if you rock up in a onesie I wouldn't mind, but I do have to draw the line at birthday suits – there are some things you can't unsee.

Setting this informal tone helps to get the most out of a relationship. It also makes it easy to create a safe environment for sharing. The questions themselves are designed to dig into how we want to work as a team and help us achieve the most honest insights. It also signals that the version of ourselves outside of work is welcome here and we are all pretty similar as humans.

A point to mention here, if you don't have the canvas mapped out that's fine. You can simply convert the canvas into a list of questions and facilitate a workshop around them. I've tested with a canvas and without, and both worked equally well. We might not have the luxury of knowing a little bit about each other before going into the DARE, so it is important that the workshop demonstrates the behaviours we want from the get-go and that starts with how we show up to the room.

DARE

1. Hard Truth

What's your bias about us?

13. Signatures:

2. Best of the best

What things do you most appreciate in other relationships?

What made them special?

What's the one feature you would like us to adopt from them?

3. Biggest ick

What things are your big turn offs? e.g. a 5pm Friday meeting

4. Fight club secrets & other things to know

Do we need to adapt for neurodiversity?

What is your biggest brag?

Do you have any dog pictures?

Do we need some rituals?

8. Past

What has been done in the past?

Why didn't it work?

Has anything similar to this been done before?

9. Present

What does the current state look like, what's the ask and why the change?

Pareto Principle: Min. effort to achieve this and in what format?

Who's our audience?

Why aren't they doing this now?

What are your competition doing?

Who are the team core and extended?

Who are the torch carriers, who needs to be on side for green light all the way?

10. Future

What change do we want to see within the business, what are the goals, how does this fit into the big strategy?

How will we measure the solution?

What is the change we want them to see?

What does success look like?

Action:

5. Success outside of delivery

Outside of delivering the project, how will we know we have created an awesome relationship?

What do you look like when everything is going to plan, are you more chilled, chatty, etc.?

6. Feedback & Red Flags

Do you have a specific feedback model to use?

How and who do we feedback to?

What do you look like when things are not going to plan?

7. Ways of working

What are the times and hours that we can work (and are there any times that are non-negotiable?

What is the best way for us to work? e.g. conditions and cadence of meetings.

How do you prefer to communicate and what are the best methods of getting hold of you in a busy world?

12. How are we celebrating at the end?

Team drinks, crazy golf, laser quest, ...?

11. Our business problem statement & our people's problem statement

In the simplest of terms, it means being switched on, curious, interested, provocative, and again just for good measure, being human. The goal at the end of the DARE is to know more about each other individually as well as how we want to work best. If, by the end of this activity, you don't know that Dave is a dog lover and Sue in finance is an adrenaline junkie, then we may not have spent enough time cultivating the relationship. So try not to shorten this activity and give it the time needed.

The order in which the canvas is mapped is by design, I would recommend where possible trying to stick to the order below. I've tried various different orders when running this, and in my experience, the order here seems to be what works best. Usually, I would first do a little activity to create a positive space, something like partner up with someone you don't know very well in the room, give everyone a Sharpie and sticky notepads. Then challenge them to draw their partner in 60 seconds without looking down.

Here we break down the 12 sections from the Canvas:

1. Hard truth

Asking a group of people who may have just met for the first time, what's their bias is a really bold question to open with, right? The reason we ask this at the start is to set the tone of 'this isn't going to be a normal dull meeting'. It highlights from the start that we all have bias and it also uproots any past experience they may have had for them to have this bias in the first place. A word of warning; be prepared for some truth serum here. I remember I once did this with a large financial services (FS) organisation – and boy, were they honest. Below is a snapshot of some of the sticky notes from both parties:

- "I think FS is an old, outdated organisation who say they want modern and new ways of doing things only to revert back to the standard dribble."

- "I think your company is very old, outdated, and not diverse."
- "If it ticks a compliance-based box it's getting through, if it ticks true change it's not getting through."
- "I worry you only want to mask the problem and not get to the root of the challenge."
- "I am worried you're here to get paid a day rate and not fix the real challenges."
- "I don't know what you will bring to the table that we can't just do ourselves."
- "Great, I can hand you over my challenges and you will go off and fix them."

As you can see, these are pretty interesting answers to one question. It's important that we acknowledge these biases, get them from their mind down on to sticky notes and out the way first. After all, how else will we be able to have an open, honest, and trusting relationship?

Remember, we are not here to dwell on those statements. Understand these questions often come from past experiences. See the answers as coming from a good place and move on.

2. Best of the best

The aim of this question on the canvas is to pull out the best elements of past relations the client/stakeholder has had before you and identify what made them the best. We have already started to identify elements that will be captured in section 7 of the canvas, Ways of Working, without actually discussing it yet.

Really try to drill down here what it was about these elements. You might uproot that one of the things they appreciate is that meetings were only in an emergency and actually the way they operate and update each other is via voice notes on Teams or WhatsApp. It is about identifying what worked in the past to make it great. As it could be something we adopt in our ways of working and approaching the question.

3. **Biggest ick**

   Here, ultimately, we are trying to identify things that our stakeholders hate and therefore we will know not to do (an ick is a noise you make when you gag, it is used to express disgust). In the past, I've seen things such as booking late Friday afternoon meetings, ass-kissing and cc'ing the boss in every email, overuse of positive language.

4. **Fight club rules (we don't talk to others about fight club)**

   This is where we blend personal and professional. The goal here is to uproot any unknowns that may help us form our relationship, it also gives an opportunity for us to share anything that might go down as a fight club rule e.g. we don't talk about fight club, it's a secret to keep within this group.

   In the past, people have really opened up about having 100 cats, having dyslexia, being slightly on the spectrum, etc. On the surface, this may seem easy to overlook but getting a deeper rich insight into why Steve might prefer calls over emails due to dyslexia is vital. Also, in the past, I've known people to talk about how their children are ill and how sometimes this results in odd working hours.

5. **Success outside of the delivery**

   Pretty simple section this one, the goal is that at any point in the relationship we should be able to identify if it's going well or not. The trick really is to understand from each of the stakeholders, what they look like when things are going well – are they super chilled, full of banter, do they talk about non-work-related things more, etc.

6. **Feedback and red flags**

   This section is the opposite of section five. Here, we want to identify when things are going to shit! How will we know on a human level, will we identify micro-managing and abruptness? It is also good here to identify how you do feedback – is there a set approach they prefer, how would they like to receive it, and so on.

7. Ways of working

By this point, if you have followed the flow, most of the early signals should have come out in the other sections of the canvas. Your goal is to distil them down and validate them.

Maybe you noticed in section 2 that one of the best of the best elements was having a group WhatsApp where every day you would do a download to the team. If so, maybe that is something you can add to this project. Perhaps you noticed Steve's point about his dyslexia and actually a voice note in the group works better for him.

Once we have completed this section of the DARE, we then move into the scoping of the project, which are sections 8, 9, 10, and 11. There are a few points to notice when it comes to these sections of the canvas.

This is still discovery, while we care about the answers they give, we also want to understand the context of it. Through these sections start to ask the Whys, Whos, and Hows, ask what they want but also what they need. We should never make assumptions about any of this. It is about us aligning on what is in and out of scope and collecting some early signals of where to look next. It is important we bring every idea, concern, and thought out in the open.

Throughout this section, ask:

- The Whys – we care about the why and why not – why did that happen, why didn't that happen, why do you think this will be successful over another project.
- The Whos – who was part of this project in the past, are they part of this project now, do they need to be, do they need to be here now, who/what are the barriers to this, who are our champions.
- The Hows – how did this project land in the past, how do you see something like this being done, how do you think XYZ demographic will look at this.

8. The Past

This section is all about us looking into the past, being able to identify what has been done like this, what was successful and what wasn't. Why will this help us avoid creating the same thing, and allow us to bring any data or insight on why that did or didn't work? This could be simple things like 'we tried but the technology was bad', 'we nailed the comms on this because we have space to do it and the comms had a real different look and feel'.

9. The Present

This allows us to get a feel on what's currently going on now. Is there a feeling of change fatigue in the organisation, what's in play at the moment that we can spring off, are any of the projects about to take flight or be grounded. This section is all about creating a current picture of your audience and the world they operate in at work, as well as identifying current barriers and champions.

10. The Future

This is about future forecasting. We don't know what any form of innovation, solution, or experience will look like just yet. But we could probably do a good job of identifying positive indicators, or the emotions/performances we want to see... this is the section to capture that.

So, we have nearly completed the canvas, only one section to go before we get to 'how do we celebrate' and that is section 11: the problem statement.

11. Problem statement

The goal with these statements is to use them as a bit of a guiding light, when we start it is not about proving or disproving them just yet. Your problem statement can often change throughout. The idea, for now, is to use it as a brief description of the challenge and keep it front and centre in our minds as a focus as we go through sense-making.

A simple Google search will give you a template to follow when writing your problem statement. In the chapter called Problem Statements, I have also gone into more detail about this specifically, however, for now I would like to break it down into two distinct points of view:

- The business problem statement
- The people problem statement

Both ask the same question, but it is good to answer them from their unique points of view. If your answers come back at the end as they did at the start then the chances are either you haven't walked in their shoes or understood your people's world enough, or perhaps the business has done an awesome job of understanding the problem from both points of view as well as the businesses.

Either way, it is worth probing a little around it to validate. I tend to ask people to write down their individual stakeholder answers on a note first then combine and condense the answer down to just one statement which gives us our starter statement. I would run the ladder of abstraction from the problem statement chapter to make sure we are going after a challenge that isn't too broad or too narrow. While doing this section, keep asking:

Q1. Who are the people facing this problem?
Q2. What is the problem?
Q3. When and where does this problem happen?
Q4. What would happen if we did nothing?

Okay, let's move on to the final section and my personal favourite which is how do we celebrate.

12. How are WE celebrating

This section is the last section for many reasons, the main one is it leaves us on a high note, it takes us away from thinking about the work and it gives us a personal North Star once the project is up. It allows us to start thinking bigger and creatively. What you want to capture here is something fun, maybe that fancy dress junkyard golf, laser quest and food, or something that feels less forced fun. Whatever it is, make sure you don't skip this step. It's important, even if it doesn't feel it right now.

Okay, so I lied, before you all high-five each other and go off into the sunset to deliver something brilliant, there is one more thing to do and that's right at the top of the sheet.

13. Signatures and action

This is a contract, it is you signing to say you will agree to what we have designed here. And while this isn't an official contract, it is more of a personal and team contract of ways of working. Please make sure everyone has bought into the concept and signs it.

Actions: Having this time together is fantastic, but without any actions it's just a nice day out. The action at the top is where you want to assign who is going to take this away and turn this into something real as well as where all this is stored. For example, let's say the team says they like to work on Kanban. Who sets that up? And you like a WhatsApp group weekly download. Who is setting up the group? I would also recommend taking a picture of the canvas and either converting it to a digital version or at the very least keeping it safe somewhere, so that people can get access to it and use it as a point of reference.

Turning this canvas into something real is where the magic happens. Now, it is easier to split all the actions up amongst the team, however, my recommendation would be to assign the core tasks of setting up to one person and then distribute the rest out after. People are busy, so reduce the load where possible.

If you don't have the canvas mapped out that's fine, you can convert this into a list of questions and facilitate a workshop around this. I've gone ahead and mapped out a suggested flow next, feel free to tweak as you like.

INSIGHTFUL INGREDIENT

Rocketbook have various dial-down days each quarter. These are days when no meetings happen, people are not expected to respond to comms, and team members can do as they like with the days. If they have a lot of work to catch up on, they can do it without distraction. If they wanted to use it as a day off they can. They can do anything they like and they have peace of mind knowing that they won't miss anything.

#DANNYDISCUSSIONS

What comes to mind when reading about this?

....

....

....

....

....

....

WHEN ALL YOU HAVE IS A FLIPCHART

Setting up a room:

Prior to the session, write each section of the canvas up on a separate flip chart and hang them up around the room (questions at the end of the chapter), each flipchart asks one question.

Intro

Invite everyone to the room, remind them why they are here, explain what we are going to be doing and the expected output from the session. Signal hard that it is about being open, honest, and transparent about the answers even if it feels awkward. Hand everyone their own sticky notepads and Sharpies. Try to use the same colour pens and sticky notes so people can't be identified should they not want to share. Take everyone over to section one – Hard truths.

Walk the group through the question (what's your bias about us/ the project) and add the extra context about this section (given above). Next, ask everyone to write their answers down on the sticky notes (one answer per note), once they have finished, ask someone in the room to collect them all and plonk them onto the flipchart. They can answer the question as many times as they wish to do so. Ask the team to first think deeply about the question before rushing in with an answer.

Once everyone is done, walk through the sticky notes asking the group to share any extra context needed about the answers. This is a facilitated workshop, 90% of it will be discussion based on the answers written down, this is where the richness lies. Follow this approach for each section of the canvas, keep people moving around the room as you navigate across the questions.

As a facilitator, feel free to start to cluster any trends you are seeing in any of the answers to the questions in real-time. One of the tricky things about not using the canvas is at the end you will end up with a lot of flipcharts. I recommend taking pictures of them on your phone and assigning one person to load them onto a virtual version of the canvas using Miro, Mural, or Figma. Where possible we want to use the canvas as a point of reference throughout the relationship, so having a digital version of it somewhere will be handy.

INSIGHTFUL INGREDIENT

Bringing a unique approach to improving schools, the Flamboyan Foundation's core focus is on building relationships and engagement between teacher and parents, this approach flipped the typical reactive end-of-year school report and instead drove for a proactive before-the-year-starts approach. The teacher would instead visit parents at their home and have a detailed discussion about the child's experience and their experience of school. No notes were to be taken, instead the focus was on the richness of the conversation. The teacher would then ask parents to sign a pledge to support their child's development in various ways.

#DANNYDISCUSSIONS

What comes to mind when reading about this?

....

....

....

....

....

....

....

....

....

....

....

....

WHY IT MATTERS

This 'heart first' approach to building a relationship and scoping out the work has proven invaluable time and time again for me. It builds rapport from the outset, disarming any potential blockers of great work and allows you to get to know the project team more informally. Using this approach has helped me avoid any trip-ups with the stakeholder. If something does go sideways, we know how to share the challenge and we also understand how to overcome it together. Don't be surprised if you find out nobody likes business as usual's ways of working, the canvas has a habit of exposing that fairly quickly.

For instance, we often make the assumption that people prefer email contact, yet, I've lost count of the number of times myself or a member of my team have heard a stakeholder say: "Just WhatsApp me as I respond much quicker there, I never look at my inbox," or "Actually, I am a bit of a control freak – could we possibly have a Monday and Thursday stand up/check-in meeting every week?" These are the kinds of insights we wouldn't find out until we either hit a friction point or edged towards a tight deadline.

This approach also helps determine ways of working moving forward, while hopefully challenging some of the bias found in the first question. This co-design, co-development approach will allow you to identify where you can be the org's biggest champion along with where and how you can challenge them to improve.

The following are some of the questions that I've found most useful, however, this isn't an exhaustive list and there may be more that you're inspired to ask:

- "What are the times and hours that we can work and are there any times that are non-negotiable?"
- "How do you prefer to communicate and what are the best methods of getting hold of you in a busy world?"
- "We use a feedback model called COIN (insert a preferred feedback model). Does that work for you and how would you like us to deliver the feedback? e.g. positive and constructive."

- "What things do you struggle with?" You can also share what you struggle with here, too.
- "What things do you most appreciate in our relationship?" You can also share the things you most appreciate.
- "What is the best way for us to work? e.g. conditions and cadence of meetings."
- "What other things should I know about you (personally)? What are some of the things you should know about me?"
- "Are there any other things about the business that may get in the way? e.g. people, process, props, places."
- "Based on past relationships, if you could purchase one big desirable or feature from us, what would it be?"
- "Based on past relationships, if you could remove one thing from our relationship, what would it be?"

SAID AND SEALED

- Investing time in understanding the wants and needs of people involved in a project can help to build strong and effective relationships.
- To facilitate this understanding, use a Design A Relationship Experience (DARE) canvas.
- The DARE canvas includes prompts to help facilitate a deeper understanding of the people involved in the project, such as "What are your communication preferences?" and "What do you value in a relationship?"
- By taking the time to understand each other's wants and needs at the beginning of a project, it is possible to create a more personalised, high-impact, and positive working relationship.

FINDING THE RIGHT PROBLEM STATEMENT

Unless you're doing some form of discovery research, doing any form of sense-making without a problem statement is a massive risk. This statement is used for various things such as:

- It challenges and aligns stakeholders on the goal
- It gives the team an anchor on what we are going after
- It enables us to focus on the actual problem vs the perceived problem
- It will either prove or disprove our bias and assumptions

The other reason, and the most important, is that it summarises the problem. This gives us something to align to. This is one of the reasons why it's so important to capture it in the design of a relationship.

Writing a strong problem statement is somewhat of an art. Go too big and you're trying to fix world hunger, go too narrow and you're not getting to the root of the issue, and often looking at a by-product of the real problem or being enticed by a solution seduction. A great model to make sure your problem statement is at the right level is called the Ladder of Abstraction and it is super easy to follow.

LADDER OF ABSTRACTION

This is a simple yet efficient mental model that was created by S. I. Hayakawa. This mental model allows us to test, as a group, if our statement is at the right level and if we are using the correct type of questions to create it. It can also produce alternative problem statements which will challenge our thinking.

A similar approach is often found in a therapist setting where the therapist will guide you through zooming in or zooming out of a tricky situation or thought pattern. I have seen this tool called various names and use various different utensils such as funnels, maps, and so on. Whichever works best go with that, however, I will stick to the original i.e. a Ladder. Regardless of which object you use, the rules are still the same.

The more you move up the ladder, the broader you go with questions, things can start to become quite abstract often resulting in rich and meaningful conversations, however, it can become too abstract to put into action. The more you move down the ladder, the narrower we get, things start to become specific and solution-focused. However, go down the ladder too soon and you run the risk of not challenging your thinking around the challenge and often go into solution mode. Please don't make the mistake of assuming going straight down the ladder is valuable, always go up first.

As we move up and down the ladder, the goal isn't to get to the solution, the goal is to create a discussion with our stakeholders to see if we are asking and setting the problem statement at the right level. If we went straight down the ladder we wouldn't have that discussion.

Below is a made-up situation of what that could look like. First, you want to identify what might be a symptom of the problem, such as:

> (Symptom of the problem) **Our people aren't experimenting in the organisation.**
>
> Then we can simply rephrase that into a starter.
>
> **Starter Statement: How to get our people in the org to do more experimenting. Put this statement on a sticky note and place it in the middle of the ladder** (seen in the illustration ahead in blue).

Below is an example of how a starter statement chat like this might go with stakeholders (SHs):

> SHs come with a statement start: How to get our people in the org to do more experimenting
>
> Dan reframes and moves up the ladder: why do you want people to do more experimenting
>
> SHs: because we need to test and learn at pace
>
> Dan reframes and moves up the ladder: why else do you want people to do more experimenting
>
> SHs: because we want to invest our resources and money into ideas that work

At this point, you can either continue to ask, 'why else?' to the original question or you can start a splinter of your ladder into the new statement:

> Statement starter: How do we invest our resources into better ideas?
>
> But for now, let's keep going up...
>
> Dan reframes: why else do you want people to do more experimenting?
>
> SHs: So we can let people be more creative with their work.

Again, you can pull that out as a splinter statement starter and create another ladder focused just on this challenge again moving up and down the ladder.

> Let's keep going ...
>
> Dan reframes: why else do you want people to do more experimenting?
>
> SHs: so we can generate more innovative ideas across the business.

Again, you can pull that out as a statement starter: How can we be more innovative and generate ideas across the business?

Hopefully you can start to see how you go from, 'How do we get our people to do more experimenting?' to 'How do we invest our resources in better ideas?', 'How do we let people be more creative in their work?', 'How do we generate more innovative ideas across the business?'. Each one of these are some suggested alternative statements we can look at.

This conversation allowed us to discuss the problem statement in much broader terms, and with more time you will generate more by simply asking why. Otherwise, unless we ask 'why' then often our initial problem statement is quite a safe statement, but it also lacks any form of imagination, it's not inspiring and often doesn't want to get people out of bed. Hold the mirror up to ask, 'Are you being adventurous enough? Can you go bigger with more impact or are you just being safe?'.

Now, let's say we want to go down the ladder and start to get more tactical.

> Dan reframes: What's stopping our people from doing more experimenting?
>
> SHs: Nobody knows the approach to do experimenting

At this point, you can either ask 'why else' to the original question or you can start a splinter of your ladder into a new statement such as: How might we share the approach on how to do experimenting?

For now, let's keep going on the chosen path.

> Dan: What else is stopping our people from doing more experimenting?
>
> SHs: Our people don't have the tools to do experiments.

New statement starter: How might we give the tools to experiment to our people?

Let's go down the ladder on that:

> Dan reframes: How do we give the tools for experimenting to our people?
>
> SHs: We could do some form of training.
>
> SHs: We could send them to a start-up or research and development function for a day.
>
> SHs: We could give them digital tools they could call on from their phone.

At this point, you can either reframe the above statement 'How else?' and this would be going more down the ladder into solutions space, or we could go back up the ladder:

> Dan: What else is stopping our people from doing more experimenting?
>
> SHs: Our people don't have enough time to do experimenting in their day.

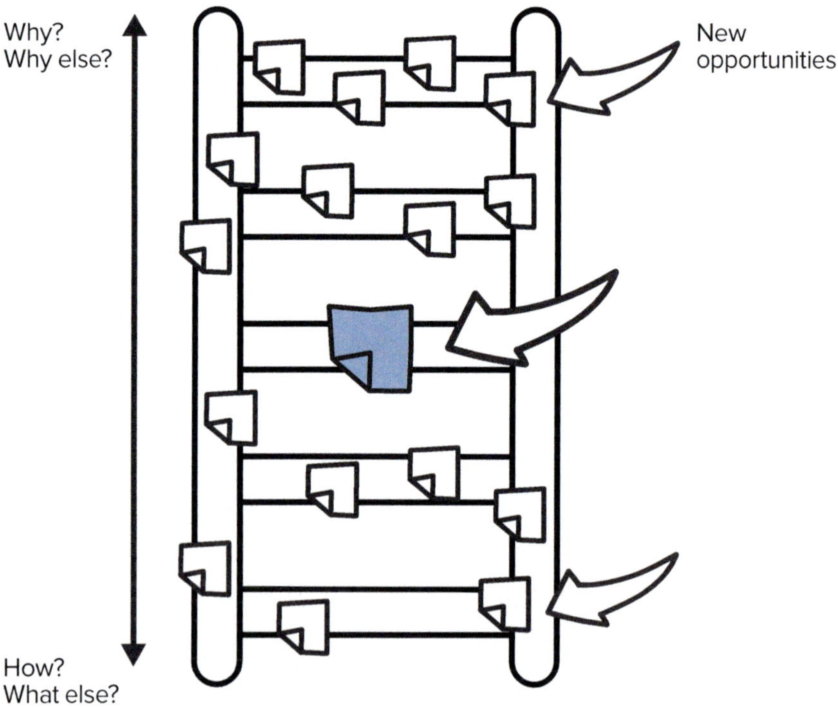

As you can see here, we are starting to narrow the problem, with what is stopping and/or preventing us/this type of questions. We have initially gone from people not knowing the approach, to experimenting, then to people not having the tools, and finally people not having the time.

Big warning here, it's so easy to get into solution mode and start generating ideas and while this is a great tool to help get the juices going for us in this sense-making phase, it is about agreeing with stakeholders. What is the right type of level we want our problem statement to be before we head off into finding the insights? We don't really care too much about solutions and honestly, we don't want to be that far down the ladder at this stage.

While you can use this tool later on in incubation to come up with ideas, it's more the splinter statement and chosen statements we want to take forward.

As a team, discuss and agree on what level you want to look at the challenge and the type of problem to focus on. As someone facilitating this, try to wear a few hats, one being a critical friend but also one who will stretch their thinking a little more and push them out of their comfort zone.

Often, when running this activity, people can get caught up in two points; when do you create splinter statements and how long do you run the activity for. The activity is designed to help you understand the problem and stretch the thinking on the challenge by asking questions. It is up to you to decide if you even want to create splinter statements or if you want to continue with just the one.

There is no right or wrong answer, it's something you as a team will identify as you go through the activity.

You will naturally find the right level and challenge statement you want to go after. The same is applied to the running length of the activity. I've run this both in 20 mins and in 90 minutes. It is about how quickly the team aligns, the appetite, and the resources the team have to go bigger or smaller on the challenge.

So, let's say as a whole, we agree on the level we want to approach this, we now need to turn this into a human/business problem statement. Let's jump into creating one.

INSIGHTFUL INGREDIENT

Helen Barnett Diserens flipped the cosmetic industry on its head, fed up with the messy experience of applying deodorant by hand, she looked outside the cosmetic world for answers. The answer came in the form of a ballpoint pen. Helen took the idea of how the pen works and applied it to deodorant. Thanks to her out-of-the-box thinking we now have the roll-on deodorant.

#DANNYDISCUSSIONS

What comes to mind when reading about this?

....

....

....

....

....

....

....

....

....

....

....

....

PROBLEM STATEMENTS

Like most things, problem statements can be written up in many different ways. In this situation, we want to make sense of the current state and give a nod to the future state. Below is a typical approach to writing a problem statement, often they don't need to be this formulaic and sometimes can't be depending on the challenge, but it will give a nice springboard for sure.

- **Current state**: what does it look like now around this challenge
- **What** is it
- **Impact**: this is causing something negative or positive
- **Where** does it happen
- **When** does it happen
- **Who** has this problem
- **Impact**: this is causing something negative or positive
- **Future state**: what the ideal outcome would feel like

Let's say, as a group, we have decided we want to make sense of why experimentation isn't being done across the business. A problem statement using the above format could be:

> **"Our people don't currently apply experimentation in their role and teams across the business in their day-to-day."**

Now let's make it a bit more meaningful:

- **Current state**: our people don't/are not trying new things out
- **What**: don't currently apply experimentation
- **Where**: in their role and across the business
- **When**: in their day-to-day role
- **Who**: individuals and teams
- **Impact**: this is resulting in us losing a competitive edge in the market and not attracting the right type of talent

- **Future state**: by next year, we want to be an experiment-first business where we can identify, experiment, and validate new innovation at record pace. This will allow us to be more focused on personal development and more efficient in business resources.

"Our people don't currently apply experimentation in their role and teams across the business in their day-to-day. This is resulting in us losing a competitive edge in the market and not attracting the right type of talent. By next year, we want to be an experiment-first business where we can identify, experiment, and validate new innovation at record pace, allowing us to be more focused on personal development and more efficient in business resources."

As you can see, the problem statement isn't too big where we are trying to change the world, however, it's not too narrow where we instantly want to go into a solution. The problem statement has an element of the unknownand states the future goal. Again, you can choose to add this to your statement or not.

Once you have done your phase of sense-making, don't be shocked if the problem statement changes a little due to what you have uprooted.

A final note on the problem statement. Often, if in some form of lab set-up or maybe just a distributed team, I tend to have the problem statement written out on the wall so that it is front and centre in the room or in the team's channel. I find it allows the team to be constantly reminded of what we are trying to make sense of and is a good anchor should we start to lose sight.

SAID AND SEALED

- A problem statement is a clear and concise description of a problem that needs to be solved.
- It helps to align stakeholders on the goal, focus on the actual problem, and test biases and assumptions.
- The ladder of abstraction is a mental model that can be used to determine the level and questions of a problem statement.
- The ladder involves asking more abstract 'why' questions at higher levels and more specific 'how' questions at lower levels.
- Using the ladder of abstraction can lead to a meaningful and actionable discussion about the problem statement and help set the scene for sense-making.

← **Scan me to be taken to resources**

This is the moment here to challenge!

SENSE-MAKING – THE HUMAN

"People ignore design that ignores people."
—Frank Chimero

The first stage of my design process always has to start with sense-making. Without it you are, as my dad would say, pissing in the wind. Sense-making is about just that, making sense of the current state, making sense of the challenge at a deep level and understanding the system at which this challenge lives in. Often the original challenge is masked by others in the system, masked by superficial problems, or wrapped in business and stakeholder bias.

Sense-making, when done correctly, is more than just empathy, it's leading with compassion and curiosity.

Not all challenges are equal, some we navigate based on past experiences, while others are so unique that we don't even know where to start. We have no benchmark to compare. I repeat WE all need sense-making ... if you're debating skipping this step then good luck.

It's worth noting here that not all challenges call for deep sense-making. Often the business has completed a lot of the in-depth analysis that will enable you to get off to a good start, although this analysis may have bias throughout it and is often outdated. The trick here is to use the data as secondary data and, at the bare minimum, challenge it to create a business case to start fresh.

In order to gain a better understanding, we can use various different types of research at different stages of the project. My go-to for all things research is Erika Hall's *Just Enough Research*, along with Sam Ladner's book *Practical Ethnography*. These books dive into exploratory research, applied research, design research, secondary research, pure research, evaluation research, market research – you name it, I highly recommend you check them out.

Ultimately, when we strip it back, research tends to fall into two simple buckets of data – qualitative and quantitative – and like anything, they form a great relationship when together.

Qualitative data: This tends to be seen as more exploratory in nature. It is less about the numbers and figures and more about understanding the ideas, reasons and motivations, emotions and feelings. There's a common misconception that this sort of data can appear somewhat 'fluffy' – however, this couldn't be further from the truth. This data is the type that allows us to bring emotion to our narrative. It allows us to never lose sight of the human involved and often will show up when we relay our findings back to the business. Using A.I. and sentiment analysis, you can pull out emotions such as joy, anger, fear, and so on from the words used. All of this is powerful, skip it at your own peril.

Quantitative data: To me, this is less about 'feeling' and more about the hard facts and figures. Again, this supplements the emotions with really hard figures often seen in the value of money, resources, and so on.

It's worth bearing in mind that one type of research isn't better than the other, often the best results come from a blend of qualitative and quantitative data. Only once we have a mix of both will we be able to gain true insight into the actual challenge and confidently tell a story and gauge a direction of where to go next.

It is not unheard of to find that clients and academic researchers prefer one data type over the other, it is important to understand both are two sides of the same coin. One gives you the hard figures, the other helps answer the why behind the figures. Usually it tends to be the qualitative data that gets dropped, often because it is misunderstood, undervalued and overlooked, usually due to cost, time, resources or, simply put, it takes effort to perform good qualitative research.

This to me seems crazy. Good qualitative insight allows us to lead with empathy and compassion and more importantly to design with it. It gives us a unique opportunity to understand the nature of the emotive response and to hear the words of people who have been through a particular experience. It also allows us to hear from the quieter voices in the room. Most importantly, it stops us from making assumptions and allows us to challenge the original thinking of the business if needed.

Having a mix of both and using some triangulation allows us to become super airtight. Later in the process, I will talk about triangulation, for now just hold on to it as a buzzword.

QUICK STORY

Barry Business: Hey Danny, we have a behaviour issue and I need you to fix it. All of a sudden, summer has arrived and a load of people like Sue are returning off their tea/lunch breaks late. It is starting to become an issue and driving call queues through the roof. I need you to basically do some form of behaviour training and timekeeping.

Danny: Okay, how do you know that's the answer?

Barry Business: I based it off what I've heard in the past and well, I've worked here long enough.

Danny: Okay Barry, Baz, the Bazmiester, how about before we rush in and create something maybe not needed, why don't we do a little bit of sense-making?

Barry Business: Sense-making, do we need that really? I know what the problem is.

Danny: Well Bazo, it will ultimately validate or disprove your gut feeling. With no human insight, how do you show you have a human problem? It will also highlight any other opportunities where you could invest resources and actually make a bigger impact.

It basically means you get to direct your resources at the things your people desire/need the most and not piss it up the wall, actually fix the problem and look good in front of the boss. Slow is smooth and smooth is fast. If we take our time here to really dig in and validate or disprove with data and insight, it means we move extra fast later on.

Barry Business: hmm am not sure it will be valuable, as I know the answer but go on then.

Now, let's pause for a minute and run these two scenarios:

SCENARIO 1:

We don't push Barry, instead, we jump to the conclusion that he was correct and that the business just needed some sort of solution to address Sue and others' behaviour. Perhaps this would take the form of a timer or alarm, or maybe you could create a mobile app nudging Sue when to come back, maybe you design some 'behaviour and timekeeping' training.

You rush off to create a little app that has a push notification telling the person when they need to return (yes, I know alarms exist but stay with me here). It has everything we want: it's simple, easy to use, and not overloaded with functionality. It's not a cheap solution either, let's say it costs £30K to build this app.

So you roll it out and notice there is a small improvement, but nothing to write home about. Barry Business comes to you and tells you that your solution hasn't worked. He suggests that Sue obviously needs some help with time management and maybe a piece of work around behaviour change.

You put together a course or training solution in response. Let's say that it costs around £60K to put everybody through this training.

When completed (assuming you didn't push back), you notice there is a tiny increase on a data point in their dashboard, but one that doesn't justify the £90K invested so far.

So far, a big waste in resources and no actual solution.

LET'S RUN SCENARIO 2

Baz has given you the green light to sense-make first, so you invest the time in interviews, focus groups, digital diaries. While going through these interviews and looking at all the breadcrumbs of data accumulated you then use the quantitative data to see if this supports or goes against the qualitative data. Just as you start to drift off, semi-hypnotised by the Excel sheet full of data and thinking about how you're going to retire early and start making jam, something eventually breaks you from this dream state and pulls you back into reality.

You see something clear as day. Something so subtle it could go unnoticed, you see it come up again in the data. You decide to go and observe it for yourself, and there it happens time and time again. Then, like a wet salmon jumping upstream, it slaps you across the face.

What we're feeling isn't a behavioural issue at all. The problem is actually down to a faulty door which each person has to go in and out of to get to the canteen. Sometimes it works and sometimes it doesn't. You follow a person out who has issues going through the door. You buy them a cup of tea and mention that you noticed they struggled with the door and ask them why that is.

As it turns out, certain people have had issues getting in and out the door with their swipe cards. Some of the cards were only provisioned to day or week access to let them through, meaning it is hit or miss whether they can get access or not. In situations where the cards don't work, reception must be contacted to let the person through.

Armed with this awesome insight, it's time to experiment. You run over to the duty manager of the team who manages the online/offline time. Next, you ask to put a marker on 8 people who seem to be consistently late back every day. Finally, you then head over to the security team, give them the 8 names, and ask for their swipe cards to be re-provisioned. All that's left to do now is to sit back and wait a few days, feeling both excited and nervous, wondering if the business is going to call you a genius or hand you your P45. After two long days of mapping your exit, you go over to the duty manager again and ask to run a report on the names you gave him.

As the system is producing this report, you cross your fingers and hold your breath. You can almost smell the jam you might be making in early retirement.

Boom: some names show green and some in blue, indicating that these employees came back earlier. In fact, it showed that they had a tendency to come back early every time.

You run this little experiment with a different sample set and again the names come back in green and blue. At this point, you push ahead and give the green light for all cards to be provisioned. However, as the problem starts to disappear you're aware that the cost has grown:

- £90k for an app and training – all proving fruitless
- 25p for a cup of tea and a chat, a bit of sense-making time resulted in the observation and solution

Waste in resources = £89,999.75

Hold on a second, because we accumulated the qualitative data at the start we also have a lot more data and actually some really interesting insight into making life better at the call centre. These insights include leadership opportunities, better rewards and benefits, and better onboarding. It also provides insight into how the business is seen from outside. Instantly, we start to really identify some potential moments where the business could actually start to reshape its Employee Value Proposition (EVP) and attract fresh new talent and fix real Employee Experience (EX) products.

The conclusion? If we don't care about the people problem at the start, they don't care about the solution at the end. We should never assume, when we do, it nearly always makes an ass=u+me.

STOP INTERVIEWING AND START IMMERSING

There is only so much you can learn from interviews. Sometimes you need to watch people in their habitat. This allows you to see and hear a lot more than what the business does. I would go as far as saying that doing any form of shadowing, immersion, digital diary, or day in the life will provide 3x more insight than a typical interview. Yet, they are rarely done.

It's also one of the most fun and challenging areas; not only does it challenge you personally and make you think more deeply about your initial thoughts, it also helps you discover any blind spots you may have in your thinking. More importantly, it gets you to the place that matters, which is front and centre of the people in the trenches in the day-to-day.

Making sense of the problem and observing what people are doing isn't anything new. In fact, many of the brands we love have been doing it for years and years. However, in a world of Google and social media, we can sometimes risk losing the human touch and that is the reason we need to fight so hard to keep it. It is nearly all too easy to pull a report of quantitative insight but quantitative doesn't always tell the full story.

I was once working with a large tech company looking at how we create better personal benefits and rewards. The customer at the time was really struggling to understand why their employees were not interested in the benefits on offer and how the business wasn't competing with other companies. The data they had collated highlighted how many people in the org were reaping the benefits and how many weren't.

The suggested solution was for us to immerse ourselves in their world for a week, giving us full access to their lives (within reason). A typical day would involve us heading over to an employee's home, observing their morning routine, then travelling into the office with them and shadowing their daily activity, then going on the commute home with them.

Now I know what you're thinking, who the hell would sign up for that? Well, you would be surprised. In fact, I've been on the opposite side of this coin a few years ago for Ford and I had a camera crew following me around. They are real people who want to make life better for everyone, they tend to be the ones who are open to being followed.

After various days of immersion, combined with the quantitative data we had requested, such as company-owned devices employees have, the demographic of employees, and so on, we started to follow the breadcrumbs in the data which lead us to some really interesting opportunities that interviews alone wouldn't have identified. For example:

- We found that most people on their commute to the office either walked or took the train
- The demographic of employees was late 20s and early 30s
- We found they took the train or drove listening to a form of streaming service such as Spotify, Audible, or Apple Music
- Not many of the employees lived within a close range of the office (5 miles) on average, they walked past 2 coffee shop chains
- Many of the employees enjoyed social drinking with friends or at home with their partner
- Many of the employees lived with a partner, often renting. Most didn't have a child
- Typical house running costs were a concern
- Nearly all the employees saw flexible working as a big tick as it helped them work from anywhere
- Holiday allowance, of course, came up as well as you can imagine

So, when you overlay that breakdown on top of the benefits that were on offer such as coupons for Christmas, private health care, and so on, it was no wonder the benefits were not being taken up. They were not targeted to the employee demographic nor were they specific to the employees' lives. I am sure that, even with just the above points, certain areas of opportunity start to show up and that was a tiny snapshot of the employees' lives.

A QUICK STORY – THE POWER OF OBSERVATION

In 1894, a discovery was made that changed the world as we know it (well, the breakfast world at least). Did you know the well-loved Cornflakes, that millions of people enjoy every morning, were created from observations (as well as a lot of failed attempts)?

Let's go back to that day. Dr John Harvey Kellogg noticed his patients were having some issues digesting the hospital breakfast (baked bread). He reached out to his brother Will, a food manufacturer, for help in coming up with a better alternative for his patients.

Will gladly accepted the challenge. Many days were then spent sitting with the patients and trying to understand their pains and frustrations with the baked bread. Once Will understood their wants and needs, he went about trying to create the solutions. However, Will became increasingly frustrated with failing to find the solution. Feeling somewhat dispirited, he decided to call it a night.

The next morning, Will was going about his usual set up ready for another day of prototyping and realised he had left out the boiled wheat from the previous night. He noticed that the wheat had turned soft overnight. Curious, Will decided to roll out the wheat and bake it. The result? A crispy flake (you see where I'm going with this now, right?).

Over time, Will went on to try this process with corn. The humble box of Cornflakes – and the Kellogg's brand – was born.

A Quick Exercise:

The image on the next page depicts a scene. Your goal is to figure out what has happened in this scene, based on the limited information you have. Pay attention to the items, the age of the items, the layout, etc. Really give it a minute or two of attention and write down all the initial thoughts that come to mind, including any thoughts or feelings it evokes.

Okay, so what are you thinking? I am sure you have many thoughts and ideas. Perhaps you have some questions. Here are some prompts:

- Is this person dead or alive?
- Has this house been burgled?
- Was someone in a rush to find something here?
- Would the curtains being closed make the situation any different?
- Is this a person so busy they haven't got a minute to clean up?

....

....

....

....

....

....

....

....

....

For the next step, do the same again but try to look at it without the feelings, thoughts, and questions you had from the first image. However, I still want you to write down the thoughts, feelings, and questions this image provokes:

So have your assumptions started to change yet? Is the story now somewhat different?

- Does adding a dog into the scene change things? Why?
- Has the dog managed to get into a room it shouldn't have been in and ripped open some bags of old paperwork?
- Who does this dog belong to: the owners or burglars?

Let's try this again, once more removing all assumptions, questions and ideas:

What do you see now?

- Has the point of view changed? Are you now looking at this from somebody else's point of view?
- Has someone perhaps already done a lot of cleaning (hence the bin bag)?
- Is the dog sitting on command for a picture to be taken?
- Does the sign outside the window change the narrative again, to suggest someone just bought the house and is cleaning up after the previous owners?
- Have the previous householders died, maybe they had mobility issues that prevented them from cleaning?
- Maybe the past owner was a hoarder?

The reality is our so-called intuition and bias will always blur a situation based on past experiences. This is why we have to take the extra step of trying to make sense of it through various points of view and not just one.

This involves using both qualitative and quantitative data. Without really taking the time to invest in a deep sense-making phase, we are simply making assumptions which ultimately end up in wasted resources and never getting to the answer of what the human pain points are. What actually is the situation with that house? What is the name of the dog?

By not taking the time to observe from the start of the suggested business problem, we risk looking incorrectly at the problem as a whole. Or worse still, looking at the wrong problem.

FOUR LEVELS OF OBSERVING

Think about the first time you ever met a hedgehog. Chances are, it was curled in a ball. Now if you didn't wait around or spy on him from afar, you would assume it was just a ball of spikes with no face. As soon as you move away and out of sight you will see that our little spikey friend not only has a face and little feet, but he's actually a fast little fellow.

Our people are no different to the hedgehog (minus, of course, the obvious).

Your people, like the hedgehog, will go about their day-to-day lives until they hit a problem. At this point, if the solution to this problem isn't clear, they will figure their own way around it over time. If you were to speak to them about the problem, they too would probably curl up and follow a process that does not work to keep them safe from getting into trouble with the 'process police'.

I have witnessed this many times before. It's very similar to the Instagram vs reality issue, where Instagram is this superficial process of what you think will work vs reality which is the process that doesn't work and which nobody is following. This then opens up a whole host of other problems – for example, security.

In order to get the right type of data and to uncover the ways in which people work around a problem, we need to do different types of research and data capture. I like to picture this as four distinct levels of observation.

Sense-making requires us to look at problems different to how others may see it. While there are many cool tools and approaches to do this at its foundation there are four lenses to it, I would recommend using all four where possible. These are:

- Intimate
- Active
- Distant
- External

Intimate

This type of approach can provide not only verbal insight but visual insight too. We get to hear from the horse's mouth their thoughts, ideas, frustrations, and often in 121 interviews, mini focus groups.

It can also be a great opportunity to hear what solution the person is already doing as a workaround and something we can present back in our findings as a potential scalable option or at least use it for the Insightful Ingredient in the incubate phase. If done correctly, it can allow a person to feel comfortable and at ease. For example, it can be done in the person's own environment if requested. It could also be done in a group as well as on a one-to-one basis.

The advantage of carrying this out on a one-to-one basis is that people are more inclined to share when they are not being judged by managers or peers. The disadvantage, however, is that it can be somewhat narrow on insights and tends to be pretty subjective. It can also prove at times to be resource-heavy. If carried out incorrectly, cues, such as nods, may cause you as the interviewer to influence the interviewee. If done in a small room, it can sometimes feel intimidating and like an interrogation.

If this insight is done as a group, be mindful of things such as groupthink and dominant voice takeover. Both of these things can completely take over and give rise to unreliable results. Being able to manage the group effectively is key to ensuring you gain the most valuable insights.

Active

This type of research and observation is great for allowing us to observe people in the flow of work or facing a particular daily struggle. If shadowing them, for example, we get to ask real-time questions such as:

- "Why did you do that?"
- "What was that action you just did?"
- "Why did you choose to do that?"

It's great for allowing us to understand people's habits, rituals, and behaviours and also puts the onus on them. Journaling, for example, is a great way to capture people's thoughts and feelings, and can be done in real time or later when at home. Using a mobile device for real time capture is fantastic for allowing us to see a full journey in action.

However, there are always downsides. For example, unless shadowed for a long period of time it can sometimes be easy for the person to act differently and mask what they would normally do with what they expect the correct 'process to be'. This is often called the Hawthorne Effect. This is why it is important, where possible, to shadow for a longer period of time. This allows any smoke and mirrors to slowly fall and trust to be built, which over a period of time will expose typical habits.

A QUICK STORY – EVP

A while back, I was leading my team on an EVP redesign for a household appliance company. The company wanted to keep ahead of the times and remain fresh in the market and wanted to redesign the EVP from the ground up. We went through six weeks of sense-making, ranging from 121 interviews, focus groups, surveys, large hotshops using AI to really understand what the current EVP meant to its employees and what makes it special to work at the organisation.

Two of the other approaches we took were digital diaries and tagalongs. Using this combination allowed us to obtain a full 360 view of employee life and gave us a clearer idea of the first-hand human pains faced by employees. The full view involved everything from getting into the office right through to the large queues at the coffee stand. We got to see some of the benefits and perks that were really loved, hear some of the stories that made them proud to be at the organisation, as well as understand some of the fears they had when it came to difficult conversations and personal development.

We were able to identify and get under the hood of some of the employees' pain points when it came to working remotely, the onboarding, and the opportunity platforms such as an internal gig platform. We found that while the business wanted a collaboration space, the narrative and processes in place were preventing them from the change they wanted to see.

We took a different approach with digital diaries, moving from a traditional approach to instead giving the audience tasks to complete. These ranged from capturing an emotion map throughout the day, turning WhatsApp into a shoutbox (think of it as a blackhole where people can vent out or share the feel good moments), recording a podcast with a friend, using Microsoft Viva as a snapshot into their digital lives, as well as breaking down their Hows (how they work), Wows (moments and things they love in work that give them energy and they truly care about), and Cows (moments and things they hate that take their energy or bug them).

When it comes to doing any form of active insight, in fact for any insight, trust needs to be established as activities such as journaling may involve logging some raw emotive thoughts and feelings. Clearly explaining what you will do with the journals, who will and will not have access to them, and how you will destroy them afterwards is critical for success. As with the intimate vision type described previously, active insight can be costly in both time and resource but can return big on insight.

Distant

This is a great way of helping to understand the interactions, not just of the person but of the environment, people, and props around them. This allows us to see the bigger picture of experiences and unconscious habits. For example, I do this whenever I put the empty milk bottle back in the fridge – I am unaware that I'm even doing it until it's pointed out to me (... various times).

Distant insight can be somewhat cheaper and can be done under the radar to remove the pressure people may feel from having someone watch over them. The downside to this, of course, is that you don't get real time feedback and you don't get to ask them why they performed a particular action. I prefer this approach when I want to passively observe and see how exchanges happen. This can be observing services, products, or information. However, be mindful that you don't want to appear as some creep. There is also debate around whether this is an ethical thing to do.

I tend to think surveys also fit in this category, even though surveys provide a weak data set. Surveys tend to be something that are sent out and completed at a distance and all you can really do is review the answers, especially if the answers are de-identified.

INSIGHTFUL INGREDIENT

This number one innovation company IDEO brings a unique touch when it comes to hiring, to make the experience a little nicer from day one. Recruiters will tease out questions such as 'What are your favourite sweets/chocolate?' in passing conversation. Should the newbie get hired, on day one their desk is covered in their favourite snacks and small messages from the team welcoming them to the company.

#DANNYDISCUSSIONS

What comes to mind when reading about this?

....

....

....

....

....

....

....

....

....

....

....

....

....

....

External

When carrying out deep sense-making, it helps to look outside of the business or industry and ask 'How are others dealing with a similar challenge?' Not only does this give you a mental rest from being deep in the weeds, it also allows you to get a perspective on the challenge at hand. Often the first thing I would see happen here is that people would tend to look externally but only ever at the nearest competition. For example, if you work for a traditional financial services (FS) company and you get asked to look at what others are doing I imagine the first port of call would be to look at the hip folk who are doing FS differently such as Monzo, Tide, Revolut, etc. Don't get me wrong, that is a good starting point, however, to really bring fresh perspective to the challenge we need to go above and beyond this a little.

While working on a culture project for a telecoms company, a couple of themes and questions started to bubble up around psychological safety, such as how to create trust, how to allow people to feel safe to speak up. Of course, to start to investigate this the first place to go would be to Google. A simple search and perhaps you would get some framework to look at which is fine. However, I first like to get some new insight into the challenge from other areas. To do this, I break down the theme into elements and questions that make up psychological safety such as:

1. How do we allow people to own up to mistakes and not be fearful of repercussions
2. How can we make it safe for others to raise their hand if they don't understand and don't want to ask what they feel is a daft question
3. How can we share learning and thoughts and failures
4. How can others share their learning and thoughts
5. How is respect, affective trust, understanding demonstrated. What rituals are in place and why

I would then map the above questions and elements down the right side of the matrix.

I then ask myself:

- Who deals with these elements in a day-to-day situatio… what does that look like
- Where outside of my professional life do these elements show up
- What other alternative professionals have these challeng…
- Who would be the subject matter experts (SMEs)

When referring to subject matter experts, I just mean peopl… have an in-depth knowledge or experience in dealing with these elements, they don't need to have qualifications coming out of their eyes. I then push the boat out and ask who may have unique experiences with these elements and questions. This will provoke a whole arrangement of different people from different walks of life. Capture a list of them as we are now going to drop them on to the Meddling Matrix.

MEDDLING MATRIX

The Meddling Matrix is a simple grid matrix like the one below. Across the top is where you would map the list you just created of people from all walks of life who may have the same challenge around how to build trust. For example, this could be:

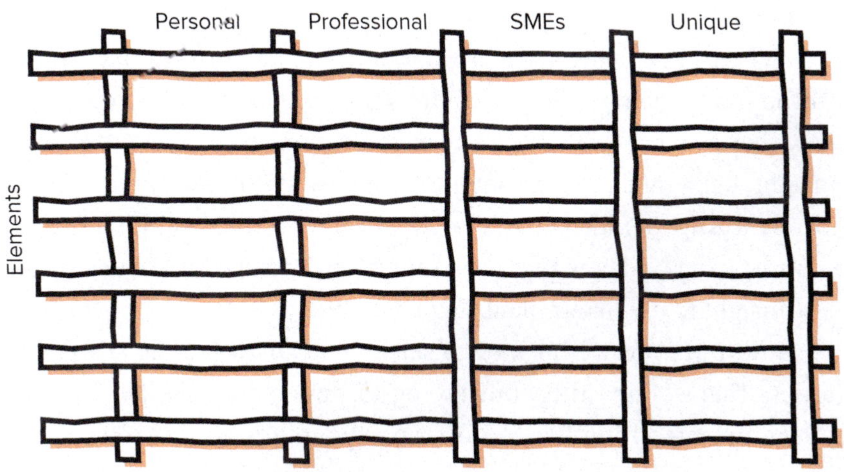

- Priests
- Soldiers
- Direct competitors
- Organisers of private sex parties
- Sex workers/dominatrixes
- Therapists
- Facilitators of meetings such as Alcoholics Anonymous (AA) or The Dinner Party meetings (a group focused on making it easier for people who are going through trauma or loss to have a safe community where they can have candid conversations and get support).

Down the left of it is the specific question and theme of the challenge you have identified i.e.

- How might we allow people to own up to mistakes and not be fearful of repercussions
- How might we share learning, thoughts, and failures

Once done, you should have a Matrix full of external, internal, and unique experts and a list of very specific questions you want insight on around how they deal with a similar challenge in the context of their world.

Where possible we want to follow a similar approach as mentioned in the immersion section, trying to walk in their shows, understand how they do what they do, try and mimic it as an experiment to get real insight. Remember, we are not going into solution mode here. We are merely trying to understand how they deal with the specific challenge you are facing, and how they overcome it, with a hope we can take away new insight to use in our incubate phase later.

Now, I am not telling you to set up your own private sex party (unless that's your thing) but trying to understand the tensions of setting up something like a dinner party and discussing some deep topics will give you bags of experience. Understanding how a priest or

AA facilitator builds up the trust, so that people can raise their hands and share how they feel, is worth its weight in gold.

(I know psychological safety is a whole big can of worms and for this activity, I have condensed the list. If you want to know more about psychological safety, I highly recommend checking out Amy Edmondson's work.)

SOCIAL LISTENING

Another option is to look at how you are perceived by external folk, this insight can be grabbed from places like Indeed, Glassdoor. However, there are various services available that will do social listening for you. This is one of the most insightful tools, I invested in building my own social listening tool that listens on Twitter, Reddit, Glassdoor, and so forth.

Using machine learning for just a few short minutes, I get rich insight into what the perception is of a brand and how people feel about them. Also, the types of words and language used, the emotions in the language, if it is envious, joyful, happy, angry, etc.

This type of insight is one of the most underused approaches I've seen, yet the insight it brings is a unique tilt to the challenge.

DESIGNING A SENSE-MAKING APPROACH

No matter which level we approach capturing data and insight, we need to be mindful of the audience, their environment, and the questions we are asking. Over the next few pages, I will share the foundation and guardrails when putting a sense-making approach in place, including some tips and tricks. The first point is ... always be thinking about the:

- Audience
- Environment
- Questions

Audience

One of the biggest tripwires when it comes to doing sense-making is sticking with what we know unconsciously. It goes without saying, we should always try to get a mixed sample audience. But what do I mean by this?

At a very high level, your audience will have its averages and its extremes. Everything that involves people will have this; think of Brexit or the presidential campaigns in the United States. Our goal is to work with them right across that spectrum to get a fair and representative sample.

This approach will give us insights into their worlds, while these insights tend to be more novel and extreme, often it is where the aha moments are. Taking a fair and honest sample rate will lead to a much more inclusive design approach down the line. Identifying extremes can be super easy, or at times, prove quite challenging. You could identify extremes via demographic for example, but I recommend taking a more behavioural approach.

Let's say, for example, I was asked to solve a problem with attrition. I would first work with the HR team and management to have a look at what their raw data is showing me. Using the HR data will not only help highlight the extremes, but it will also slowly start to shine a light on any unseen patterns such as a large percentage of people leaving one specific area, function, or even manager.

I would also look for the people that show great behaviour with attendance, as well as those who have not. Any form of recent data (last two months) is vital. As well here, I am thinking, pulse check data, great place to work data, Glint, and CultureAmp are all great tools that provide this, but it could be as simple as survey data. (Remember before you check the data, check the questions asked were not leading the witness to answer in a certain way.)

Using the data collected will hopefully allow you to zoom in to see which area, function, or manager is doing well to keep a low rate of attrition, while another manager or function seems to be doing the opposite. Here we can start to ask ourselves 'why': how is it that one person has managed to come up with a way of successfully addressing this problem while another hasn't? Then use this to slowly direct where to look next.

This will allow us to start asking bigger questions about the patterns we are seeing. We can now look more closely at another selection of our audience via the different types of roles, i.e. managers, customers, and stakeholders. Interviewing the general audience as opposed to the extreme will help uproot some insight for sure, but this insight is of course ... well, general. This isn't necessarily a bad thing, especially if the same thing keeps reoccurring.

If I was to look at the attrition rate of a business struggling to keep its staff, a simple early start sample of people I would want to look at and speak with could look like the following:

- People who never have a day off and have been in the business a while, what makes them different to everyone else, is their working world different
- People who are pretty much never in
- Past leavers – regretted and non-regretted leavers
- Manager who demanded their team to be in the office
- Managers who work hybrid

Environment

Picking the right environment is just as important, if not more so, than picking the right audience.

If you're doing face-to-face interviews, I have found walking in nature to be a massive help. Alternatively, you could go with an environment of their choice. Just make sure it's not too distracting and that it's somewhere they feel safe to share insight (with no fear of being overheard by surrounding ears).

In the past, I have seen people not wanting to share insight in a room booked out by the business, only to find myself tapped on the shoulder later by those same people explaining that they didn't want to be too specific as the walls in the meeting room are thin. They've informed me that they didn't want to be overheard in case the powers that be were in there.

No matter how much you set the scene at the start of interviews, be mindful of the space where they are happening and ask yourself: if this was you, would you be comfortable enough to share specific details on systems, processes, and even people in a room like this? If there is any doubt that the environment would prevent people sharing, then there is no doubt you should look at changing the environment, even if that means taking them to a coffee shop away from work people.

Depending on the project and the insight you're wanting to capture, sometimes the environment can't be changed (for example, a home or social space). Also, depending on the type of observation we want to do, actually not changing the environment is the very thing we need to do when it comes to active and distant observation, especially if we want an honest representation of what it is like in their world. If people are fearful of being overheard or of certain meeting rooms because of thin walls that observation wouldn't have been captured if we had taken them out for a walking interview.

A QUICK STORY – MOUNTAIN GORILLAS

In 1973, *National Geographic* released its documentary The Mountain Gorilla, which told the story of zoologist Dian Fossey's observation, understanding, and interactions with the great apes of Central Africa.

This study ran from 1967 to 1972. Dian spent over 2,000 hours observing these gorillas in their natural habitat, understanding their unique personalities by mimicking their daily routines and actions, and examining the social dynamics and hierarchy at play. She was even known to beat her chest like the apes.

Unfortunately, Dian also observed the dark side of this experience: the ongoing battle between these apes and poachers. She got to understand the frustrations of the animals, the poachers, and farmers alike.

Dian was known to have some very unorthodox and at times

extreme approaches to scaring off these poachers. One of my favourites of these tactics was that she would wear a mask and trick them into thinking she was a witch to scare them off. She'd clearly acquired a great understanding of the poachers to know exactly what would freak them out.

Sir David Attenborough, who was part of the filming of the original documentary, has gone on to say: "If anyone could say they have saved a species, I think Dian could."

Thanks to Dian's infinite patience, hard work, and detailed notes we have come to know a lot more than we ever did before about these beautiful beasts. It also set into action a blueprint of deep observation and understanding which, even to this day, we see on programmes such as Blue Planet and Seven Wonders: Our Planet.

While I wouldn't go so far as to call us all silverback apes, the power of observing people in their environment is critical to understanding any pattern and frustration that may not be seen at first glance.

Questions

One of the biggest skills in any role (or life in general) is questioning. When it comes to trying to make sense of a challenge and trying to understand where your people are struggling, questioning is the biggest yet one of the most under-practised skills. I personally think we lose this skill over time due to two key experiences:

- **Curious child** – throughout school, we have a deep desire to make sense of the world around us. One of the fastest ways to do this is through experimentation. That is, until a child learns to speak then they use the next power sense-making tool, asking 'why?' ... a lot.

  I imagine this could be annoying for some teachers and parents when asked 'why?' for the 100th time. Unfortunately, not all teachers are given the luxury of time to feed this courageous curiosity (one of my many hates about the school system) and often I can imagine this why, why, why can wear thin for parents when they are trying to cook dinner, pay the bills, work longer hours ... It is not unusual for parents to cut the 'why' conversation short with a 'it just is' response. As time goes by, if we are not careful, this courageous curiosity slowly starts to disappear as we move into adulthood.

- **Annoying adult** – then we get into our work lives and what little curiosity is left with us we don't apply at the risk of annoying the people in the room. We don't want to look daft or seem like we don't know what we are talking about to other adults in the room, so we avoid asking why. It amazes me how many people will leave a call and suffer in ambiguity rather than just asking why.

We should all get back to feeling comfortable and empowered enough to ask the question as often as needed to gain the insight.

Questioning is a huge skill and, like any other, it needs to be practised a lot and be refreshed even more so. In fact, people like Warren Berger are now classed as a 'questionologist', which is basically a person who has mastered the art and science of questioning. Warren in his book of beautiful questions covers the many different types of questions which I would highly recommend. However, when we talk about questioning, I always try to revert back to some simple principles:

- Keep it simple
- Keep it conversational
- Keep it honest

KEEP IT SIMPLE

While we know there are many types of questioning such as probing, checking, clarifying, multiple, rhetorical, open and closed, using them correctly and branching them together is where the magic happens. When I say branching, I mean follow ups.

The last thing you want to do is craft a question and have a sneaky second question slide in before the interviewee has had time to answer the first ... sounds simple eh? The difference in any good interview is how they structure questions one at a time and wait for an answer before they follow up and ask a second one.

I would bet a chocolate bar that it happens on nearly every podcast as well. The majority of question types we would find ourselves using would be open, closed, probing.

Let's break these down.

What do you think of open questions?

Like what I did there? Open questions are a great question type to obtain a broad perspective on things. They can provide the first layer of how a person engages with the world and the challenges they face. These questions tend to lead to a wider conversation and are a great way to start building rapport with your people. After all, it is near impossible to say 'yes' or 'no' without the conversation feeling awkward, unless that initial rapport hasn't been established.

Open questions tend to be used throughout a conversation but are particularly effective when used right at the start. When it comes to open questions and simplicity, I like to use the analogy of six bums on a goal post:

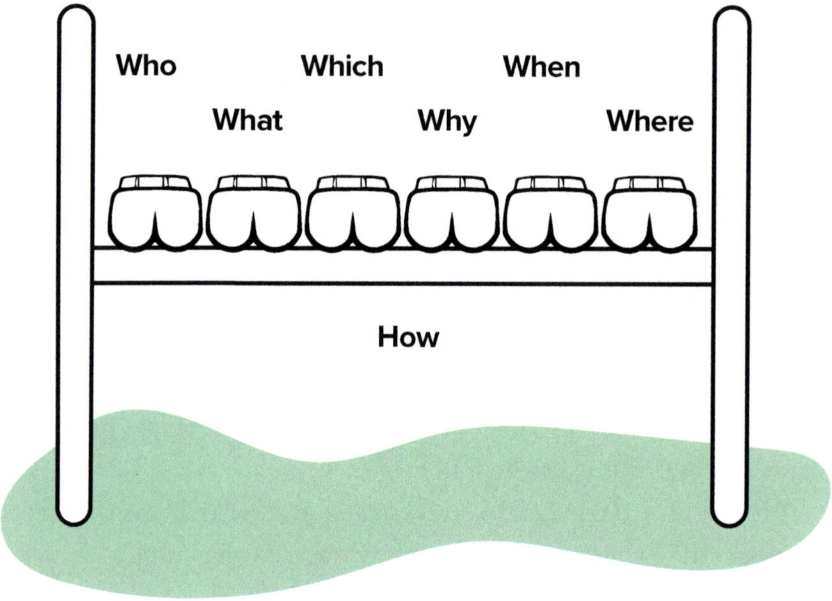

Who, What, Which, Why, When, Where ... and then, of course, we have How.

You can use these simple types of questions in any form of interview and it will provide a much richer and fuller answer from the interviewee than a simple one word. For example:

- **What** does your typical day look like
- **Why** did you decide to apply for that role
- **How** did the experience feel

Probing questions

These do pretty much what they say on the tin: they allow you to focus and dig a little deeper into an aspect of the conversation. This slowly moves us from a very broad understanding to a narrower understanding of a certain area. Again, we need to keep things simple.

These fall into TED questions:

Tell me, Explain to me, Demonstrate/Describe to me.

So, following on from the question where we asked:

"What does your typical day look like?"

A great follow up to that could be:

"Tell me more about your commute to work."

Perhaps a follow up to "**Why** did you decide to apply for that role?" might be:

"Explain how you applied for that role or describe to me a little bit more about the interview process."

I love using TED questions because nearly every time the response is rich in data, what they are seeing, doing, feeling. All these little data points are breadcrumbs for you to pick up and follow. This is why actively listening is vital.

You don't always have to start with TED. In fact, another quick tip I picked up if you want to dig in more without saying 'tell me, explain, describe' is simply by saying the last few words back to them or the impactful words. For example, they may say something like:

"Yeah the interview process was quick and stuff but I left the room feeling a bit daft."

Simple following up with: "You left the room feeling a bit daft?" signals you want more detail.

Closed questions

Closed questions tend to be answered with a single word or very short phrase such as 'Yes', 'No' or 'That's correct'. These are great questions to use when needing to check or clarify something or when collecting data. Be careful, however, if used incorrectly they can be an instant conversation stopper.

So, to continue the example above, where we have asked them about the experience of the interview, a simple closed question could be:

Would you want to go through the interview process again?

Hopefully, you see that the start of the funnel is big open questions, but as we move down the funnel with the conversation, we start to be more specific with the TED questions. And finally, we have some closed questions to finish it off.

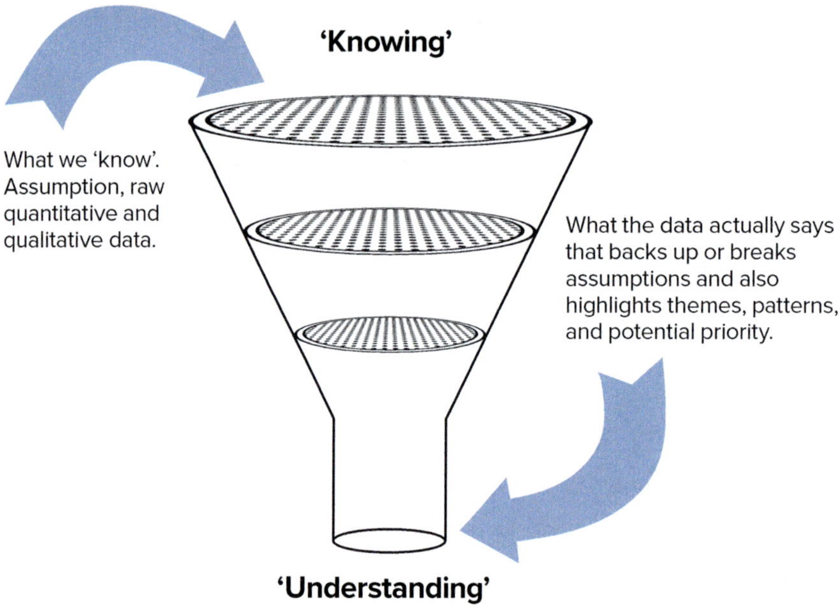

In the real world, true organic conversations don't follow a linear process. If anything, they ebb and flow and move between the open, closed, descriptive type questions. This is the reason why we must get out into the field and apply the skills. However, to get a feel of people who are great at this, grab a piece of paper and put on your favourite podcast. Now, actively listen and write down the type of questions they ask. I bet you a mixed bag of sweets, it will be a selection of the question types mentioned above.

QUICK ACTIVITY

1. Write down on a sticky note the name of someone famous.
2. Now, do it again on another sticky note.
3. Without showing the sticky note, ask a friend to play two games of 'Guess Who'.

4. Explain to them that in round one, they can only ask you questions. Time how long it takes for them to get the answer by answering with closed answers i.e. 'Yes', 'No' or 'That's correct' and how many questions they had to ask to get there.
5. Now with round two, using a different famous person, explain that they can use both open and closed questions. Again, your task here is to answer the questions and time the activity and see how many questions it takes. The only thing they can't ask, which is fair game, is 'tell me who you are' – that would spoil all the fun, right.

KEEP IT CONVERSATIONAL ... BUT HOLD A PAUSE

As mentioned, if you listen to any good podcasts or interviews, the chances are it doesn't sound like an interview but more like a story. A lot of the time, this is down to time served in honing their skills. I can hear it myself when I listen to the first few episodes of my Mindchimp podcast in Season One compared to episodes in Season Two: it's worlds apart.

While this isn't a book on how to create a podcast, I do think that there is some value in sharing what I've learnt so far in how to make an interview feel more like a lovely conversation. The reality is that with most conversations it tends to be a two-way street, where people share ideas, views, and opinions. However, when doing this type of sense-making, we have to be careful not to lead the people we are chatting to with our own ideas.

I have found that great conversations in this type of situation consist of:

Trust

It's a really easy one to overlook, but let's just walk in the user's shoes for a second. Perhaps the business sent them an email or DM about them being interviewed for something the business is working on and their name is being put forward.

It's the same with podcasting – I ask the guest to come on the show sometimes out of the blue. However, I tend to send them over a document them prepare. This document script is something I use for build-rust with interviewees before we get into the interview, I have apted the approach here for you to apply in a work situation:

- I thank them for agreeing to be part of the interview or letting me shadow them. I then ask them if they know much about me and why I am here ... they always say no!
- I explain that the business is looking at 'X' or how to make 'X' and that they want true insight that isn't biased. I will explain a little about me and the person who may be taking the notes in the room.
- I get consent to record. If they say no, that's fine. If they say yes, that's fine too. I will then explain that we are using this to help make sure we capture everything that is said and it allows us to be more present in the chat. I send a clear cue that the business will not see this video footage (pre-agreed with business, never ever break this agreement).
- I explain that the transcriber is taking notes, but that these notes have no names or distinguishing details. This is about capturing as much honest and open feedback as possible. I let the interviewee know they are more than welcome to see the notes when we have finished.
- I then hand over to the notetaker in the room, who talks a little about himself. I explain he may have the odd question too.

I then drop in a joke about me being from up north, or the UK, and explain that I do speak fast, so not to worry if they need me to repeat anything or reword it. This patter does change a little sometimes. I often find myself introducing my dog Rufus or how it always rains in Manchester. You will find a way to make this your own, it's just about making them feel at ease and that they can trust you but also letting them know what is going to happen.

- I then go on to ask the guest about themself. Usually, I use this statement: "So yeah, enough about me ... tell me about you?"

Using this question stops it feeling like a work interview and more like a chat. Try it and let me know how you find it.

Genuine interest by pausing

If you are not interested in what what your audience is saying or doing, or you find yourself getting fatigued, your audience will see it a mile off. I would recommend swapping roles with your note-taker for a mini breakand never ever do back-to-back interviews.

So what's the difference between listening and active listening? Well, it's a bit like reading, for example did you notice in the last paragraph I use the word 'what' twice? Maybe that is because you will skim-read, however, if it jolted you then chances are you were actively reading.

Listening and active listening is no different. Let's assume you're in a little office or meeting room. It probably feels quiet, but if I ask you to stop reading for a second and listen, perhaps you start to hear the noise from the aircon. In that moment, you've moved from listening to active listening. Often interviewing is as much about good questions as it is about actively listening to the answer and knowing when to hold a pause or not.

You will need to get comfortable with being uncomfortable, not to rush in to fill silences. If you listen, often it flows as question › answer › question ... however, with active listening it tends to be question › answer › active listening and pause › more answer › question.

Have a listen to any podcast or any great TV interview show and listen for the silences: we all want to rush in and fill it as we perceive any lapse in conversation as awkward, but it really isn't. A lot of the time your audience is perhaps going through some internal dialogue. Maybe this person is thinking: "Do I share this or don't I?" By rushing in to fill that silence, you could have missed out on some vital insight. Bear in mind that sometimes people just need time to find and form the answer.

Getting in the field and practising is something you must do, you can't simply read a book (like this) and think you've mastered it. I honestly believe one of my show's strengths in getting people to share more than normal is just down to not filling the silences, using active listening and simple language – that's it.

Be approachable and honest with your team

Be you ... that's it, honestly. Don't go in pretending to be some hotshot researcher or cool consulting hero. Go in and have fun with it. Don't be afraid to show some personality (unless that personality is one of a 5x5 piece of timber; in that case, you'd better get someone else to lead on the interviews).

Just be you, be accountable and have an agreement with your scriber in the room. There are times when you're in such rapport with someone that you can end up leading them: it could be simple things such as nods on cue, leading with questions or things such as saying, 'I agree'. If you want to see this in action go to any coffee shop and watch two people (who aren't playing on their phones), and you will see it by the bucketload.

Prior to any interviews, set up a simple agreement with your wing person, agree they have a job to do, and if they notice any leading happening then implement things such as a 'safe word' or perhaps suggest a 2 min break, or a simply a loud chair move. Whatever it is, set it up before the interviews.

INSIGHTFUL INGREDIENT

Dyson has teamed up with Warwick University to offer a unique opportunity for aspiring engineers! This 4-year programme combines an on-campus academic study with real-world experience at Dyson's headquarters. While you're there, you'll work alongside experienced engineers on exciting projects and get paid a salary that increases each year. Plus, you won't have to pay any tuition fees. This programme is a great way to kickstart your engineering career and get connected with the Dyson brand.

#DANNYDISCUSSIONS

What comes to mind when reading about this?

....

....

....

....

....

....

....

....

....

....

....

BRILLIANT BASICS

Okay, buckle up as I am about to give you what I would say is the most basic in sense-making that I've seen done wrong so many times. Get these right and you will become a master sense-maker.

Intimate – Interviewing

Ever been in an interview and the person across the table has asked you a question like, 'Tell me a time when (insert something competency-wise)?' In that minute, your brain decides to reboot and it feels like an eternity before it fires back up and you can answer.

What can you do as an interviewer in order to not make it awkward or painful? It's all about having some structure in place but allowing the flexibility for the conversation to go where it needs to go. Before going into any interview, first I step right back and ask myself some simple questions. What's the stuff I don't know about the situation, what's the stuff I don't know the answers to, what's the output I need from this interview. When you start to reverse engineer the potential interview experience, questions will slowly start to bubble up.

My approach is to never go in with a list of questions from 1–20 and just work through them. It makes the conversation feel transactional and very robotic. Remember, this is supposed to be a safe space, not an interrogation. I try to go in with a cluster of questions, key points, and themes. All spread out, visible for me on a Miro board as a form of mind map. This allows me to naturally bounce across different questions and topics, should the interview go that way. (Interestingly, this is also how I prep for when I am getting interviewed). I have tried various ways to map out my interview questions from lists, bubbles, ladders, and mind maps. Go with whatever approach works for you as long as it keeps the conversation feeling natural.

Be mindful of the situation and context and adapt the interviews accordingly. Perhaps you're looking at recruitment, a checkout experience, wellbeing, or onboarding. I like asking about past experience first. Usually, I will use a simple tool that presents a timeline and emotion map like below. This timeline would consist of key milestones, so for something like onboarding that might be from job acceptance to the end of three months in the business and everything in between. I present the timeline at some point in the interview and ask them to plot how they felt throughout the onboarding.

Emotional Map

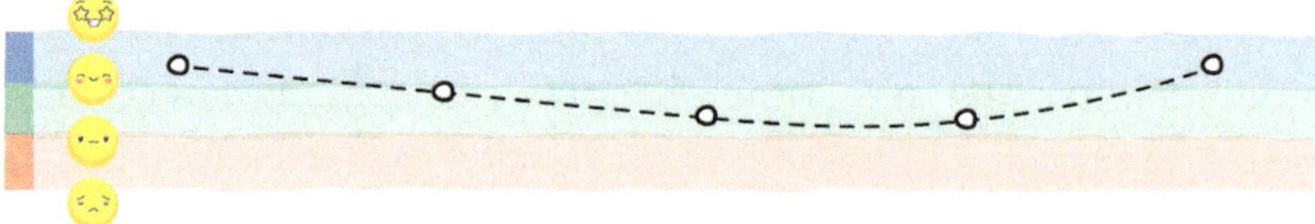

Below is a 101 checklist approach to setting up and getting the best out of your interviews. Of course, I haven't added specific questions because this ultimately depends on what you are interviewing for.

Pre:

- Pick the right sample of people (including extremes and stakeholders)
- Decide on the environment (e.g. meeting room, out on a walk, own environment)
- Adjust for natural lighting and heating (in the case of the meeting room)
- Change furniture layout to feel less formal and more conversational
- Decide on the key touch points the conversation should cover
- Agree wing wo/man's role (including what action they should take if they notice any 'leading' or tiredness during the interview
- Set up and test video and audio recording equipment
- Ensure you have a supply of spare chargers, batteries, and memory cards
- Turn phones off, or put them on silent – remember, full attention is needed here
- Pen and paper (taking notes in this way is less distracting).

The conversation (Stage 1)

- Welcome the person
- Introduce yourself and your wing wo/man
- Ask if they know why they are here
- Explain the reasons for the interview
- Explain how the conversation will go, including how long it will take
- Confirm they are okay with video and audio being used
- Reassure them that they will be able to view any notes taken at the end and that any identifying details will be left out or removed
- Ask if they have any questions.

The conversation (Stage 2)

- Ask them what a day in their life looks like at the organisation. Note their reactions when talking about processes, rituals, and experiences (remember to ask open questions – what, when, where, who, which, why, and how)
- Guide the conversation through key points using open and TED (Tell, Explain, Describe) questions, displaying curiosity throughout. The trick isn't to 'lead' the interviewee, but to guide them to one of your key points for discussion
- Use closed questions to clarify and confirm.

The conversation (Stage 3)

- Finish on a positive (e.g. "I really appreciate and value your time and support on this.")
- Ask your wing wo/man if they have any follow up questions
- Ask your interviewee if there is anything else they would like to add that may not have been covered
- Ask the interviewee if they have any questions they want us to clear up
- Ask the interviewee if they would like to see the notes taken
- Ask if you could follow up with the interviewee later
- Give the interviewee your email address in case they wish to add anything later
- Confirm your next steps.

Immediately post-interview:

- Get outside for some fresh air, especially if you have another interview soon
- Discuss with wing person anything they found interesting (including whether they was any leading or tiredness showing)
- Back up digital copies of audio and video
- Set up for the next one.

Note: While this is based on an in-person conversation, it doesn't mean that this can't be done virtually. However, bear in mind that things such as screen sharing, recording, data capture, and note-taking will all need to be facilitated using applications such as Zoom, Google Drive, or OneNote and Teams. The interviewee will be able to choose their own environment in this context, but make sure you advise them to select somewhere quiet and free from distractions.

INTIMATE – JOURNALING/DIARY STUDIES

Would you look at someone's diary if it was just left out and there was no chance of you getting caught? Oh I know you would, you devil you. Well, in some way, Diary Studies are just like that only you have consent to do so.

It is one of the quickest ways to understand someone's inner thoughts and feelings, expressed in their own words and sentiments. Plus, you not having to be there also makes it pretty easy to scale over time with a larger audience. Oh and it's less costly than other approaches. It is important to know that the real value in these studies is the length of time in which they should run. Ideally, if you're trying to track if something happens over time, aim for days and maybe weeks rather than minutes and days.

I find journaling a great way for me to look at something over a set period of time, for example whenever I start a new role, I always capture the first few months and use this at the end of a three-month period to determine how happy I am in the role, how my emotions have been, and if I want to stay. Now imagine if I had to capture that every day with someone sat over my shoulder watching me.

There are various ways to journal, and of course they don't always need to be pen and paper – a private blog or app are also ideal. The key, I find when using journals, is to be very clear from the start about what it is you want to capture versus not capture.

Depending on what I am capturing, my typical approach would involve setting up some agreed guardrails and ways of working with the participant. We will look at when and how to capture, how we will communicate, as well as tools to log the data. The tools could be a notepad, an actual diary, or something more digital – usually, this is all set up in a 121 beforehand.

I also like to include some challenges in the journal approach. This could be taking pictures of X, Y, Z. It could also be what your calendar looks like, your working space, desktop layout. After all, a picture is worth a thousand words and you will be amazed what you can pull from it later on in the interviews and debrief.

You could use apps such as Google Drive or OneDrive and set each participant up with a unique document for them to sign into and capture their thoughts. You could even fill that document with prescribed questions to trigger their reflections. Being clear from the get-go on how you are going to use this insight and who will have access to it is vital for establishing trust. Once the period of data capture has passed, it is worth booking some time in to go over it.

However, as with most other tools, capturing data from your audience via a journal does have its downsides on an individual level. If we explain in too much detail, or not enough, then there is a risk of adding bias or failing to offer enough context on the task at hand. Without sufficient reminders, there is also a risk that our audience may forget the task until the last minute and then quickly fill in the gaps. By not explaining that a journal can be done via bullet points, emoji reflections, or drawings, we could be indirectly adding pressure on to someone who isn't as comfortable with writing or is a person with dyslexia, for example.

It is worth pointing out to the participant what will happen to these journals once they have served their purpose at the end. The next big task is pulling all the data in and looking to see what trends are happening across our participants. How to do that is coming up in the next chapters.

Below is a simple checklist on setting up the journal so you get the biggest bang for your buck:

- Set the scene of the challenge and provide sufficient context
- Explain who will see this insight and who will not

- Explain how the insight will be used and how the journals will be destroyed or stored
- Choose the methods of journaling (e.g. pen and paper, blog, drawing, shared drive)
- Set a clear period of capture and end date (e.g. 3 days, 2 weeks, 1 month)
- Add prescribed questions or a guide on how to fill out the journal if confused. Reassure the individual that there is no right or wrong way to capture
- Set up regular nudges if activity is not completed and check in regularly
- If the journal is completed in a traditional manner, make sure to get the delivery address and return postage if required
- Make sure the individual is aware of who to contact if a journal becomes lost or damaged, and for any other business regarding the task

ACTIVE – MOBILE CAPTURE

I love mobile capture, for me it blends some of the best bits of the intimate lens while also being able to have some fun with it. You can suggest the usual stuff like tracking how tasks and activities are done but it can also be less about tasks and more around understanding their work over a longer period of time similar to journals. The strength of mobile capture is its flexibility and the data is often received in real time.

Using a mobile-first approach is the way to go, mainly because in this day and age everyone pretty much has access to a smartphone and that tends to be where their eyes are fixed if not busy with something else. 'Fishing where the fish live', so to speak, tends to be one of the easiest ways to get something done – in this instance, capturing data.

Allowing your audience to use their own devices removes some of the friction that can be found in a more traditional approach. It allows people to capture their thoughts, ideas, frustration, and pain points in real time and in multiple ways. Mobile capture allows people to use the phone apps they are already using; for example, to take pictures of touch-points in their journey or to make videos of a day in their lives.

If set up correctly, you can make use of tools such as WeChat, WhatsApp, Facebook, Instagram, Twitter, Pinterest, Microsoft Teams. If you go down the route of a journal-type response, making use of applications such as Office 365 or Google Suite can not only make your life easier by keeping track of who is engaged and who isn't, but it will also allow people to quickly record information without disrupting their daily lives. While this approach can be scaled fairly easily, bear in mind that the greater the number of participants in an app such as WhatsApp, the higher the noise.

Top Tips on using Mobile Capture

1. Be clear on what data you want to obtain and even clearer on what you want your audience to capture. For example, if you want insight on one part of a user journey, you may only need people to record moments within that section. Not being clear on what you want your audience to consider could result in a lot of irrelevant data.
2. Ask your audience what applications they would prefer and if they say 'any', ask them to show you their front screen apps. The chances are, any app that is on their front screen is used a lot. Try to capture any mobile interview and journal within one of these apps, ask if they would be happy to use their device and this app of choice in a private group.

   Examples of groups might include:

   - Facebook – handy for group chat, one-to-one chats, private groups, and chatbot nudging
   - Instagram – perfect for pictures and text, stories, following hashtags, and short daily videos
   - Pinterest – useful for private boards based on interest or touchpoint
   - WhatsApp – great for community insight, reflection journals, private groups, and one-to-one chat

- Office 365 – includes video conferencing (Teams and Skype), cloud sharing, OneNote, OneDrive and forms
- Google Suite – pretty much the same as Office 365; this is just an alternative option.

A great mobile app I recommend is Daylio which is a bullet journaling app for self-care which allows you to add things such as goals, mood diaries, and a happiness tracker. It's a great app which I highly recommend, whether you want to track daily or just for supporting you during a new experience e.g. the first 90 days in a new role.

Once the tech has been selected, make sure you set up the various access rights. For example, you could have five groups of people using Google Drive which would require you to set up five separate folders, each with a digital journal. This could be a Google Doc or a form, all asking fixed questions.

Perhaps you'd like to include a link to a private Instagram account you've already set up that the user can use to capture images and videos throughout the day. How about a private WhatsApp code too? This could be used to bring users into a group, where they can freely ask any questions. This can also be used to nudge people if activity is slow or to discuss any repeat questions or pain points being mentioned.

Once all the data is in, you can start to map out any trends and patterns that occur. There are many tools and tech to use for this which I will provide at the end, but of course, feel free to map this out using a whiteboard, sticky notes, and pens if that's more your style.

ACTIVE – DO THE JOB

What people say they do vs what they actually do can often be very different. This isn't on purpose – it's just human nature to play things up or down. I find, in most cases, the best way to overcome this is to 'get in the weeds'. By this, I mean either shadowing the person or trying to walk in their shoes and do the job for a day. Thinking, feeling, and doing the things your sample audience would see is what we call 'contextual inquiry'.

The contextual data will bring in another level of detail, which allows you to not only understand your audience's environment, but also the experiences that occur within it. It brings with it the flexibility to ask questions in the flow of work and allows you to see first-hand how things are actually done.

The next level to this is to actually do the role and carry out tasks as a complete newbie. This is something I did at my previous employer when trying to understand customer complaints and at which point within the journey the call went from a mild call of displeasure to one of severe displeasure. This not only allowed me to get a better understanding of the role and the tasks that fall within it, but also made me experience similar emotions such as frustration, anger, and happiness just as the call handler would go through. It all comes back to having empathy and compassion with your audience and the customers.

It's important to note when shadowing that we are mindful of the 'Observer Effect' or 'Hawthorne Effect'. This is the risk that the person being observed changes their behaviour simply because they know they are being watched. It is always good to make clear who you are, what you're doing and why at a high level. After all, you don't want to tell them what you're looking for as this could cause their behaviour to change. You want a clear picture of the challenges and not one that is clearly exaggerated or based on Goldilocks, when everything is just right but nothing ever is.

Explain to them throughout that you may ask them various questions on why they did certain things and that you want them to simply do their role as they normally would. Your role here when researching is trying not to have an influence over the situation.

INSIGHTFUL INGREDIENT

Ben & Jerry's ice cream has a global activism strategy that aligns with the values and behaviours of their employees and addresses current politicised and social impact events. They have a dedicated team, led by a Head of Global Activism, who are always discussing the current social climate and taking action when they believe it is necessary. The team, made up of former non-governmental organisation (NGO) employees, uses their marketing expertise to support and amplify important causes. This strategy is also designed to appeal to and align with the values and behaviour of their future Gen Z employees.

#DANNYDISCUSSIONS

What comes to mind when reading about this?

....

....

....

....

....

....

....

....

....

....

....

....

DISTANT – SURVEYS

Surveys are great for targeting a large audience at a low cost, however, the data off the back of them rarely tends to be valuable. At best, it's a nice temperature check. A rule I follow is to use surveys when you have nothing else. They can provide a mixed bag of questions ranging from multiple-choice, open and closed questions, or those that involve a degree of measurement e.g. Net Promoter Scores (NPS).

However, as with most things, there are always weaknesses as well as strengths. This is why you should try to complement these with another form of insight, such as group interviews. In many organisations I've worked with they have suffered survey fatigue ... basically Microsoft forms now allow any person and their dog to create a survey. After your 10th survey around Susan's leaving do, it is fair to say you would be done with surveys. It's always worth asking yourself first; is this survey valuable or is it just pissing people off?

Below are a few tips on how to create a survey that won't trigger a mass brawl:

1. **Respect people's time.** It's likely that, like me, you feel as though you're getting pestered for surveys and reviews all the time (I have three in my inbox right now, in fact). If we're going to ask a customer to fill one out, we need to make damn sure we are efficient with their time, so make it short and snappy.

2. **Make use of data before deciding to write a question about it.** If you didn't know already, I have a podcast. I host it with a provider and they charge me every month. Now, if I was to do a survey to understand what my audience likes, I would be wasting their time by asking them questions such as, 'How do you listen to my podcast?' The reason?

   I can already find that data out on my dashboard provided from my hosting site. I didn't need to ask this question to find that out. Your audience's time is valuable and their attention span will be short with other distractions so don't waste it by asking questions you can get answers to elsewhere.

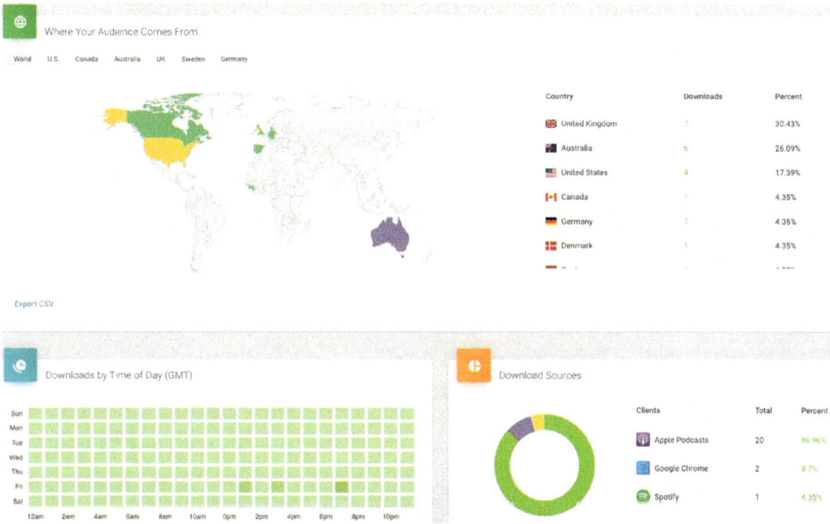

3. **Only ask the questions you actually want to know and that provide value.** Valuable vs interesting are two very different things when it comes to data collection. If it doesn't add value or if you're simply unsure, don't add it.

   A survey with 5 killer questions is better than a survey with 10 weak questions.

4. **Chunking.** Sometimes, being sent a survey containing 10 questions can be a real pain. However, if you send the same questions in smaller chunks through the day, it doesn't feel like as much hard work, especially if all they have to do is give numbers or one-word answers (e.g. NPS type questions, such as 'rate your advisor out of 10' or 'rate how happy you were with the service out of 10'). Chunk the questions up using a chatbot to push one question out a day. It instantly doesn't feel as time-consuming for the person filling out the survey again. Though don't assume you can just set up 20 questions now.

5. **Be clear.** Being clear and concise is key. Not only does it reduce an unnecessarily high word count in the survey, but it makes you more focused on what you're asking. Also be clear on the scoring system. Never change it mid-way through the survey e.g. asking someone to score the service from 1–10 with 1 being the worst and 10 being fab, then asking them, 'how would you rate the burger with 1 being the best and 5 being the worst?' It causes your brain to do mental gymnastics and often results in the employee answering the question wrong.
6. **Layman test ('Leah' test).** My niece Leah doesn't work in my industry at all but if I have to do a survey, I will always test it with her first. If she gets through it with no questions, then the chances are that an engineer filling it in about their industry shouldn't have a problem. Use simple language.
7. **Think of your audience**. Don't create surveys that aren't mobile-friendly (honestly ... don't). Most surveys like Google Forms, Microsoft Forms, or Survey Monkey are mobile friendly, but always check first. I did one a few months back where I had to keep zooming in and out. How is that even a thing in this day and age?
8. **Say thank you.** Thank your user for the time they took to fill out the survey. Whether it's 2 minutes or 10 seconds, show that you're grateful for them giving you their attention and try and leave them with a smile (I tend to leave them with a picture or a GIF, or a code to get a few coffees ... but don't tell them about the free coffee till the end. You will be amazed at how many people who are not important to your survey will fill it out for a freebie.

BUILDING A RESEARCH REPOSITORY

When it comes to sense-making, before you do any form of research you want to make sure you have a research repository set up. This might seem like a no-brainer right, but it is the one thing I've seen let research down more than anything else. Often, user data and insight is stored in an Excel file somewhere on someone's desktop.

Excel data also tends to be pretty static and hard to keep up to date or you may just be like me when you watch someone on it and think you are witnessing black magic for the first time. Your data and insight are not a one-use only kind of thing. You should be able to return back to these and use them to challenge future projects, identify themes between data sets, and so on.

What is a research repository?

Think of it as a one-stop shop for all your research data. Depending on how you set it up, if you are a consultant, an internal team, or a stakeholder, having a research repository is something you will come to love. The idea is to create this one place where all your research sits.

The research is organised often by project and mapped out by tags, it allows you or a team member to get to the past and current insight in quick time. It's also valuable when you have a stakeholder who is being restrictive on how much time you can invest in sense-making as it becomes the place to go for great secondary research for other projects later down the line.

However, it is only useful if it's set up right. Set it up wrong and you can find yourself in a rabbit hole worse than the ones you find yourself in on YouTube at 2 am. The good news is it isn't too hard to set one up that is useful from the start, you just need some good guidelines, principles, and of course governance. It's pretty straightforward to set up and the tech to do it is found in nearly every org around the world.

Tech needed to set up a research repository

I have played around with a few different research repository set ups. I've used paid for tech such as Dscout and Dovetail, I've used tech that the org already had in place such as Microsoft Teams, and G-suite, I've also used tech such as Notion and Obsidian. Each of these tech set ups has its pros and cons. If you have the money to spend, I recommend you check out Dscout and Dovetail, both are fantastic and not all that expensive. But for those who don't have the money let's jump into how you can create one.

Creating a research repository

First things first, when building a repository from scratch, all you really need to remember is that when stripped right back a repository is a journey with a folder structure similar to how you might set up folders on your desktop or mac. In order to have these folders, you're going to need a decent amount of storage to save all this good stuff too.

Your repository is going to hold lots of different types of data and insight such as videos, audio files, images, notes, prep docs, reports, etc. The last thing we want to do is build a repository and then release it, only to realise it can only go so big due to the storage capacity. Building it on something such as OneDrive, Gdrive, or any other cloud storage will allow you to scale up the space when needed without any backing up etc.

Having a good backend step up is vital for a repository but it's all a waste if the front end is ugly and hard to use.

The front end needs to allow people to come into the repository and get to where they need to go fast. This could be anything from Wiki pages to Sharepoints. If you're using something like Obsidian or Notion, think of it as a big landing page. The front end of any repository should really share what the repository is for, what you can do here, and some direct links to get to the big stuff.

It is easy to drop a lot of stuff on the landing page but honestly give it some thinking time and think about the people who will use this a lot. Why are they coming here? What do they need once you have them answered? They should become your main links.

Spoiler alert, often the links tend to be:

- **How to use this repository**
  This basically is what it says on a tin. Some brief copy about why this is here, how to get the most out of it, as well as who to speak to if you're struggling or bump into an issue/error.

- **Projects**
  This page should have all the completed or inflight projects.

With tools such as Notion and Obsidian, you can do some wizardry, which will allow you to turn this page into a nice landing page which gives you everything you need to know at a glance in a table e.g. who, what, when, and how.

Microsoft Teams roll-out of Loop will make the UX of building out a repository in Teams much slicker. As someone searching for the insight, you want to try and give them an update on its lifecycle, who was involved, the name of the project and any tags e.g. financial services, big pharma research, as well as tags showing the research type such as interviews, focus groups, and so on.

As someone coming to the repository, I should be able to find everything I need such as videos, audios, deliverables, notes from interviews, the interviewer's questions, and the research approach taken all in just a few clicks.

- **Guidelines, principles, and templates**
  This is more for the research team when they start a new project. Everyone using the same templates will allow the shelf life of the repository to last longer. I won't go into details of the templates to use as each business will do it differently, but having a good template for people to follow and as well as some guides and tick lists will make all the difference. Don't get caught short by not creating the resource your people will need to stick to a certain approach.

- **Tools and approaches**
  Again this is more a resource of guidance, but having a simple breakdown of the research method you use as well as a step-by-step guide on how to run them will help newbies when they come into a team and help keep a consistent approach. Anyone who isn't in the research field but wants to understand an approach taken on a past project can instantly make sense of it.

The biggest search engine in the world has one simple search bar. Where possible, try to make the experience as slick as the tech you use outside of work.

Couple of things to be mindful of when creating a research repository:

- A research repository is for everyone, not just the design team. The more research that goes in and follows a standard approach the more value that will come out ... so give access to others.
- As much as I've seen these repositories work, I've also seen them fail due to poor management and poor hygiene factors. Don't overlook that in your thinking.
- While the research and insight from past projects is there, it doesn't mean it is valid forever. As time moves on, your research and insight will start to become dated and less relevant and valuable. Often this means it either moves to archive or at best becomes a form of secondary research.
- Tags can make or break this, select the tag that can be used wisely. And for the love of god, use them but, and it's a big but, don't create hundreds of them.
- Have a community manager who, over time, will constantly check the health of the repository and manage any anomalies.

SAID AND SEALED

That was a lot to take in, right!

- Qualitative and quantitative both have their place.
- Use internal qualitative data to see if it supports the quantitative data.
- Observing can be done in many different ways; one isn't better than the other.
- A fair audience sample should be taken, including the extremes.
- The appropriate choice of environment will allow a better and more honest conversation.
- They are many tools to get deeper understanding and empathy, but don't be blinded by the lights, nearly all tools and functions are built around the core approach already mentioned.
- Create a research repository, it can be so much value to an org but it has to be designed and more importantly well managed.

← Scan me to be taken to resources

MAKING SENSE OF IT ALL

Assuming, at this point, you've done the interviews, focus groups, surveys, digital diaries, and so on. You are more than likely looking at all this collected data thinking: what the hell do I do now? The answer is simply to make sense of it all and squeeze every ounce of insight from it in order to present the opportunity areas back to the business. At this stage, depending on the structure of the project and sprint set up, the conversation can go one of two ways. You'll find one of two things:

- The business will see you as the expert, thank you for identifying these areas, for proving/disproving the problem, and allow you to progress to the other phases of design.

Or

- The business will allow their egos to step in the way, they will choose to ignore your findings and insights and insist they know better, tell you to stop all progress or, worse still, progress with the original challenge (that isn't actually a challenge and build what they want)

The decision is sometimes out of our hands. Our job is to create the best narrative and insight story possible so that they choose option A. Often, option B happens when ego appears, either stakeholders don't know what you're doing and see you as a witch casting black magic, or they don't understand or can't relate to it. The bias is often ego stepping in to save face.

This is why the DARE is so important. Often, this makes it easier to overcome situations like this but it also highlights the importance of breaking down design language into simple terms and overcommunicating the approach. Let's have a look at how we can put the best foot forward and turn these data points into insight that everyone can get behind.

The first thing we want to understand when turning this data into insight is how we actually present this back to the business. Often when working with EX products the typical stakeholders are people who nearly always fall under the HR/People Team. You could hedge your bets and say the people in these teams often (not always) tend to care about people; they are very 'hearts and minds' type folk.

In order to help bring them along, it helps to lead with emotion, identify the human friction and pain points to really give the insight meaning. Over time this has become BAU for anything I am designing. So if you're sitting there thinking, 'well I work in tech so this doesn't apply here', think again. Based on experience, backing up hard facts with human emotion will get you moving a lot quicker towards success.

Knowing we need to make the story impactful, and visceral before going into this makes it easier later on down the road. Before we get to all that, I guess it makes sense to cover how I differentiate between data, finding, insight, and opportunities.

WHAT'S THE DIFFERENCE – DATA, FINDING, INSIGHT, AND OPPORTUNITIES

Data

This is everything that came out of sense-making. It's the breadcrumbs you heard and saw, it's the word-for-word statements, actions, and emotions you observed. At no point can or should you add your bias to them, right now it's all just raw data.

Finding

This is where the data starts to show itself in repeating streams of connection. Finding could be around certain experiences, touchpoints, products, and so on.

Insight

It's something that comes out of challenging the data themes and streams. Often you start to think, 'hmm there is something around x or y'.

MOO

Where everything comes together. It has identified the themes, turned over new insight, and exposed a MOO (Moment Of Opportunity). These moments could be a way to take an EX-product to the next level. Be mindful that just because we see an opportunity doesn't mean we should jump at it. However, it is something we could perhaps take forward to ideation and experimentation.

Burning Platforms

These are the MOO that we identified as areas for radical change and innovation, either in a proactive sense or sometimes in a sense of urgency.

Remember when it comes to us presenting this back, the goal isn't to have answers ready, the goal is provide enough narrative that provokes and stirs enough of the powers-that-be to want to know more and for them to see there are many areas of opportunity that can be explored. Ultimately, it is about making the decision to move on a no-brainer for them.

INSIGHTFUL INGREDIENT

At the time of writing this book, VaynerMedia has a special role called the Chief Heart Officer, whose job is to get to know every single employee at the company and help create a culture of empathy and understanding. This person, (currently Claude Silver), believes that we should all treat each other like human beings rather than just employees. As Chief Heart Officer, Claude works to understand the unique challenges and vulnerabilities of each employee and turn them into strengths for the company. This role is all about supporting and developing the talent and people within the organisation.

#DANNYDISCUSSIONS

What comes to mind when reading about this?

....

....

....

....

....

....

....

....

TRIANGULATION

Triangulation is one of the things that unfortunately gets overlooked, usually because to do it often means more time in the sense-making to get the data needed. However, an ounce of prevention is worth a pound of cure, and if the risk or unknown is big enough then it's something we should invest time in doing where possible.

Okay, so what is it?

Triangulation is a method we use to confirm our conclusions, but rather than relying on one approach, tool, or perspective we combine various different ones. This also removes any bias we may have in a certain approach. Try and think of it as simply cross-checking your data to make sure it's accurate, while removing any confirmation bias (when we only pay attention to the things that support our beliefs and ignore everything else).

A great example of Triangulation is *The Goonies.*

The movie *The Goonies* has a simple story about a group of young misfit kids who set out on a quest to find the treasure of One-Eyed Willy. While using a map and following the clues, along the way they go through various challenges and obstacles all validating that they are on the right track leading to the treasure.

Using the same story of a treasure hunt, and let's call your group of misfits the Rebel Alliance (shoutout to the group), you would follow the map and clues to find the treasure. However, when you think you are at the spot where the treasure is hidden, rather than assuming it is all there and jumping into hours and days of digging to find nothing, perhaps you would use a metal detector first, then a ground-penetrating radar to double-check your findings.

Maybe you would ask a few of the other Rebel Alliance members if their own methods have brought them to the same point. Only then would you think about digging, this in a nutshell is Triangulation.

If using various techniques and POV to confirm something, there are many ways to do triangulation depending on what you are looking at.

The main four, often used are:

- **Data triangulation** – this is comparing findings from data obtained from different sources and methods
- **Investigator triangulation** – involves using multiple researchers to study the same topic and compare the findings
- **Method triangulation** – rather than using different research to study the topic, we use multiple methods to study the issue
- **Study triangulation** – involves using multiple subjects or groups to study the topic

I get it, triangulation can be a little confusing but stripped back it is something we naturally do in our personal lives when trying to make a decision. In fact, you probably performed triangulation back in the day at high school when trying to make sense of if you should split up with your high school love (should you have been so lucky). Rather than making the decision you would maybe ask various people what they think, would they do the same, give the data.

There are many experts in this field who can go into detail around triangulation and bias, and rightfully so, especially with misinterpretation and bias that can sneak in. It's always best when doing this user research that you pair up with a great data scientist (if you don't have one of them, get one). Think of it like having a whole team of treasure hunters working together to find the treasure.

Rather than just relying on your own approach, the findings from this extra step will help you be more confident that you're going to strike it rich and find the gold (it also means the effort of the digging is going to be worth it).

Get the right people in the room to sense check.

"One man's terrorist is another man's freedom fighter."

—Unknown Author

Okay, so how the hell do we get you into a good place to be able to present all this good stuff to your stakeholders? Well, step zero is to have a quick look around the room. Who are you going to go through this data with and does everyone look the same as you? Fix that first, the last thing you want is a room full of people who all look the same as you. Let me explain.

Throughout the end-to-end flow of the sense-making, incubating, experimenting, and designing experiences, we constantly need to ask what the perception and perspective of this challenge and the people who are facing it is. Perception, to me, is how we individually look at the world and challenges, perception is our reality, our coding of the world, unique to only you.

I like to see ourselves as empty jars full of space and opportunity. Over time, we as humans, fill these jars of empty space with sticky notes full of thoughts, moments, memories, experiences, beliefs, bias, and so on. This becomes our human operating system if you like, to make sense of the world, we often call this gut feeling or intuition.

Ultimately, we use these jars as filtering systems when it comes to looking at things such as data, challenges, and so on. However, as discussed, the jars are unique to us and somewhat distorted. For example, if we were looking at a challenge such as restaurants and one of the unanswered questions was 'what time do people like to eat dinner (or tea if you're northern)? If you were to ask me, an English male, what time I eat dinner I would say around 7-8pm. However, if I ask my Spanish friend what time they eat dinner they may say around 10pm.

If we looked at a challenge around creating a new business model in property buying, but you only asked a group of white British people about moving out, the answer you get might be: 'We want to move out as fast as possible once we turn 18 onwards.'

Because that's the 'normal thing' to do. Now if you were to ask my Indian friend Raj, he would perhaps say his approach is to not only live with his parents but also his grandparents as that's the 'normal thing' to do.

It is why we need to constantly challenge the data and so forth with different perspectives, looking at the challenge not just from your point of view but seeing it from others' point of view.

The last thing we want is a group of people looking at the data with a collective 'normal thing' perception. We want different people from different backgrounds and walks of life looking at the data. If, when you look around the room, all the people looking back at you look like you.... then you have to ask, how much are we doing a disservice to the challenge and also potential solution? A great music video that captures this is from the artist Joyner Locus called *I'm not racist.*

Okay, once you have challenged the people in the room and made sure you have a more honest and diverse spread in people and thinking, now you have to start turning all that data into finding and insight.

It is possible to create this level of insight in many ways. The simplest approach I find myself coming back to is below.

TURNING DATA INTO AN OPPORTUNITY

We have a high level of understanding of what we mean by data, findings, and insight as well as what the MOO and Burning platforms are. Now, let's turn all that data into finding, insight, and opportunities (MOOs).

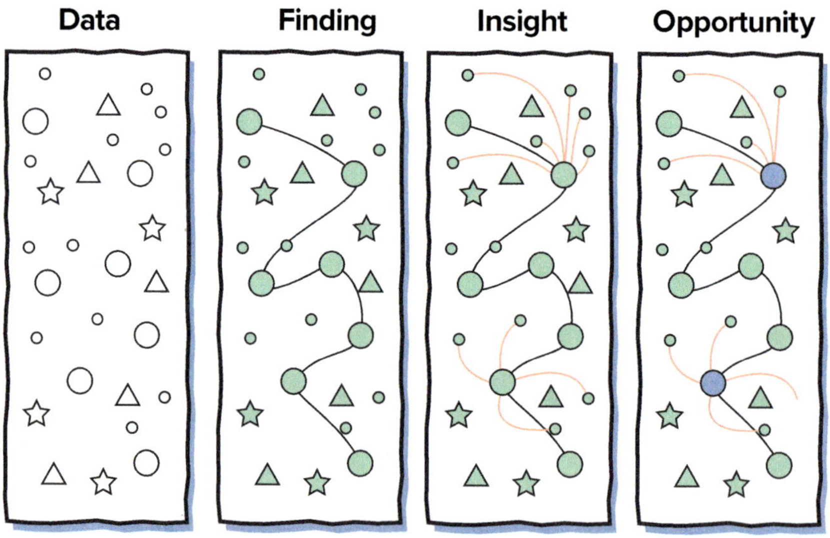

- First, we look over all the data collected.
- Second, we identify the themes coming together such as relationships, interactions, etc.
- Third, we challenge and question these themes to uproot new insights.

- The final step is to create moments of opportunity and Burning Platforms to present to stakeholders.

Let's jump through each step in a bit more detail. Next stop for us is looking at data and finding the themes.

MOVING FROM DATA TO FINDING

At this stage, hopefully you have a research repository full of data. The job now, with your team and some other SMEs, is to look at the data. At this point, it is about finding patterns, themes, etc. Remember the Design A Relationship Experience we did earlier? Now we get to bring it out and pin it up on the wall. We will use this as our North Star when looking over the data. It helps as a reminder of why we are there, what we are looking forward to, and the ultimate test if the problem statement still stands true.

There are many different approaches to turning data into themes, but I love nothing more than being manual hands-on with it. While it may be a bit more time-consuming, I find it allows the space for people in the room to discuss and challenge in a safe environment.

The first step is to convert all the data points from the audience insight into their own unique piece of content. This could be statements made, visible reactions, suggestions made – each one needs to go onto an individual sticky note.

Hopefully now you see why having a research repository and a process allows you to get ahead and move at a faster pace, by simply being able to separate, tag, and log the insights somewhere after each interview allows you to identify insight quicker later down the process.

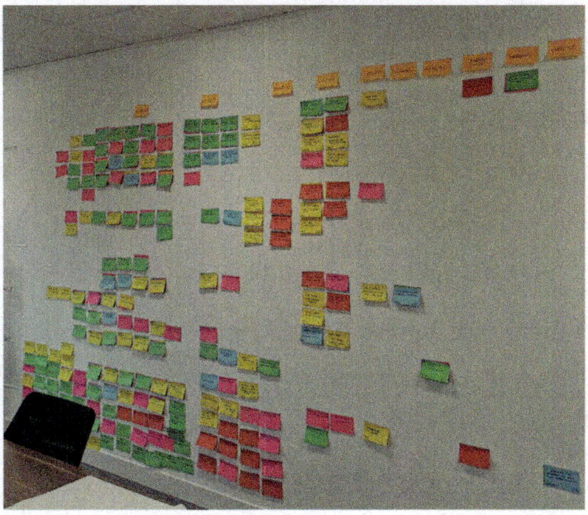

At this point, you should have multiple data points depending on how much sense-making you did. The second step is to find patterns and themes in the data, these could be points of friction, joy, opportunity, and any big observations. Once you go through your data points and cluster them you may come up with a theme highlighting larger areas such as wellbeing, but equally you might also find smaller areas, such as finding a Mental Health First Aider on the Intranet. Don't worry too much about how big or small these themes are, the goal is to just find them.

MOVING FROM FINDING TO INSIGHT AND MOOS

So you have your finding. At this stage, you want to discuss and challenge them as a team, ask 'Why do you think this is a finding?', 'Are there any gaps in our data to prove or disprove this?'. This stage tends to be largely discussion based, lots of back and forth.

You may be looking at a wall of sticky notes that have been clustered, rearranged, clustered again. There may be arrows linking one cluster to another. Don't be worried if, at this point, you feel drained of energy, it can be super hard work and at times frustrating. By investing the energy here in checking for blind spots and challenging any gaps in thinking or data, it will allow us to form better structured MOOs and Burning Platforms.

The next step is to pull fresh new insight from these clusters. The insight is a capture of the collective, it is the essence of what we are seeing in the clusters. It's also what else is showing up in that cluster when we look at it in isolation, this is where some opportunity starts to show.

If you have a wellness theme, but upon closer examination of the data points within the group and across different clusters, you may start to uncover new insights. While wellness may be a prominent theme, analysing the other themes bi-directionally can reveal additional findings. Such as pressure to meet expectations, reports of burnout, lack of time for personal development, and high turnover rates for new hires. These emerging insights can be transformed into key strategic priorities or MOOs (Moments Of Opportunity) and Burning Platforms to address these critical issues.

To create a MOO, I like to have a set structure to form them. I have seen in the past where things such as MOOs become a massive dump of words. These MOOs should be small concise captures. The insights here are to provide new opportunities and a lens to a challenge, it is about finding the diamond in the rough.

If we go back to the business and say we have discovered that your people want better wellbeing and they don't like the learning platform you have, the chances are the business will respond with 'Tell us something we don't know'. However, it would be different if we go back to the business and can demonstrate that due to the high delivery needs of the business, people are working longer hours including weekends to get the basic work done, and so learning just isn't a priority for them. This starts to unfold into a much richer piece of insight which we can bounce off.

I also like to try and write the MOO in the tone of a customer or employee. It is worth mentioning the Burning Platforms are structured in the same way, the only difference is that Burning Platforms are areas that need a sense of urgency or radical change and disruptive/innovation.

Depending on the business some stakeholders will ask to see all the MOOs while others will ask just to see just the Burning Platforms. Either way as a team, you will need to identify which of your MOOs fall into the Burning Platform category.

Each MOO is broken into five key elements:

Title

Each MOO needs a memorable name, make it catchy, give it a hook. Ask yourself, how would a documentary-maker write some clickbait for this? Be mindful that you don't go so far where nobody knows what it means if you are not there to explain it.

Insight

This is the essence of what you've found and the opportunity you have identified. When writing this statement, capture the who, what, which, why, when, and where. But make this human, use the emotions and descriptive words lifted from the data – don't water it down.

Themes

These are the themes that come out in the cluster perhaps it is burnout, technology, boundary setting.

Breadcrumbs

Here you want to put in a few of the data points you found exactly as it was said. Don't edit it or condense it, I tend to find and use the more hard-hitting data points to add richness to the MOO.

HOW MIGHT WE (HMW)

Writing a couple of How Might We (HMW) statements at the bottom, not to drive the solution but just to get the juices going of what sort of questions and possibilities could come next.

Typically, I tend to create a one-page template for each MOO ready to present back.

Building out these MOOs isn't something to do in silo and job done. In the past, I have played around with asking the team to go away, write in silo, then come back together to challenge and build on each other's MOOs. Then remix them together to create one we all feel is the best. Other times, I have the team create them together and bring an outsider in to read over them with a fresh eye (as I would when clustering).

When it comes to writing these MOOs, I would recommend trying both methods and seeing which works. Although, sometimes time and resources will make that choice for you. It can feel hard to get going with this. However, sit with the tensions and I promise you will hit a flow with it.

At this stage, we can often get caught out by Apophenia, which is where we can start to apply/force our imagination into the process and start to identify patterns or meanings in our data which are not there. You perhaps have done this in the past where you see a shape that looks like a heart in the clouds, or one of my favourites, the drunk octopus wanting to fight.

If you ever have the time type 'drunken octopus' in Google image search and nerd out on what comes up. Warning, you won't see the world the same again.

THE EMPATHY MAP & PERSONA

An empathy map is a staple tool out of any design toolbox. It's a great tool when you want to bring together what you've identified in sense-making while creating the MOO.

Similar to the DARE, I like to use empathy maps as focus points so we can come back to them as a team. It allows us to immerse ourselves in how people are feeling in the current state and stops us forgetting who we are here to serve, it is usually at this point you hear people suggest personas. I prefer an empathy map over a persona for many reasons, the main being that empathy maps are built on qualitative data we have seen and heard pulled from sense-making. At no point do we add our own bias to it, unfortunately that can't be said for personas.

With empathy maps we also remove the risk seen in personas where we fill it with fluff and non-tangible data. Also with empathy maps we tend not to see the flaw we see with personas where people start to think they are real people.

Let me try to bring to life the flaw of persona in a simple activity, below is a breakdown of information. All I need you to do is read the bullet points and write the name that comes to mind:

- A man born in 1948 in England
- Loves dogs
- Very wealthy
- Has a couple of kids

Okay, so what name have you got in mind?

The reality is that this breakdown is describing King Charles, but it's also describing the king of rock, Ozzy Osborne and in fact probably many others.

Personas

Same but different

I think we can all agree, these are two very different people once we see who they are. BUT if we looked at the persona breakdown above it, it could be easy to suggest these are the same. It's for this reason that, at this stage, I tend to avoid personas and look at what will bring me the biggest impact and for me, I always find myself going back to the Empathy Map.

The Empathy Map I use is the tweaked version that comes from Paul Boag, his format is one I have found to be the most successful and valuable. It is broken down into 5 simple quadrants. We will give this a bit of context using an example of something I am sure we have all faced while purchasing a festival/gig ticket. The first thing we need to do before creating an empathy map is first refresh ourselves on all the data and insights and capture on sticky notes tensions identified from the human point of view.

TASKS

What tasks are trying to be completed? What questions need answering?

Using the ticket purchasing example, tasks involve:

- Pre-registering months ahead of the sale
- Log into my PC, phone, and laptop
- Sign into the website ready for 9 am
- Have many treats next to me
- Stock up with water
- Open up six other tabs to the website
- Hit refresh constantly

FEELING

How are they feeling while in the experience, what really matters to them?

What impact does that challenge have on them, how does it make them feel? Often you will see words such as worried, excited, joy, sadness. Ultimately, here is where you capture what a person is feeling and more importantly why and what matters to them.

INFLUENCE

What may influence them, who are the influencers: people, props, places, profit.

Perhaps, it's what they are seeing and hearing, an advert on the radio, maybe they are hearing how some of their friends and work buddies are going, perhaps their favourite band has just announced they are going to be playing. When it comes to getting the tickets, be mindful that influences don't have to be people, it could be posters, comms, or even subtle nudges on email signatures.

PAIN POINTS

What pain points could they hit? This could be the website timing out, the forms are too big to fill in, the limited tickets, the system that decides who gets one and who doesn't, not being able to buy tickets later. Buying a ticket and finding out the line-up is poor after the fact.

GOAL

What is their ultimate goal, what are the things they are trying to achieve.

What's the end result? Ultimately it is getting a ticket from the website and being able to watch Daft Punk play on the pyramid stage at Glastonbury with a beverage of choice in hand.

A top tip which me and my team have used with clients is turning these into full framed images. I have also had success in the past with life size cut-outs of customers with all the above attached to them. Again, this isn't to replace personas but it's a true reflection of the hearts and minds of your customers and often your comms team can use them in some way.

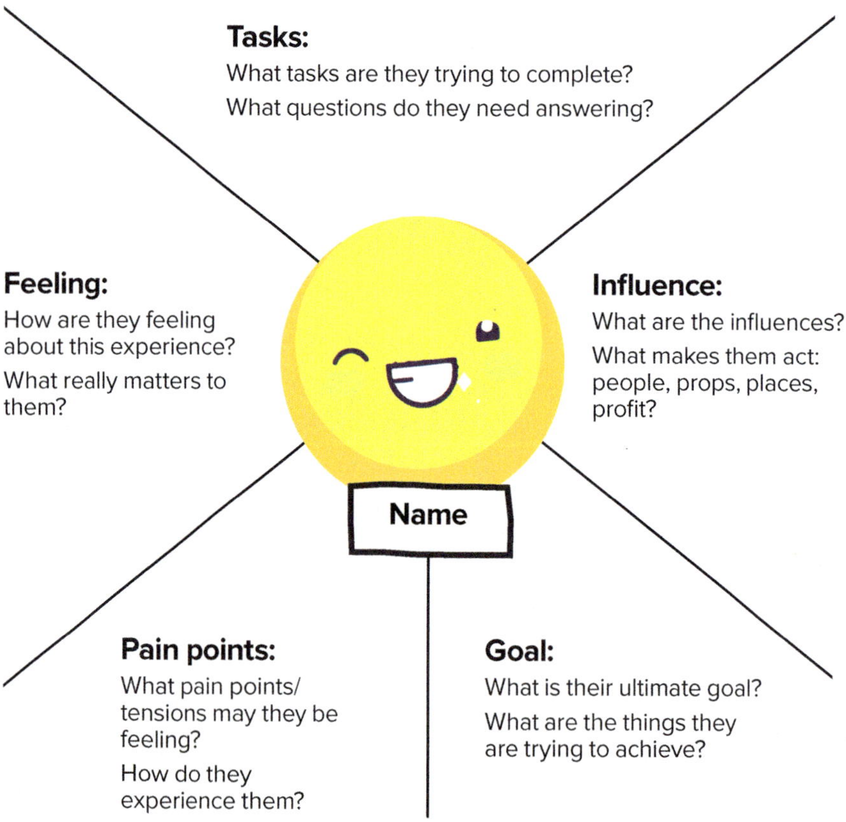

INSIGHT CANVAS AND PLAYBACKS

There's a time and a place for messy, and a time and a place for neat and tidy. As we move on to the Insight Canvas and playback, it is time to fix up, look sharp, and get a little neater.

The goal of the Insight Canvas is to bring all the MOO, Burning Platforms, empathy maps together on one page, ready to present back to the stakeholders. By following the steps above, you should have everything to simply drop in here and have one single chain of evidence that allows you to fill this in pretty quickly.

I have had mixed output presenting this to stakeholders, some love it while others get too in the weeds and open up a whole can of worms. It provides the richness of insight data and really brings everything to life. But it ultimately comes down to you knowing your stakeholder and what they would prefer. Again, revert back to DARE.

When presenting back, I try to avoid PowerPoint at all costs, the Insight Canvas can be presented back in various ways (discussed in the Incubate phase). When designing it, we may want to make use of imagery as well as certain colours and fonts to really bring them to life. Feel free to add your own creativity to the Insight Canvas. Just be careful not to lose any narrative over a bias to make the Insight Canvas more aesthetically pleasing.

Ultimately, people buy the stories we share.

Insight:

I love working at (company x), it is caring, has a can-do attitude and goes above and beyond for the customer. This is the only metric my boss uses. I know this because I spend more time on the customer stat. metric and none on my personal dev. ones. I keep hearing of all these courses and opportunitites and I've looked on X learning, which was clunky, but ultimately my boss doesn't value my development.

Early Ops

Early Ops

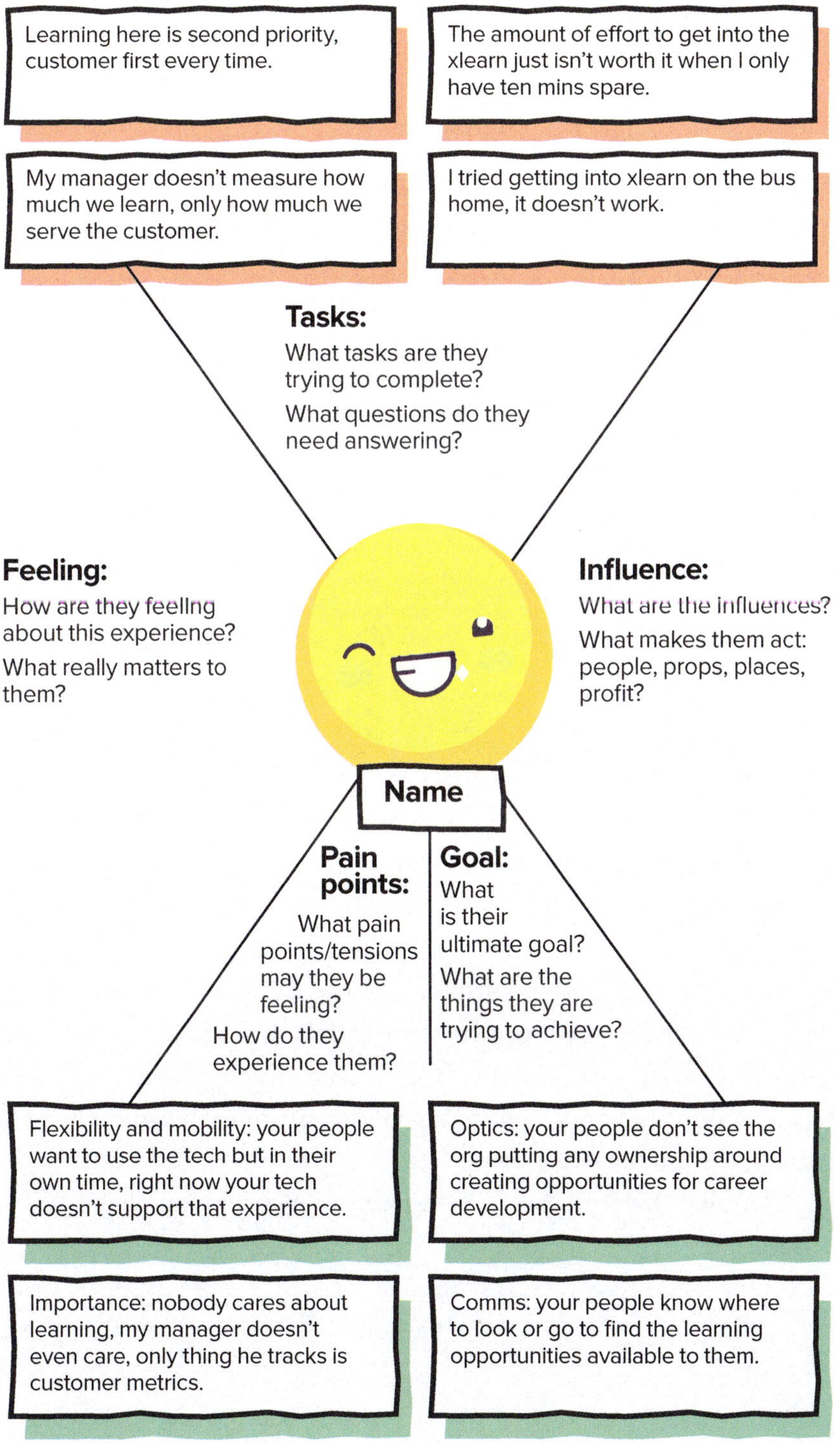
Learning here is second priority, customer first every time.
The amount of effort to get into the xlearn just isn't worth it when I only have ten mins spare.
My manager doesn't measure how much we learn, only how much we serve the customer.
I tried getting into xlearn on the bus home, it doesn't work.
Tasks:
What tasks are they trying to complete?
What questions do they need answering?
Feeling:
How are they feeling about this experience?
What really matters to them?
Influence:
What are the influences?
What makes them act: people, props, places, profit?
Name
Pain points:
What pain points/tensions may they be feeling?
How do they experience them?
Goal:
What is their ultimate goal?
What are the things they are trying to achieve?
Flexibility and mobility: your people want to use the tech but in their own time, right now your tech doesn't support that experience.
Optics: your people don't see the org putting any ownership around creating opportunities for career development.
Importance: nobody cares about learning, my manager doesn't even care, only thing he tracks is customer metrics.
Comms: your people know where to look or go to find the learning opportunities available to them.

SUMMARY BOOTLOOP

I want to highlight the need for patience. Sense-making can feel like you're constantly going round in a loop, over and over, theming and re-theming, writing and rewriting. It can often feel like you build them just to tear them down, then build and tear them down again. It is hard work, it's exhausting and sometimes you feel like you're stuck in this groundhog day. You're not, I promise.

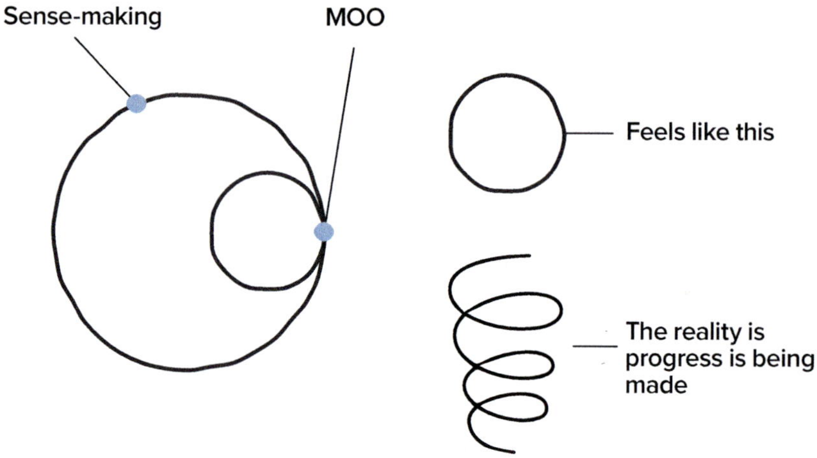

Collectively, every time you break and reassemble these themes, the hive mind together is identifying better opportunities together. If you step away, you will see you are moving in circles but you're slowly making smaller circles and getting the MOO tighter.

There are many different tools, methods, and approaches to find sense-making, many of which will appear in future books. However, my goal here is to share the core foundation that will allow you to take any future tool and not only apply them but understand and identify which work best given the situation.

Okay, let's move on to the next part of sense-making which is the service.

SAID AND SEALED

- Sense-making is the process of understanding and giving meaning to new developments and experiences.
- It involves empathy, compassion, and curiosity in order to gain a deep understanding of the challenge at hand.
- Research can be qualitative (exploring ideas, emotions, and motivations) or quantitative (facts and figures) and a mix of both can provide the best insights.
- Triangulation involves using multiple research methods to confirm findings.
- Sense-making is an important first step in the design process and should not be skipped.
- It helps to uncover the root of the problem and avoids making assumptions or falling victim to business bias.

← **Scan me to be taken to resources**

SENSE-MAKING – THE SERVICE

The term Service Design (SD) is somewhat of a new term when you apply it to EX products. From what I can see, I am one of the first to bring this in and adapt it to the EX space. However, I am merely standing on the shoulders of giants of experts outside our space. So what is Service Design?

I imagine in your life, at some point, you have used some good and not-so-good designed services. You just wouldn't have seen or known at the time that it was good service design.

- If you have ordered a taxi through Uber, you would have been involved in it
- If you had to use the gov site for taxing your car, you would have been involved in it
- If you bought a ticket for a concert, you would have been involved in it.
- If you were going to an amusement park, you would have been involved in it.

It's fair to say that, every single day, you are involved in some form of service design and every well designed service uses human-centred design to make it. You might be thinking how does this link to EX? Well, in order to create more human-centric products (i.e. anything that's in the end-to-end employee experience) you need to create a service behind the experience that supports it.

As mentioned in chapter 3, at a high-level, service design to me is an approach used to understand and map out the whole end-to-end of service. This tends to look at the touch points of a journey between the customer and the service they are using, looking at the people, the process, the props in the service as well as the channels the customer goes through.

Let's assume you are part of the 40% of the world's population that drinks coffee every day and let's pretend you go to your local Starbucks every day before work with the ideal end goal that you end up with a hot coffee in hand.

Now, even at a high level (we will get into deep blueprints later) there are a few touchpoints between:

Start: you want a coffee
Finish: you have a coffee in hand

Touchpoints include how you get to the coffee shop, joining the queue at the store, choosing the coffee, placing the order, paying for the coffee, coffee being made to spec by a highly trained coffee artist, coffee being served. All of these interactions are part of a service design blueprint. However, there are many elements of the service that you can't see, these fall behind something called the 'line of visibility'.

The line of visibility is a SD term that is used to describe all the things that happen in order to make this service work that are unseen by the customer but critical to making the service work. This could be anything from the tech used to place the order and take payment through to ordering and receiving the right kind of beans so the store never runs out. Anything that supports the actions seen by the user is part of the service design.

I haven't introduced other channels such as the customer ordering through a mobile app or subscription services for the coffee shop, but as you can see, a service can start to grow legs very quickly. That's the idea ...

By designing a service from A to B, and everything that happens in between, we help create the structure from which we can build great experiences.

People > Touchpoints > Channel > Ecosystem

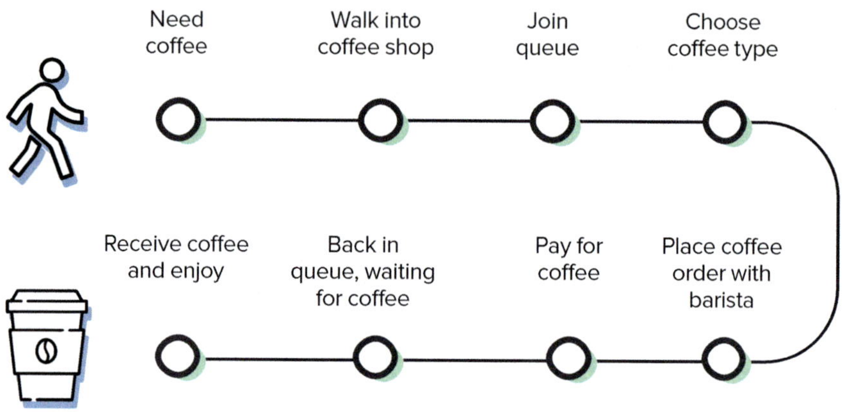

Now, lucky for us we have some principles and methods to help us design this service and remove some of that daunting feeling if this is new, but it also starts with sense-making. If you have got to this point of the book and are like, 'What the hell is sense-making?' then stop reading and revert back to chapter 1.

Okay, so perhaps you're thinking, 'What the hell has this coffee shop got to do with the employee experience?' Well, as mentioned, great experiences are built on the structure that service design gives.

Behind every great scaled experience is a great structure of service holding it together.

INSIGHTFUL INGREDIENT

Tudder is an app that helps farmers find mating partners for their cows and sheep. It uses a detailed profile system and has connected over 42,000 farms in the UK.

#DANNYDISCUSSIONS

What comes to mind when reading about this?

....

....

....

....

....

....

....

....

....

....

WHY UNDERSTANDING THE SERVICE IS NEEDED FOR EX PRODUCTS?

I hope you're now able to look at my definition above and are starting to see the value this could add to the employee experience. I believe that service design's biggest value is when we start to look at the service structure that underpins the employee experience. Particularly when we zoom in on the areas that drive friction or are disconnected, often because things don't seem connected in order to deliver a consistent service.

When people say a company has a poor employee experience, when you drill in a little more, often what really gets exposed isn't a poor experience but a poorly designed service to deliver it. The reason service is mentioned in the sense-making phase is that in order to design better EX products we need to know what the current service looks like, how it's all held together, and where the dependencies are.

Throughout the next few chapters, we are going to zoom in and take a look at what the service is and its importance, why it's vital in helping us identify potential barriers to delivering an innovative EX product. Each of the tools and principles mentioned below can be used to make sense of the current state but also to help design for a future state. Allow me to explain what I mean by example of poor service and the value we can gain from taking some time to look at it.

Let's look at attracting new talent for an open position. Now assume everything behind the line of visibility is done in order to get the role out to the public. The new talent, Helen, sees the role on LinkedIn and decides this is perfect for her. Helen clicks through the link to apply for the role. The tech platform then asks Helen to upload her C.V. (This is never the easiest thing as some don't take PDF, others do, some have to be below 2mb). Anyway, Helen does the typical gymnastics of uploading her C.V., then moments later the platform informs her that she now has to manually add all the details from the C.V. on individual sections of the platform.

It's at this point your service has broken and here is why ...

- Adding friction and duplication to something that should be simple.
- Most people applying don't have the time to do this, often applying for a job that catches your eye is in the moment and fleeting.
- Most people apply via mobile.
- If you do go through this crap and get to the interview, interviewers tend not to have a C.V. in front of them because often they can't print it off from the system to which it was uploaded.

What do you think Helen will do? Will she continue to struggle to upload her C.V.? Will she use a PDF shrinker to then upload it again? Will she jump through daft hoops of copying and pasting all the sections after she just uploaded her C.V.? If Helen doesn't do all the hoop-jumping in the moment will she return later? More often than not these basic tensions are seen and felt in most first-stage applications because the services aren't well designed and connected. The bigger question to ask is how many talented individuals has the business lost due to a poor service failing?

When a service fails, without some form of intervention, an experience inevitably fails but an intervention shouldn't be needed in the first place. The goal is to create EX products that are suitable, work at scale, and can be automated as much as possible. In the past, when I have personally applied for roles and found myself in a situation like Helen's, I choose not to continue for many reasons. Often, I think, rightly or wrongly:

- You as an organisation don't care about my time.
- You can't thread a simple process like this together.
- I am applying to other organisations that have their shit in order and don't add unneeded friction.
- If my first experiences of this organisation are terrible, imagine what working there is like.

For me, if a company is changing the service this should be the first thing they change because of the strong positive and negative signals it can give to potential new talent.

Now, let's be honest, I have pulled just one tiny moment from the EX journey, but there are many situations like this. For example, onboarding people not receiving their tech, new hires being force-fed training either too late or too early, updating my pension internally, opting in and out of rewards and benefits, finding support with personal situations when needed.

I once had a three-month back and forth with an ex-employer while starting a new job because they owed me over 2k in expenses, the failure came down to a poorly designed service. Sometime after the three months of effort and finally getting my expenses, someone reached out to me asking if I would recommend them as a place to work. What do you think I told them about? I told them about the shocking experience I had and the constant battle to make simple things work, such as the service of expenses for me.

Okay, let's break down service design into some simple terms, for this I am going to introduce the analogy of theatre, here is the basic concept:

Customer Journey

Often in service design, this is a collection of key touchpoints the customer will have in the service. In book two I will show you how to design much richer experience-led journeys. For now though, understand customers will have various touchpoints in their journey, some of which we can design for others, some of which we can't.

Front stage

The front stage is what the customer/employee sees. Imagine you went to watch a show at a theatre, here you would see the show and the audience around you but you wouldn't see anything going on behind the stage, that leads us to backstage.

Backstage

Backstage, as mentioned, is invisible to you sitting watching the show, it is everything that helps us create the front stage. Without the rigour and foundation of the backstage, the front stage wouldn't happen. Often the backstage consists of processes, policy, props, people.

Channels

Throughout the journey, the customer may make their way through this 'theatre' analogy through various channels, maybe they ordered the tickets online, maybe they picked the tickets up from the box office, and so on. We must not lose sight of channels, especially in this multi-channel world which we live in.

The Roles

This is the role each individual is playing, for example backstage: Dave is playing the sound engineer, Rachel is clearly calling the shots backstage as the theatre manager. Steve is playing the lead actor front stage.

Explaining service design could be a whole book on its own, of which there are many. These core basics as a foundation will give you what is needed to progress forward. For now, if you can take one point away from this, it knows that you need to look at the service in sense-making, underneath experience design is service design. Service design brings structure and rigour underneath an experience.

Designing a new EX product without looking at the services is like trying to understand how your iPhone (or Android) was made and how it's in your hand now without looking at the supply chain.

Okay, so hopefully, you know under every EX product there is some form of service design going on, let's have a look at some simple guiding principles of what makes a good EX service:

DIFFERENCE BETWEEN SERVICE DESIGN AND EXPERIENCE DESIGN

A quick note on my take on the difference between SD and XD, we now know that service design often has a journey map, under that is a frontstage/backstage, and so forth (which we will come to shortly). You could be forgiven for thinking that the journey map is experience design, it's not.

In my experience, often the journey map is a high-level overview of touchpoints, what experience design (XD) gives is a level above the journey map. It applies a very specific lens to design from the employee or customer's point of view looking at the nano, micro, and macro of the experience.

We will get into what is clear, the difference between service and experience in future books. However, if you take one thing away from these chapters on service design it is the fact that service design is not experience design. Without a solid structure of designing the service, most experiences can't be sustained or they fall over pretty quick. If these terms and concepts are new to you my advice would be don't sweat the small stuff, even the industry of service design, experience design, UX, and so on can't come to an agreement on what it is and isn't.

Principles

When it comes to rules and shortcuts for service design, I have a few that I use every time when designing a service of some kind. If you're new to this space or in your career you may struggle to put these in the context of your world, please try to sit with them and frame them in your context.

Dumb Design, not Dumb People:

Linking to the very start of this book, human-centric is vital. You need to care deeply about their pain points because if you don't care about their pain points, chances are they won't care about your solution.

Services that don't work will often drive friction and tension, your goal is to identify what and where these tensions are in that service from the employee/customer's point of view. I am not saying you need to fix the whole service end-to-end because that often needs more resources. However, if you can identify just a few little touchpoints that are causing friction then you can get a pretty big bang for your buck.

Simply put, if people are not using your service right, it is not because they are dumb it is because your design is dumb and you haven't cared enough to understand the problem or how people typically overcome it. Think about any tech platform you may have introduced, ask why your people haven't returned or used it in the first place ... Have you really cared enough to design it, or have you gone into 'I know better' mode?

Good services are need to haves:

Chances are most of the services that employees or customers are involved in exist because they are deemed as necessities i.e. they need to exist in order to achieve or overcome something.

Often, good design is about helping people get what they want/need in as few steps as possible.

Again, I have this test that I do when helping companies design products or services, I call it the 'Leah test', basically I bring my niece in who has no clue about the industry and I test the EX product with her. I then simply observe how she uses it, the questions she asks, and identify where she gets stuck.

All of this ultimately allows me to test the language used, maybe it is the UX or something else. Every time I have run the Leah test it has always identified a blind spot. But why bring in someone who doesn't get it? Well, revert back to point one on dumb design:

If someone who doesn't understand your world can still get it, you are moving in the right direction.

It's also about consumer grade which comes next. How many times have you tested your product, service, or experience outside with someone who isn't the perfect person?

Make it CG (Consumer grade)

Nobody ever really taught you how to use Google, Instagram, or TikTok, yet the chances are you use many of them with ease. The reason is due to their near frictionless designs. I don't mean just from an aesthetics point of view (that's nice too), I mean in day-to-day life, it's also very simple to know how to use them. All services should be like this.

In fact, Jacob's Law states as human beings we tend to prefer things to work the same as the other things we have, if not they tend to drive friction which ultimately drives frustration and maybe even fear. I firmly believe that is why people move from Apple to Android and quickly move right back to Apple. It is down to the simplicity of design, Apple makes it effortless, you don't even need a user manual, and even toddlers can quickly learn how to use it. Unfortunately, that can't be said for Android (I am biased).

When it comes to designing a service, ask yourself 'Is this simple to explain? Easy to use?' While the example used here is more product and UX-focused, the basics of it can be applied to the design of better services, design them like you're designing a great product.

This doesn't just apply to digital either. Think about how Amazon has set up their service so you are constantly aware of where your parcel is, now apply that to how you received your employee onboarding kit on day 1. Both are providing the same service but often feel very different.

INSIGHTFUL INGREDIENT

Airbnb partnered with journalism start-up News Deeply in order to increase diversity and inclusion in their company. News Deeply helped Airbnb understand the social issues surrounding them and created three guiding principles for the company to follow: Balance Your Bias, Consider The Opposite, and Embrace A Growth Mindset. These principles will hold the company accountable in all of its decision-making and design moving forward.

#DANNYDISCUSSIONS

What comes to mind when reading about this?

....

....

....

....

....

....

....

....

....

....

Language

In Lou Downe's book *Good Services*, she shares a story about a man who walks into a local police station and drops a dead badger on the desk. When the police ask what he is doing, he explains that he couldn't find on the government website what to do with roadkill.

Lou uses this story to signal the importance of language. Again, another reason to do the Leah test to see what non-HR, non-corporate jargon she would use to find an answer. Nobody is ever going to search for a 'Loc0202' form but they will search for 'how to change my name'.

Language comes up a little later in a personal story below, however, it is worth mentioning great services you use tend to have clear simple language throughout and help redirect you should you not use the right spelling or get lost. Cooking these fail safes into the design is a godsend, so run the Leah Test a lot.

Google mastered this, nine times out of ten when I spell a word wrong it prompts me with 'did you mean: xyz?' This simple touch is something, as a dyslexic, I appreciate every day, it makes my Internet browsing much more frictionless and enjoyable. Remember, clear beats clever every time when it comes to writing and helping your people navigate the world.

Bloat formation

If you find yourself designing and uploading content and resources to any internal platform, pause and ask yourself this ... am I part of the problem? We live in an information-rich world. While this is wonderful, it also makes for a very noisy place.

One thing I have seen time and time again when working internally and for clients is bloat formation (think I've just made that up). We have become so good at producing information that we often forget to take a pause and remove the old information it is replacing. Look at any internal Intranet, LMS, LXP, or EX platform and you will see it. We have to get better at removing when we add.

I once had a manager called Bronnie who used a little saying which has stuck with me. She would stick her hands out and say: "These things are hands and fingers, not wands, if you want me to pick something up then what am I dropping?" We need to use this approach when it comes to bloat formation. Before we add, what are we removing, what links do we need to change before you add any more content? Step 1 should always be, what we are removing first?

Let me know what's going on:

Most services are analog or digital, often like the basics of how to get help, simple things such as contact numbers are often missing. It is fair to say, at some point, the employee will get stuck using your service. A simple example is raising an IT ticket internally, often the ticket is submitted through a form and 9 times out of 10 disappears into a black hole never to be seen again. Only when you check the system, it says it has been resolved.

Adding essential contact information such as phone, chatbot, WhatsApp, all help to create a better service. Sometimes something as simple as having a chatbot that hands over to a human could be the difference. A company that does this really well is Publicate. I know who's online and when I move from chatbot to human, I also know when they are away and when I can expect a reply. These simple bits of information allow me to get on with my day. It is the same when waiting for a parcel, there is a big difference between waiting for a parcel from Amazon and one from a courier service. Amazon allows me to track the driver and gives me a short time period of when to expect my delivery vs the courier who says, 'we have your parcel and it will be with you tomorrow'.

Ikea lets you know what parcel they are working on when you go into their stall, this allows you to relax and know how far away you are from being served. Even fishmongers use it with ticket numbers. Again, be the human in the service you are designing and ask yourself 'if I am a customer or employee, do I always know what's going on, what's expected of me at each point, is it clear in language and what I need to do next?'

Stackable and Connected:

Goes without saying, but services move across various channels, from physical to digital. Using the coffee scenario from earlier, let's add a channel to the situation. The customer could have ordered a coffee via the app, and then walked past the queue feeling all smug to pick up their hot cup of coffee.

To make that simple app service work, the service has a lot to do, it has to work on all devices, the app needs to be able to take the payment, add the customers rewards on to their account, and then send the instruction to the coffee shop telling the coffee artist when the customer is due, the coffee artist then needs to follow the same process mentioned earlier.

The instructions from the app need to then connect to the rest of the service. Maybe one of the connections in the service is the system that keeps track of the stock of coffee beans, the ordering process, and so on. The person who uses the app doesn't see any of this. Below is the app channel added on to the coffee shop experience from earlier.

People > Touchpoints > Channel > Ecosystem

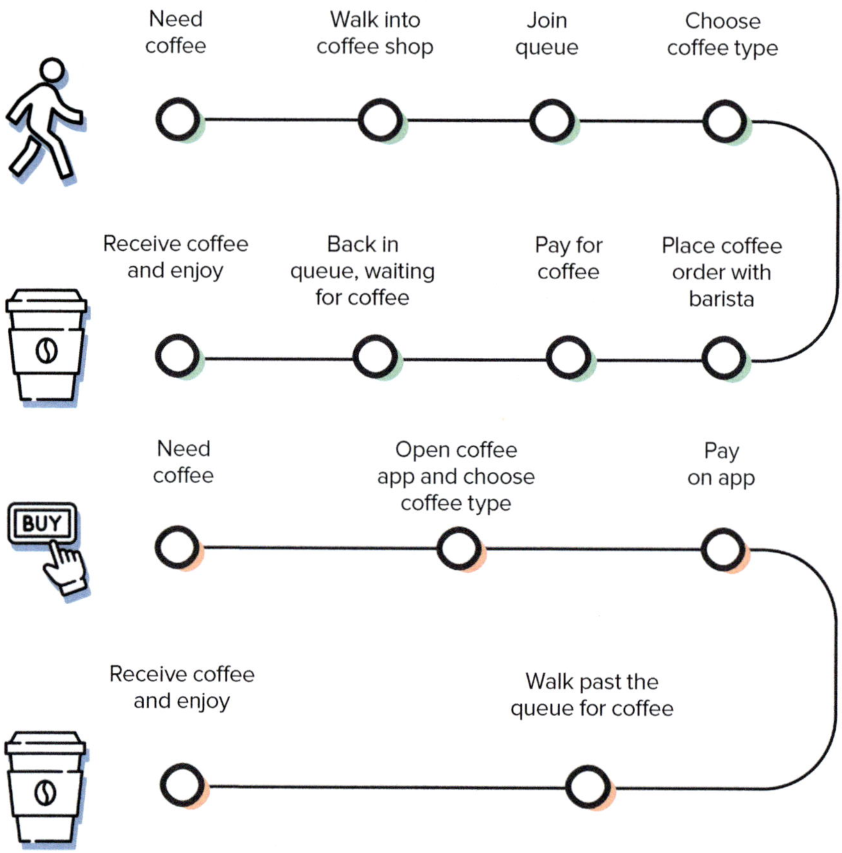

I have seen in various orgs where each part of the business operates in a silo manner, each bringing their own supplier in, and so on. The challenge is one silo isn't aware of the impact this could have, and the result is a disconnected end-to-end service.

This is why companies often bring in MLS (managed learning services) and outsourcing of HR work. It is because the MLS wraps their arms around it and stops people just running off doing their own thing, the goal of an MLS is to standardise quickly with a connected service.

Nudge and prompt when needed:

Sometimes, humans can be like moths. One minute we are deep in focus and the next some dust passes our eyes and takes our attention with it.

To me, a good service should always prompt you, keep you updated on where you are in the journey and most importantly tell you if something goes wrong.

Great service design should also slowly but surely nudge you through the journey.

I don't mean it should constantly demand your attention but should you incorrectly fill out a form, not action something, or not attend somewhere, then a well-designed service should attempt to try and help you.

There are many great examples of where this works, for example, my dentist service is pretty slick. It tells me about when I am due my next appointment, after I have been it will nudge me to book another, a week prior it prompts me to change the appointment if I need to via an SMS, a few days beforehand they will call up to confirm and so on. What makes this service work is that if I don't make an appointment it will let me wait a few weeks then prompt me again, informing me that I need to book.

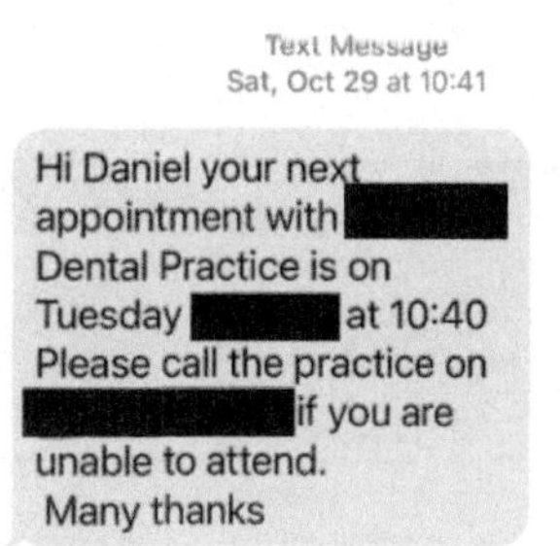

Build for a human and their quirks

As I write this, I am currently looking at the process of having a new driveway done. I live in a little cul-de-sac and the street is really tight. Now, I have two options at this point, I can be a law-abiding citizen and seek the right information and go down the right process to make it happen or I choose to just do everything without checking in with the local council.

The two main things I need answered are:

- Dropping the pavement – in order to get on to my new drive I need to have the kerb dropped so the car can get on and off smoothly.
- Replacing a street sign – the street sign is currently attached to

my front garden wall, part of the new driveway includes a new wall around the house and so the street sign is going to need a new home.

(Two things I wouldn't think I ever needed to know the answers for, but hey we are where we are, this is middle age for you ...)

I headed over to the government website and typed in 'lowering my curb' (notice the spelling error), followed by 'lowering my pavement'. I received 65,231 results back, the top one was 'child maintenance' (I have no children), along with claiming universal credit, again, not what I was aiming for. As I scrolled down, thinking something useful would pop up, I found other links such as 'managing the pandemic in prison'.

I came away knowing jack all about getting my pavement sorted, however, I do know that the prison system created an additional 1,200 temporary cells to limit the spread which was interesting.

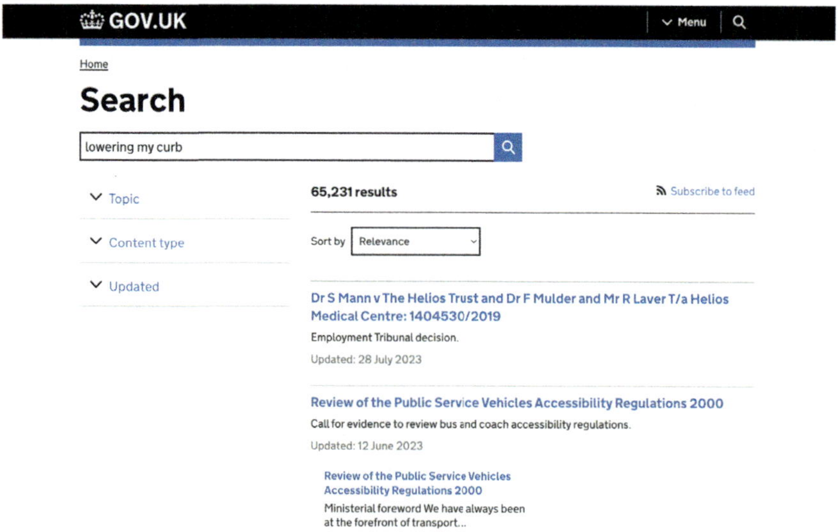

I type in 'replace street sign' and I am presented with 79,706 results, none of the top ten have anything to do with my challenge.

After lots of searching and time wasted, the outcome may well be to watch this space. Given the GOV site was useless, I may well be off to

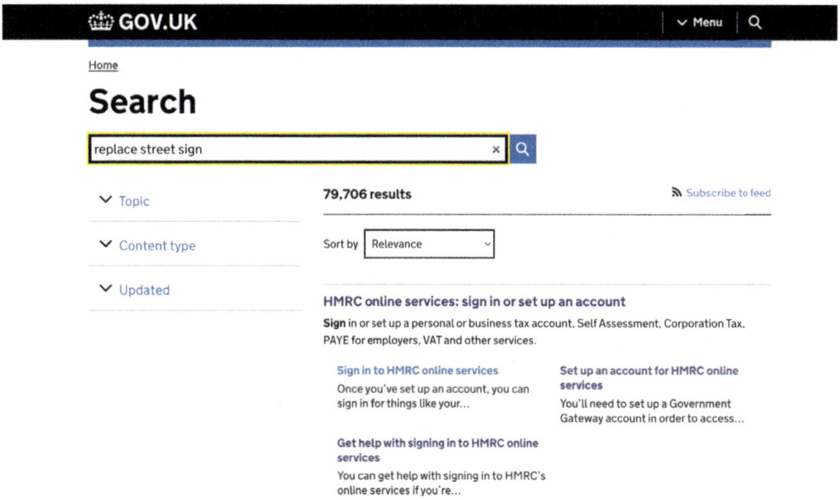

the pub later tonight to see a man about a dog. When I say this, I mean seeing a man about lowering the pavement illegally. As for the street sign, well good luck Mr Postman.

Of course I am joking, I would never intentionally break the law, but it does highlight a challenge. As someone with dyslexia, spelling is a daily challenge for me. The fact that the government site doesn't recognise that when I say 'curb' I mean 'kerb' is a challenge, but even when I changed the word to 'pavement' I still retrieved nothing. The golden search term was: apply for a dropped kerb.

Note: no pavements or street signs were harmed in writing this book.

Acknowledgement of a service failure

Any service you design will fail, that could be a taxi service, Spotify, your Intranet and so on, however, not acknowledging it drives more frustration leaving the human on the end of the service feeling frustrated.

When a service fails, it's a unique opportunity to get feedback from a customer/employee on where it failed and also how to overcome it.

Yet, when most services fail, the typical approach is to stick your head in the sand and pretend it doesn't exist. One of my favourite stories about someone who not only mastered the acknowledgement of a service failure but also turned it into a delightful moment is Amazon with its Amazon dogs.

Having a service fail isn't great for someone who is in it. However, acknowledging it and closing the loop off is still a lost art. Amazon found a way to turn this failure into a nice, cute moment. Many moons ago when a 404 error on a webpage used to be a thing (when the page no longer existed or a redirect wasn't set up), Amazon came up with a cool way to acknowledge the error but still put a smile on customer's faces, they presented a page with a picture of one of the employee's dogs.

This unique twist on the service failure actually drove a spike in the usage of the site as people constantly refreshed to see what dog they would get next.

Unfortunately, 404 errors are rare now so seeing the dogs is a thing of the past. Feel free to scan the QR code to find out about how it all started with a dog called Rufus (side note: also the name of my dog).

← **Scan me to be taken to resources**

INSIGHTFUL INGREDIENT

The mobile network provider Three have won awards for their wellbeing solutions. Every Wednesday, the whole business would take part in Wellness Wednesdays where no meetings were allowed to take place between 12pm and 2pm and everyone was encouraged to take the time to participate in activities.

#DANNYDISCUSSIONS

What comes to mind when reading about this?

....

....

....

....

....

....

....

....

....

....

BLUEPRINT

Okay, so we know the importance of service design. We know it's a critical part of sense-making and it allows us to really look at the current service in place and to identify the disconnects and tensions, but it can also help later on when wanting to design the future state.

However, often everybody is working in their own function and not looking at the wider end-to-end service. One of the most used tools for service design is the service blueprint, this map allows us to connect the dots and elements of the service together.

It brings people, such as your stakeholder groups, together and creates a visual representation of the end-to-end service. It allows the group to discuss and zoom in on any areas of the service to understand it and challenge it a little more. It's built on insight gained from the sense-making phase. Hence the importance when in sense-making that we identify customers, tech used, stakeholders, processes, etc. and really dig deep to uproot tensions and insights.

I have tried various different approaches to service maps. Often, the end result of my maps tends to bring in elements of experience maps, the journey map, and then under it all, is the service blueprint.

One of the most notable outcomes of a service blueprint is when you bring together an org that is working in a silo and show them the impact they are having on the customer/employee by not having a constant approach. When you see the revelation moment in stakeholders when they realise it's all connected, like the circles of life, life gets much easier at this point. You start to cement the team together and people all tend to start moving in the same direction rather than in silos.

A note of caution, service blueprints tend to grow legs very quickly so don't be surprised by the scale that can come from this. It is worth discussing as a team the level and scale you want to go to with this beforehand.

Let's go through and apply some of SD terminology and use it in a blueprint. An important point to mention is that blueprints are not just for current state, you can also use them to map a future state again to help expose bottle necks or potential future tensions.

Using the concept of the theatre from earlier, let's jump into what it means on a blueprint. Zoom in to just one small and simplified part of the blueprint, this will provide a little more clarity on how a blueprint could look.

Imagine an employee has a technical issue and needs to raise a ticket with IT support.

JOURNEY MAP

Remember this shows the end-to-end moments the employee goes through. Often they are also accompanied by some narrative and mapped to the stage of the journey.

Using our example, this could be that an employee hasn't received a keyboard with their kit or that it doesn't work.

As you can see on the picture overleaf, the pink and green channels on the map show the narrative (pink) and the journey (green). If we were to map this in a real situation, the narrative, as well as some of the tone and emotions, would be found in the insight from sense-making.

FRONTSTAGE

This is everything the employee would see and engage with when raising the ticket; people, process, platforms, and props. In our example, perhaps the employee has to follow a set process online (process and platform), after this they may need sign off from the manager via a face-to-face chat or via email (platform and people) and so on.

LINE OF VISIBILITY

Unfortunately, we don't all get to wear Harry Potter invisibility cloaks here. However, what this means is that from your employee's point of view anything that goes on here isn't seen by the customer. Therefore, once the employee raises a ticket on 'report my IT' they then won't see anything that happens backstage.

BACKSTAGE

This is everything that happens but isn't seen by the employee. So they raise the ticket and receive a case number. After that, all things cross the line of visibility and move backstage. This is where Jeff and Sarah, our IT gurus step in. Here, you will also see if any backstage interaction connects with front-stage action and often these connect via arrows into process documents, other teams, etc. (If this is starting to feel confusing, stick with it, when you see the map overleaf it will make sense).

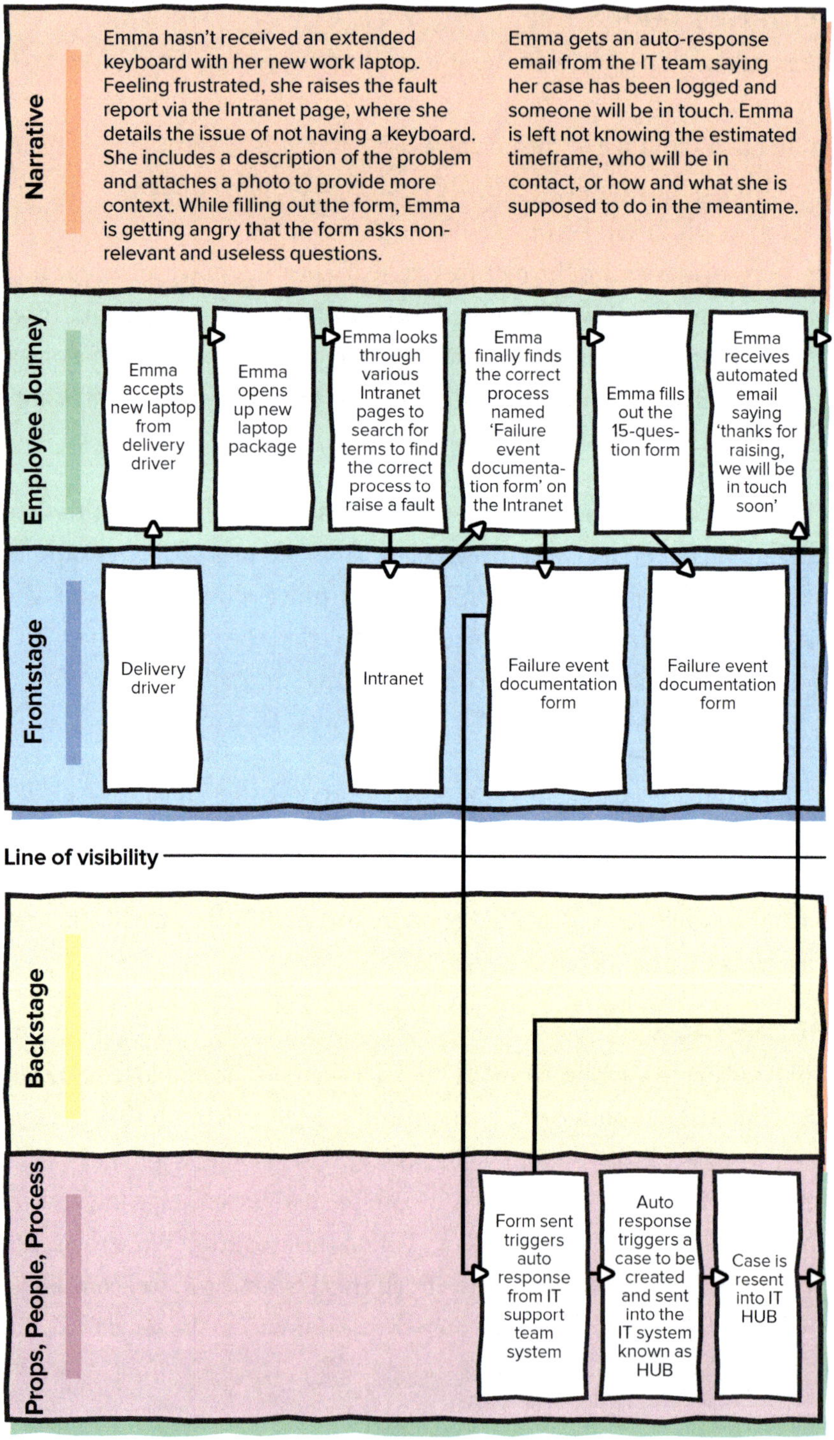
Narrative
Emma hasn't received an extended keyboard with her new work laptop. Feeling frustrated, she raises the fault report via the Intranet page, where she details the issue of not having a keyboard. She includes a description of the problem and attaches a photo to provide more context. While filling out the form, Emma is getting angry that the form asks non-relevant and useless questions.
Emma gets an auto-response email from the IT team saying her case has been logged and someone will be in touch. Emma is left not knowing the estimated timeframe, who will be in contact, or how and what she is supposed to do in the meantime.
Employee Journey
Emma accepts new laptop from delivery driver
Emma opens up new laptop package
Emma looks through various Intranet pages to search for terms to find the correct process to raise a fault
Emma finally finds the correct process named 'Failure event documentation form' on the Intranet
Emma fills out the 15-question form
Emma receives automated email saying 'thanks for raising, we will be in touch soon'
Frontstage
Delivery driver
Intranet
Failure event documentation form
Failure event documentation form
Line of visibility
Backstage
Props, People, Process
Form sent triggers auto response from IT support team system
Auto response triggers a case to be created and sent into the IT system known as HUB
Case is resent into IT HUB

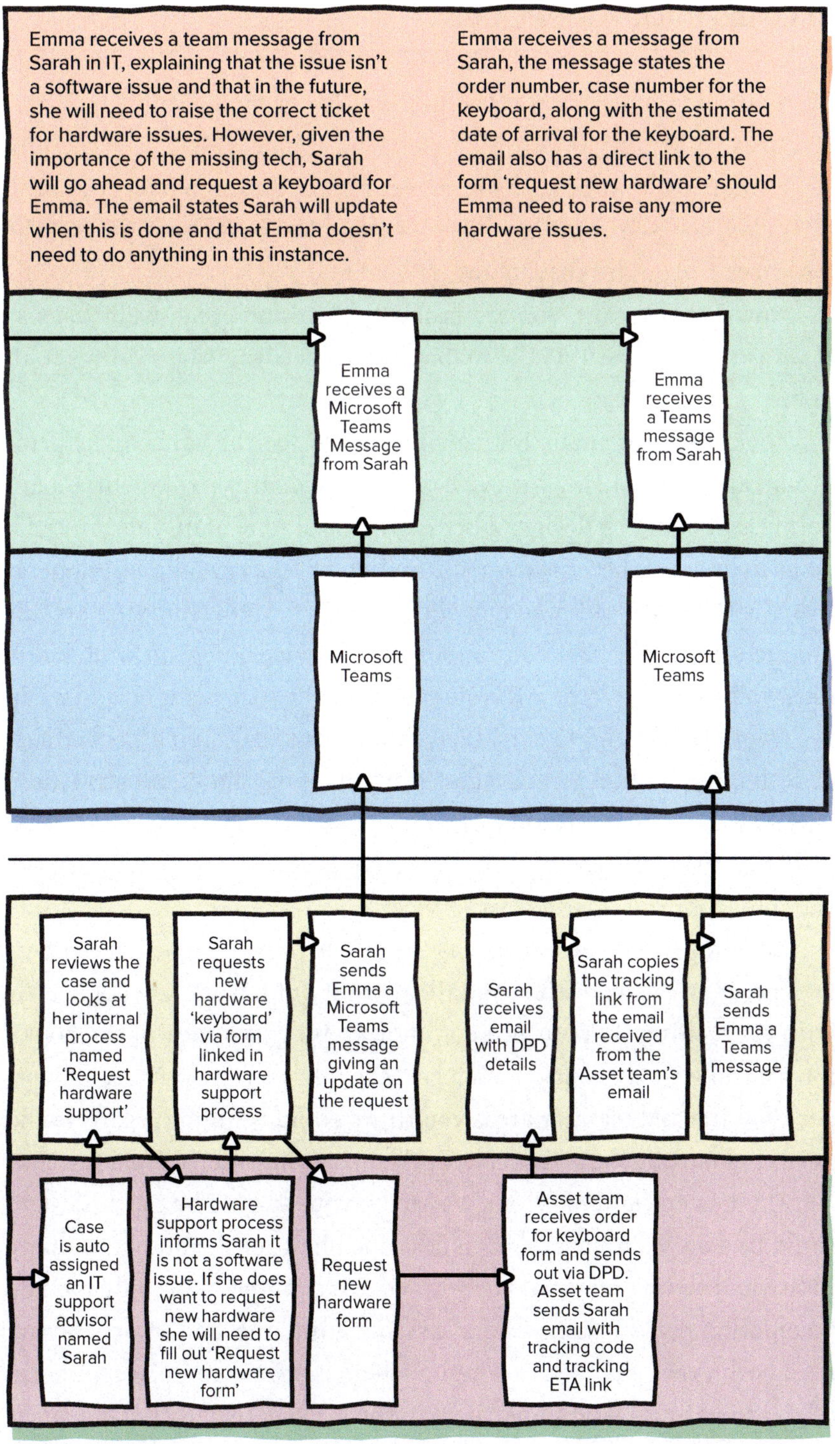
Emma receives a team message from Sarah in IT, explaining that the issue isn't a software issue and that in the future, she will need to raise the correct ticket for hardware issues. However, given the importance of the missing tech, Sarah will go ahead and request a keyboard for Emma. The email states Sarah will update when this is done and that Emma doesn't need to do anything in this instance.
Emma receives a message from Sarah, the message states the order number, case number for the keyboard, along with the estimated date of arrival for the keyboard. The email also has a direct link to the form 'request new hardware' should Emma need to raise any more hardware issues.
Emma receives a Microsoft Teams Message from Sarah
Emma receives a Teams message from Sarah
Microsoft Teams
Microsoft Teams
Sarah reviews the case and looks at her internal process named 'Request hardware support'
Sarah requests new hardware 'keyboard' via form linked in hardware support process
Sarah sends Emma a Microsoft Teams message giving an update on the request
Sarah receives email with DPD details
Sarah copies the tracking link from the email received from the Asset team's email
Sarah sends Emma a Teams message
Case is auto assigned an IT support advisor named Sarah
Hardware support process informs Sarah it is not a software issue. If she does want to request new hardware she will need to fill out 'Request new hardware form'
Request new hardware form
Asset team receives order for keyboard form and sends out via DPD. Asset team sends Sarah email with tracking code and tracking ETA link

PEOPLE, PROPS & PROCESS

This often maps out any documents, processes, or assets that are pulled from our employee actions; the manager(s); or by Jeff and Sarah, our IT gurus. When raising the IT ticket, the collateral could be the processes required to follow, the manager required to sign a form to raise the ticket, the platform they raise it on and the forms they fill out, the resources and guides they follow.

Now at this point, you are probably thinking great, well that's as clear as mud. Hopefully, the map on the preceding pages brings it all to life.

Looking at this map, I hope you start to see the value a blueprint can bring to visualising a service, as well as identifying potential pain points that could be designed better. In one simple map, you can track what happens, where it happens, and what is seen, felt, and done. It really is the circle of life map when it comes to understanding any EX products. Imagine what your onboarding service blueprint would look like, what about how the HR system works, who it depends on and what.

Over the last eight years, I have used service design as a core part of design. I have had great success from mapping out talent attraction, onboarding through to graduate and apprentice programmes, new leadership solutions, EVPs, and so on. I have even used it to map out the end-to-end journey of a dentist service.

Mapping out services isn't easy, it can be fairly complex and tiring. I've met many people who can talk about it but have rarely done it. As with everything (hopefully a common trend you notice in the book), roll up those sleeves and give it a go. Map out a service you use in your personal life and identify areas you think could be improved. A simple one is to map out your Uber ride, or the pizza you ordered from Just Eat.

There is no right or wrong way to do your service blueprints, there could be a very simple approach described here, or it could have many individual swim lanes that are detailed. For example, you could include an emotional swim lane, a data insight swim lane, and so on. Having used both types – details vs simple – there is a time and place for both, often I sometimes land somewhere in the middle. Usually my blueprint has an emotional map on there, as well as a qualitative user insight lane to add some richness to the story (gained from sense-making).

However, we have to be mindful that we do not get seduced by creating a super sexy blueprint. The goal is to identify the service, the pain points, and bottlenecks in the system, and use these to design from there or use the blueprint to spring us into what the future could look like.

9 times out of 10 a simplified blueprint will hit the spot, it will also allow you to move faster when time is tight.

'Don't let perfect be the enemy of good enough.'

INSIGHTFUL INGREDIENT

Schneider Electric identified a lack of opportunity and awareness of untapped potential as the main reason for employee turnover. To address this, they implemented global benchmarking to identify unknown skills and then created an internal marketplace where employees could showcase their skills and experience. This was intended to increase opportunity and awareness of potential within the company and help employees identify their next internal career move.

#DANNYDISCUSSIONS

What comes to mind when reading about this?

....

....

....

....

....

....

....

SAID AND SEALED

- Service design is the process of understanding and mapping out the end-to-end journey of a service that underpins everything.
- It involves designing the structure and experience of a service, including touchpoints, people, processes, props, and channels.
- The line of visibility refers to elements of a service that are not visible to the user but are critical to its functioning.
- Service design principles and methods can be used to create a structured and well-designed service.
- In the context of employee experience, service design can be used to improve the employee journey and create a positive experience for employees.

← **Scan me to be taken to resources**

SENSE-MAKING – THE SYSTEM

"Pull a thread here and you'll find it's attached to the rest of the world."

—Nadeem Aslam

Okay, so far in this book we have looked at sense-making for the human, sense-making for the service, now it's time to go big or go home and look at the sense-making of the system.

The system, as the name suggests, is a beast of a thing honestly, and while I say the blueprint from service design was the circle of life for bringing people together to see a service, the system is the circle of life for the whole of the EX.

The Lion King nailed it with the circle of life, which ultimately is a system. Now, unfortunately, me and Simba are not mates, I did once sing Hakuna Matata in high school (you're so cool Danny! I know thanks.) but let me take you out of the world of Disney and talk about the system in the context of life and the employee experience.

Let's start with a definition of the system and what we mean by system thinking. It is important to note that system thinking is more of an overarching lens on my design. It is more about awareness, having deep and meaningful conversations, and a lot of mapping to really make sense of the systems we operate in.

WHAT IS A SYSTEM & SYSTEM THINKING

The good news is a system isn't some unicorn or some mythical thing, we are part of many in our personal and professional life. The company we work for is one. Same with our close and wider family, healthcare, and education. Often these form a super system which is a whole thing by itself, for now, let's keep it to a system level.

They are usually made up of sub-systems, elements, and sub-elements, all of them are connected to each other in one way or another. These all work within the bigger system, a change in these parts and sub-systems can start to affect the whole over time.

Now you may be thinking what is going on here, do I need to go off and research all of these? Not for this book no, your body is a beautifully complex system, the eco-system we are in is another beautiful one that's as complex as it gets in this book. Now let's put it into an EX setting.

- System – let's assume the organisation is the system that we are looking at
- Sub-system – these are focused department areas such HR, Learning, Account, EX, Procurement, Marketing, etc.
- Elements – this is more looking at teams within the sub-systems and looking at the technology and physical items that are connected (props)
- Sub-elements – as you can guess, these are similar to elements but at the individual level

As with anything, the question must be asked of where the tipping point is with something like system thinking and where the value and impact is. It can become tricky, as humans we have a tendency to value quick wins and rewards over longer bigger rewards. Look internally and you will see this show up in annual performance reviews, especially ones that are mapped to a monetary reward, often every object needs to be finished by the next review else you won't get the bonus. Often, this just simply drives people to game the system:

At one place, we would need to get feedback from other colleagues to show where we have added value in order to get the bonus. So everyone would send each other the feedback ahead of putting it on the performance system and ask, 'You cool with this? You want me to add anything in before I post it to the system?'

The recipient of that feedback would do the same. Pulling myself out of this rabbit hole of flawed performance reviews I could see that it is a simple example of a business that wants to 'change the system' but rewards the opposite. All this type of performance review signals to someone is:

- Don't do anything too complex or that might take longer than the time period of your next review e.g. quarter or annual
- Don't go big with your objectives and truly try to create some form of change because the chances are it will take longer than your next review

The result is that year after year orgs spend fortunes fixing the symptom, plastering over the cracks, and never changing anything too much. Another point to mention here is that the more we move up the system, the harder it is to produce a tangible thing such as a product. Going too far up the system and you lose sight of the initial challenge but often end up looking at the thing causing the actual problem which are often big meaty complex challenges.

Picture this, when you're in sense-making, you stand at the bottom of a river. The current of this river is powerful, coming down that river at pace is the tension, challenges, and problems your people are dealing with. You hear this in interviews, immersions, and so on.

If you swim further up the river, you would get to the point where you can identify the systems, sub-systems, and patterns that are causing this output. However, this is a challenging struggle, you're not the best swimmer, the current of the river is strong and you don't know where the top of this river is.

Should you choose to be a brave human and go for it anyway, you may find yourself at the top of the river looking at sub-systems... you think eureka, time to fix/redesign these challenges. It is only at that point when you finally think you are there, you identify the headwater (this is where the water starts to flow, often from mountains or rain), aka a bigger system at play. It's at this point you realise you're not in the weeds of the original challenge i.e. creating tangible solutions. You are so high up that you're looking at an area where a simple solution can't be built, it is much more complex and needs a lot more design and thinking to overcome.

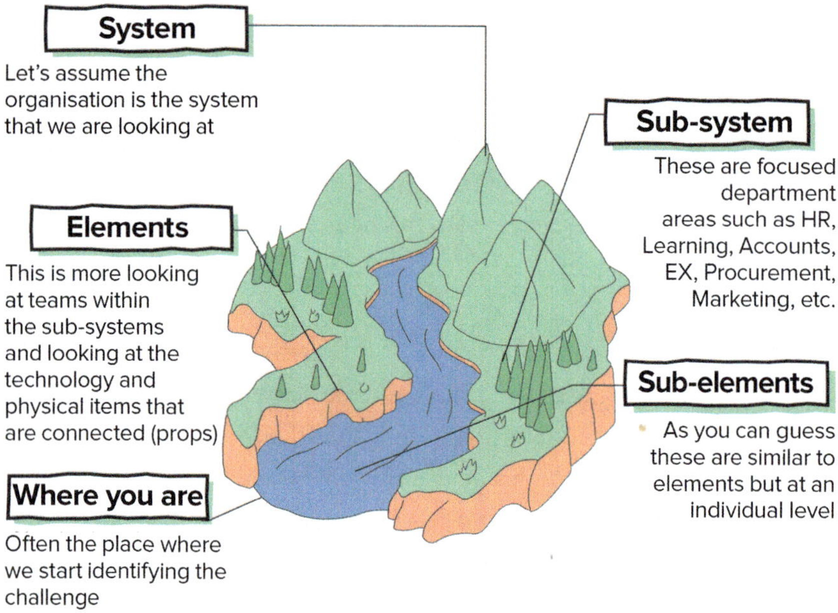

To apply system thinking, you don't have to be in a certain role. Don't get me wrong, system thinking is often discussed when talking about big strategy (even if they don't use the term system thinking). For me, it's about having a mindset that can be rebellious and curious by nature but can also apply logic and reverse engineering. But be mindful that it is hard to do because often the system that you are in doesn't want you to change it. I think that's why I apply system thinking as a lens over my work to help identify problems but I am mindful that I won't always get to change the sub-system or systems as such.

INSIGHTFUL INGREDIENT

Emperor penguins use sound to communicate with each other, as they all look similar and so rely on unique voices to recognize their mates and chicks. They use vocalisations to attract mates, warn of danger, and give directions to other penguins.

#DANNYDISCUSSIONS

What comes to mind when reading about this?

....

....

....

....

....

....

....

....

....

....

....

....

SYSTEM THINKING, EXPLAINED IN MAXIMS

So we know what a system is, it makes sense to move on to talk about what system thinking is (the inner child is screaming at me to write it's 'thinking about the system' but I won't, well, I will but let me try to explain a little more).

System thinking came about in the 1960s, it is a way of zooming out from the weeds and looking broader. You're ultimately trying to remove the blinkers you have on to look at how things work with each other, see the patterns and ultimately identify levers we can pull to see how changing one thing may help to change another. How changing something in a sub-system may help to change the result in another.

I am now going to share how I think of system thinking with maxims. There are many great books about system thinking from experts in this field. Should you want to dive deeper into system thinking, I highly recommend you check out the reading list I keep updated on my website. Use the QR code anywhere in the book and it'll take you there.

A SYSTEM IS A LOT LIKE A WIDGET MACHINE

If our machine (system) is built to produce widgets, the inputs to this machine are values, behaviours, policies, processes, incentives, and guide rails. You can't be angry with the machine if it produces a widget you don't like, the machine is producing the output based on the input.

On Feb 13th 2006, Malcolm Gladwell wrote a piece for *The New Yorker* sharing the story of Murray Barr, an alcoholic homeless man living in Nevada. In the story titled *Million Dollar Murray*, Gladwell shares how two local police officers tracked the drunken acts of Murray. The police officers identified that just one of the many drunken acts ran up a hospital bill of over $100,000.

Over the years, the same thing would happen time and time again, Murray would get drunk, the police would arrest him, he would be placed in a cell for the night to sober up then be released back out the next day. Gladwell goes on to write there was a time when Murray was put on a treatment programme, like most detox programmes Murray was taken out of the real world and put into a space where everything is set up for him to be successful including getting a job and managing to collect some savings.

Unfortunately, Murray graduated from the programme and was

placed back into the real world with all the structures now non-existent. Over time, Murray slipped into his old ways: more arrests, more hospital visits, more jail sentences. The two police officers over time totalled how much Murray cost the state, taking into account all the emergency services, treatments, and treatment centres, and so on.

The police officers found that by not putting Murray into the system and the sub-system, over ten years, it cost the state over 1 million dollars. This led to a wide study being done and results showed that it cost the state around $24,000 a year per homeless person to give them a shelter bed. After digging into the data, the study found that if you instead take a proactive approach, and don't just drop people into the system, they could give the homeless person a house and all they need for much less than $24,000. In fact, at a maximum, it would be a third of the cost.

Output: It's funny, when I read this all those years ago, I couldn't help but make the connection of how orgs spend money and resources on fixing symptoms without looking at the system. I imagine how many orgs and functions, if they sat back and totalled up the cost, would realise they had also spent more effort, time and resources on fixing the symptom but not the problem. I wonder how many have been caught out by the Million Dollar Murray problem by simply not looking at the bigger picture.

INSIGHTFUL INGREDIENT

Disney views hiring as casting people for a role, whether it be a performer at Disney World, a shop assistant in London, or back-office admin staff. Everyone, regardless of whether they are on stage or backstage, plays a role in making the show happen.

#DANNYDISCUSSIONS

What comes to mind when reading about this?

....

....

....

....

....

....

....

SPEEDY SYSTEM THINKING IT IS NOT

One thing though, system thinking is not fast. I think this is one of the reasons many orgs have chosen not to use it. Thinking and looking at a system is fairly complex work. If you tried to map a simple system that you know really well, it would still take you time to do it and even then there will be lots of unknowns that you need to know about. However, the value in taking the time to map out a system is worth its weight in gold when you see patterns forming.

When I created a transformation design team at a large consultancy one of the core principles I put in place was to first zoom out before zooming in. Based on what I had experienced in the business before creating this new team they were very quick to rush through to traditional solutions yet our clients were needing more.

When a large consultancy of over 300,000 people reached out with some pretty unique challenges, I immediately saw this as a good case to show how system thinking works. The client had a few challenges, their sales team were not selling enough Amazon or Google cloud services, their people were not getting certified in these areas fast enough. Now, it could be super easy to suggest some form of learning solution here and the job is done.

However, I helped remind the team of system thinking. I tasked them to first zoom out and map the system, challenge the assumptions, and see what patterns they could see. Mapping just a few of these sub-systems took over ten weeks, looking not only at the element and sub-elements but also identifying the relationships and how things work together (in system thinking terms this is called Synthesis).

We uprooted that the client did have a development problem; it was tiny in comparison to some of their other system challenges. We identified where the relationship between various tensions was working to produce an unwanted product or response (in system thinking terms, this is called Emergence). For example, a tech expert whose day-to-day involved getting their head down in doing in-the-weeds tech work, then a salesperson who was heading up building relationships with their clients. The tension happened when these two parties had to interact together, two different types of language resulting in one party not knowing what the other was saying.

The result is that the salesperson would be churning out jargon to a potential new customer that they had received from the tech experts.

Other areas also came up such as incentives, tech, comms, team silos, poor processes, and so on. One of the key things we shared was that the system is producing perfect output based on the way in which it's built. When presenting this back to the client they were blown away at the work we had done as a team. Stating they had never seen it done like this before. What this allowed us to do is go back to the client, have a much richer conversation and redirect the resource to some of the areas we suggested to look for potential experimentation.

Output: Take the time to slow down and zoom out, identifying the relationships of a system rather than just the elements. If you have a high turnover don't rush to fix the onboarding. The turnover is potentially based on some other upstream challenges, so make sense and understand how these various relationships and patterns work. While onboarding may be an issue, so might be the shifts, the manager, the culture, and so on.

TAKE NOTE OF THE UNSEEN

Measuring system thinking is tricky, I am not talking about measuring the change of elements or sub-systems that are pretty well established but actually measuring the invisibleness of system thinking. I was once chatting to my partner's grandad Derek over a cup of tea one morning. Derek, a police officer in the '70s, told me a story of how young police officers would often game the system a little to speed through the ranking as it all came down to numbers, the more an officer made arrests the quicker they flew up the chain of command.

Derek gave an example of how a young police officer could make friends with someone who works for an electricity supplier, over time the officer would ask this new friend whose electricity was unusually high or low. The electricity supplier would hand over the address of the customer and the officer would go round to do a 'routine check' with the hope that their house was illegal, maybe wired to the grid and avoiding the metre, or find that the high usage was due to them growing cannabis and the associated lamps required for this. All the police officer would need to do then is simply arrest the customer. Derek explained that young police officers would do a lot of these routine stops throughout the day over the course of many months to get their arrest rates higher.

When I asked what the not-so-new officers were doing, he mentioned they would be doing street walks, being visible and building relationships in the community and with low-end criminals. Derek explained that by being present on the street, it allowed him to keep his ear to the ground, criminals knew him by name, as they saw him patrolling the streets and were less likely to do these illegal activities such as growing cannabis or wiring up to streetlamps.

On paper, if you compare the young officer to Derek you could make the case that the first officer had the largest impact, but did he?

How many offences/crimes did the street walking officer stop before they ever actually became an offence? What's the measurement of his presence walking up and down the streets? Goodhart's Law states when measurement becomes the target, it ceases to be a measurement.

Output: measuring tactical output like the new officer is easier to do but should that be the measurement of success? By this point, often the measurement is on a crime that has already happened. The richer question to ask is how do we measure the impact of the more mature officer that walks the streets and stops things happening before they even start? What indications can we track? Ask ourselves what are we not seeing, what else may be helping or hindering success? Will we ever truly start to measure the right kinds of things? Which leads me to Cobras in the next section.

INSIGHTFUL INGREDIENT

After the initial training and induction period, new employees at Zappos are offered a 'bribe' of $3000 to leave the company if they don't feel that it is a good fit for any reason. This is seen as a small investment to ensure that only committed employees remain with the company. Less than 2% of employees have taken up this offer.

#DANNYDISCUSSIONS

What comes to mind when reading about this?

....

....

....

....

....

....

....

....

....

Watch out for ~~Cobra~~ Rat effect

Cobra effect is the term used when applying incentives to a problem only for the incentive to drive a less desirable and often unintended consequence. Often we add an incentive to a system in the hope it will drive a result and rarely do we give enough thinking time to what might happen if we do. In layman's terms, every action has a consequence and often this consequence results in the opposite of what you are hoping for.

The term 'Cobra effect' comes from an unproven story that happened in India during British rule, however, because this story is unproven I propose that we change the name to the Rat effect, a story that has been proven. Perhaps I am being pedantic, but here's a little more about the Rat effect. In Hanoi, Tonkin French Indochina (now known as Hanoi, Vietnam) the French government was overrun with rats, they decided they needed to get a handle on it and they did what all governments do and chucked a load of money at it. They opted into incentivizing and rewarding the hunting of rats, as the Pied Piper wasn't available, and we hadn't grown a love for 'Ratatouille' yet.

The government decided to reward people for killing the rats with a pretty simple set-up; for each rat killed they would get 1 cent. Not wanting to be left with lots of rat bodies, the government decided that for rat hunters to claim this 1 cent per rat, they would only need to show the severed tails. At the start there seemed to be a noticeable decrease in rat sightings, however, over time the government started to notice a sharp increase in rats, what was more peculiar was that these rats had no tails.

What was happening was simple, rat catchers realised that there were no long-tail wins for them, if they killed rats then over time they could be out of a job. So they chose to game the system and stay in work for as long as possible. These rat hunters were instead capturing the rats, cutting the tails off and letting them loose so they could produce more rats. This resulted in the government being left with more rats than they originally had and a lot of financially better-off rat hunters.

An experience I recall many years ago while working for a telecoms provider, the company had a sharp increase in call volumes for various reasons and predicted they needed a higher headcount for around six months. They were not able to fulfil the volume of calls with fantastic advisors because their high standard recruitment process was taking too long, so they decided to bypass the process and opted for a quick recruitment model that rewarded internal recommendation.

Unfortunately, they didn't take into account when launching this incentive that:

1. Local students were on break from university and looking to make an easy bit of money for two weeks before going back to uni.
2. Demographics of employees recommending people were also younger 18-23 years old
3. T&Cs of getting the incentive for a recommendation.

This resulted in a high application rate of students pretending they weren't students and wanting a full-time job and a big drive on the internal L&D to support the new recruits with consistent onboarding cycles (two weeks in length).

The incentive was rewarded once application passed initial interview stages which meant that two weeks would pass and everyone would leave the business to return to university. In the end, the rapid hire resulted in more people leaving the business, stating they felt the business had lost its way, it didn't feel like it used to, plus simple things that maybe the existing employees felt valuable, such as 121 meetings and coaching, were being pulled so the employees could stay on calls longer.

Output: When we think about internal performance reviews, benefits, and rewards, it pays to ask how this can be gamed. What's the rat effect that could happen if we build it?

INSIGHTFUL INGREDIENT

Unfortunately before my time there, '?What If!' founders would take all new hires on a magic bus tour where they would stop at some of the company's historic landmarks. The founder would share how the business was created and what makes up the DNA of someone who works at ?What If!

#DANNYDISCUSSIONS

What comes to mind when reading about this?

....

....

....

....

....

....

....

....

....

....

....

....

....

....

ADDING BALANCE

There are certain tools and approaches to use when looking at journeys and complex systems, such as the feedback loops.

Throughout any system, there are many feedback loops, these show the relationship between two or more things and help identify potential leverage points in the system that could have the biggest impact. There are two types – balancing loops and reinforcing loops.

Reinforcing loops are one part of the outputs of the loop that reinforces the other, these often drive growth or decline. I try to think of it as an action and effect. A typical example is the population:

- Population impacts births – more population = more births (effect)
- More births impact population – more births = more population (action)

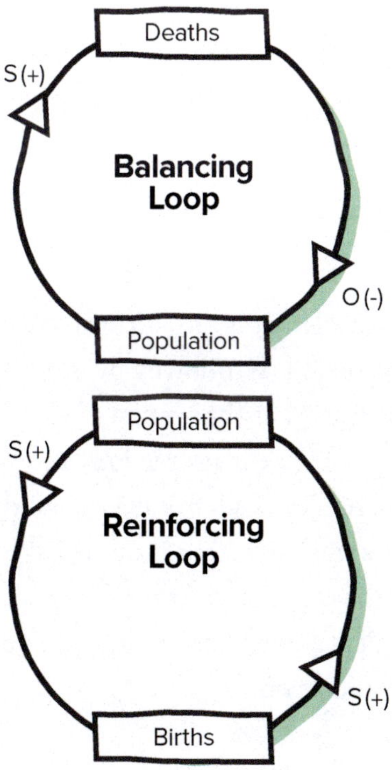

The little 's' or sometimes seen as (+) to the sides of the illustration show the relationship between each is similar. So one goes up, the other goes up.

Balancing loops are loops that add balance to the system and stabilise it; they don't allow it to overgrow in any one direction. They are like the doormen at a fancy bar, they make sure the bar has enough people in to make money and thrive, but not too many that it overflows and ends in a mass brawl.

Now, with population it clearly doesn't go just one way, death also happens. When the population increases, deaths increase. When

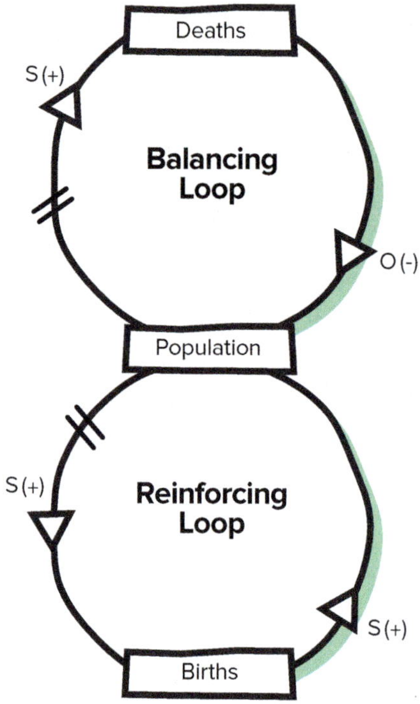

deaths happen, this decreases the population. This type of loop keeps the balance. The O or sometimes seen as (-) shows it has an opposite relationship.

An important note in this type of loop is the fact of time and often to see the loop in action there will be a delay in time between each point.

Time between each point can be seen by a marker of double lines in this illustration:

As soon as you start to scale this process out, you inevitably start to see the bigger system and identify where to zoom in. Mapping simple feedback loops for any EX product is often one of the tools I turn to straight away when wanting to identify where the moments of tension are and which areas are ripe for me to challenge.

WHO OWNS THE SYSTEM

Often when mapping out a system, there will be a wow moment. The sheer vastness of the system, sub-system and elements are a thing of awe (well, I think so anyway). This moment tends to be followed by a swift dose of doom, when you realise nobody really owns the system as such.

It's easy, when in a complex system, to think it's somebody else's challenge and not yours. Identifying stakeholders and influence is vital but they don't own the system either, it's something that is owned as a collective. For example, mapping something out like the hiring process, you will be amazed by the many stakeholders and people involved alone before looking at elements, process, tech, and so on.

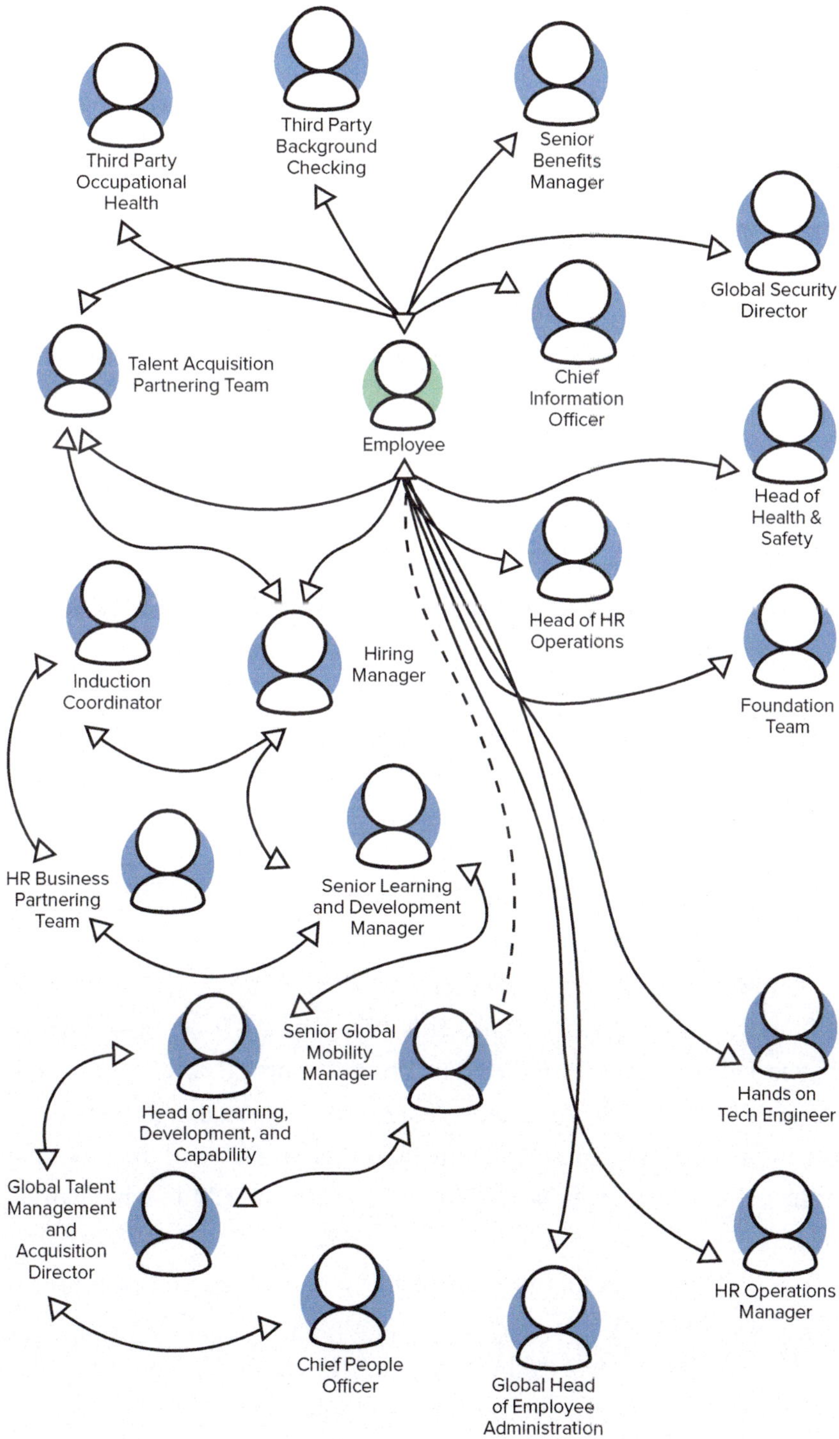
Third Party Occupational Health
Third Party Background Checking
Senior Benefits Manager
Global Security Director
Talent Acquisition Partnering Team
Employee
Chief Information Officer
Head of Health & Safety
Head of HR Operations
Induction Coordinator
Hiring Manager
Foundation Team
HR Business Partnering Team
Senior Learning and Development Manager
Senior Global Mobility Manager
Head of Learning, Development, and Capability
Hands on Tech Engineer
Global Talent Management and Acquisition Director
HR Operations Manager
Chief People Officer
Global Head of Employee Administration

Next up is an example taken from a client I was working with, looking at onboarding and induction.

Just look at how many people were involved, each bringing with them barriers, process challenges, and so on. Also, think just how much overload in noise and interactions the new starter is having. It is no wonder there was an inconsistent and disconnected onboarding experience across the company.

As you can see there is a lot of one-way traffic going from the business to the newbie. Another map taken from system thinking is the stakeholder map that allows us to really start bringing the people together who have the influence to make the change but who will also take individual ownership. Before we get into it, you might be asking, 'Why is stakeholder mapping here and not in the service and human parts of sense-making?'

Well, it kind of is, you will interview various stakeholders throughout sense-making the human, asking simple questions like:

- Who else needs to be part of this?
- What clout and influence do they bring to this?
- Who are the three people I need to talk to?

These will all help to slowly bring this type of map to life. It will also help you when it comes to designing a relationship experience.

From my perspective, a stakeholder map starts in the human touchpoint of design. However, this type of map is often linked to system thinking and it makes sense to put it here. Like all tools and methods in design, they are somewhat fluid in nature, don't get stuck to just applying them here. Test them out in various different touchpoints of the journey. This approach is yours to remix and edit to what works for you.

Okay, let's get mapping, first thing to do is draw out a bullseye diagram (see below).

Place in the centre of the bullseye what the challenge is, for example, to understand the hiring process of new employees, place this challenge bang centre of the bullseye.

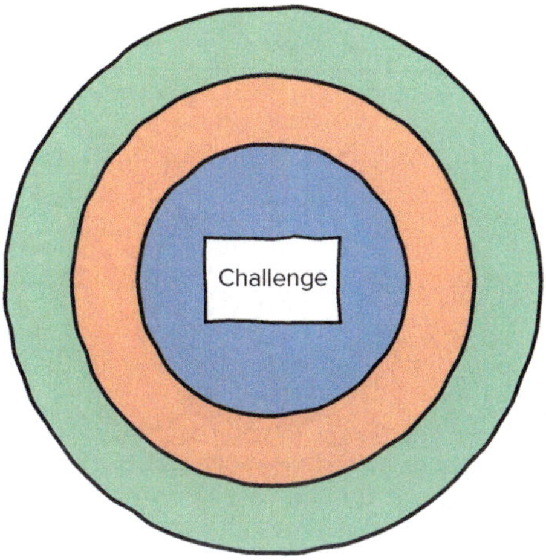

By this stage, you will have heard of lots of names from interviews. From the DARE, who are important to the hiring process? These are the names that will have influences in the hiring journey, a non-exhaustive list may look a bit like this:

- Hiring managers
- Recruitment managers
- Recruitment team members internal/external
- Function leads
- Employees
- Knowledge SMEs
- Project manager
- EX lead

There are many ways to now prioritise the stakeholders, some may do it through the level of influence, contact, engagement, etc. if you struggle here ask:

- Who needs to be kept up-to-date
- Who will feel the pain and gain of this
- Who has skin in the game to want to make this work
- Who actually has a legit real interest in it on a personal level

By now, maybe you have twenty names. The next step is to map these on the bullseye, the more important they are to the challenge, the closer they are in the centre.

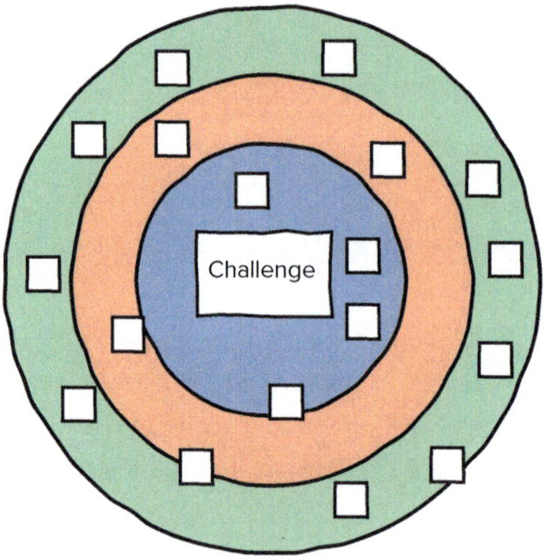

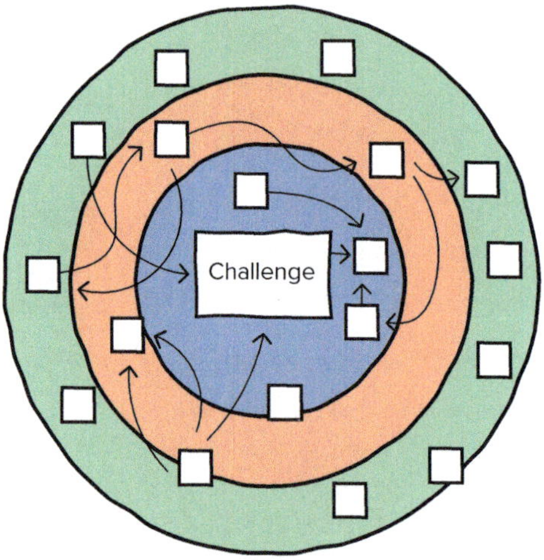

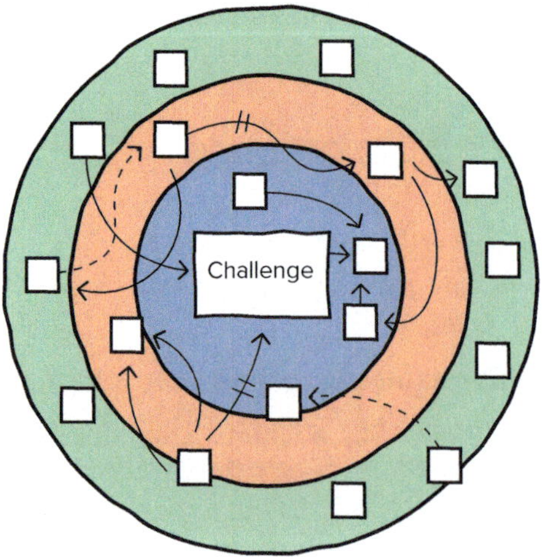

The core stakeholders identified in the DARE should appear here, often in/around the centre.

So, at this stage, you can start to see the importance of all the stakeholders who are vital vs the ones we just need to keep warm. The next thing to do is map out how they are interlinked via relationship.

To do this, think of it like an exchange. What is exchanged between them? Use simple arrows to show this and the direction the exchange happens. As you can see (left), some have one arrow going out while others have a two-way arrow. This is normal, like all good relationships it's a two-way street, stakeholders are no different.

What this gives us is a visual representation of how the exchange happens, as well as a list of people, for example looking at the hiring process through the eyes of the employee is very different to looking at the hiring process through the eyes of a recruiter, and so on.

You can also take the

stakeholder map up another level in detail if you so wished, simply by identifying where the delays in the exchange happen. Similar to feedback loops, mark this with a double line break through the arrows. Where tension may show up, I often use a dotted arrow.

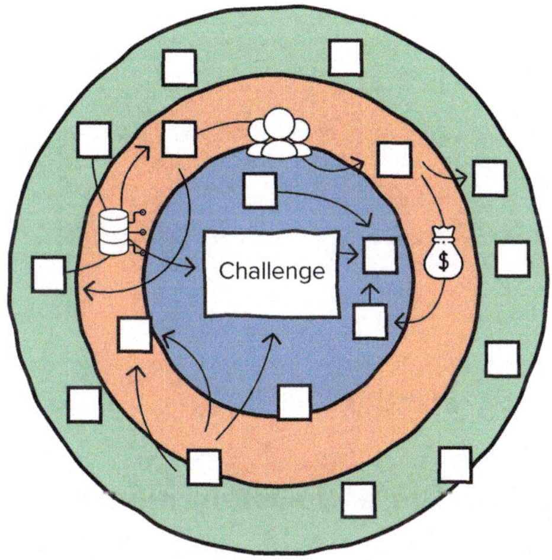

We could evolve the map once more, adding in an exchange layer which shows the form of exchange between stakeholders. This could be knowledge, resources, data, etc. As you can see here, one exchanges funding, and another exchanges data.

Often when getting into complex systems and challenges, it is easy for the blinker to come on around looking wider. The stakeholder map allows you to zoom out, see the challenge from a bird's eye through various angles, and then zoom in to look specifically at any identified tension points, as well as the value of exchange between them all.

INSIGHTFUL INGREDIENT

Thinking bigger, Robert Wagner came up with the idea of an escape fire. Trapped by the Mann Gulch fire on Aug 5th, 1949 with only minutes to spare, Robert lit a small fire ahead of him so that the flammable ground burnt out and he could jump on it. Once the Mann Gulch fire got to him, with no fresh ground to burn, the fire burned around him saving his life.

#DANNYDISCUSSIONS

What comes to mind when reading about this?

....

....

....

....

....

....

FIRE STORM

Tubbs fire and system failure

In October 2017, Northern California was victim to the worst wildfires on record (a year later being overtaken by the Northern California campfire) record shows over thirty lives were taken by the fire, many hundreds were burnt, and thousands of buildings were burnt to the ground.

In a report done by Reveal, they walk through a thread of events that led to the destruction and loss of so many lives. Signalling to me at least the importance of system thinking and looking and thinking broader than just tactical and silo. Throughout the report, you can hear what becomes a series of reactive system failures.

The story began with someone calling through the emergency service stating they had witnessed the strong winds blow over a powerline into a tree causing the powerline to spark out. This started a chain of events. When a powerline sparks out, it drives a power surge down the line, causing the transformers to overload and blow which then creates a domino effect, driving too much power onto other transformers and causing them to blow.

The emergency service, following procedure, calls the energy service and asks for a patrol to go down, put out any fire, and fix the power lines.

In the report, you can start to hear the demand increase as emergency services take more and more calls about fires happening. The power stations are not the only thing pushing the fire at this point, the strong winds are picking up hot embers from the ground and blowing them across dry woodland causing more mini fires. As these fires start to become aggressive, picking up momentum from the wind and taking anything down in its path, the fire starts to make its way to the city of Santa Rosa with a population of over 178,000 people.

One of the key points of failure, and something we touched upon in the service design chapter, was the importance of language. At one point in the report, you can hear jargon get in the way of communication as emergency services call local Santa Rosa emergency services asking for a reverse 911. You can hear the Santa Rosa advisor say, "Sorry, I don't know what that is?". This turns out to be simply jargon, where both emergency services have this tool but it goes by different names.

Once the communication breakdown is overcome, the next failure comes as the tool used to send the evacuation messages to locals is an opt-in service that only alerts people via landline, which many people don't have or stopped using many years ago.

You can't help but think adding a simple change to default and having people opt out could be easy here. The report also highlights another service that could have been used (a text evacuation service) however, it seems nobody wanted to step outside the process to do this. Due to the overwhelming calls and communication breakdown, you can hear some emergency services tell people to actually stay in their homes until told otherwise.

This is just a snapshot of some of the system failures heard in the story. Without looking at the wider system and where it failed, it could be all too easy to just focus on one aspect of the failure and misjudge that as being the root cause rather than an effect of a bigger failure.

Jack Cohen, a system thinker and now retired fire scientist was looking at the behaviour of fires. One area he zoomed his focus on was he wanted to understand how the 1980 Panorama fire had caused so much damage, especially given their prevention tactics were so good.

He went on the journey of sense-making. This involved listening to hours of emergency call recording from the day of the fire to really piece together what went on. Jack started to notice various patterns but the one that jumped out the most was why were so many people calling in about their houses being on fire when the actual fire had not reached them yet.

Jack started to notice some similarities with these houses and buildings:

- They were downstream of the fire's direction of travel
- These houses all had similar types of roofs

What Jack had identified in his sense-making was most of the houses were catching fire, not from the major fire but actually from the hot embers the wind was picking up and travelling downwind. These hot embers would then fall onto these properties with wooden roofs and slowly set the house alight. Jack's curiosity triggered. He set out to prove or disprove this and test his finding. He didn't need to look far.

When he took a walk to where the fire had passed through he noticed a stark difference. One side of the street was burnt down, while the other street was perfectly fine. The only difference being one side of the street was modern with slate roofs while the other was wooden roofs, these modern houses were able to withstand the fire and were left untouched.

This aha moment took Jack on a journey of deep sense-making, not on how fire works, but more importantly on how houses are built. In a child-like, dream mindset Jack went about understanding the ins and outs of how a house is built, the materials used, and the process it goes through. He even went on to do various experiments to test his assumption, one famous one is when he actually set a forest on fire.

His findings helped identify many systems and sub-system flaws. He suggested many proactive changes to the system ranging from redesigning property layouts, designing where things such as trees should go in relation to each other in the garden, right through to replacing roof materials, adding ground stones to the property, and so on.

Unfortunately, Jack's research and system thinking approach didn't land so well, with many people not taking it seriously. This could be for many reasons such as experts not wanting to be challenged on their thinking, through to the impact this thinking may have on the infrastructure such as firefighting services, the jobs, and amount of spending that goes into it.

Jack's story is a cautionary one, that we can all take something from. Which is, for as long as we build reward systems or services that fix the after effect of a problem we will never truly address the wider system problem. While we may have all the will in the world to completely fix a system, you have to be mindful of people, sub-systems, and elements in play. And while we may want a full system change, there are various roles and people that rely heavily on the system not changing whatsoever.

Output: While you may see the value in system thinking, others may not. At which point, you have a choice to look bigger and wider and identify bigger areas of impact or get more tactical on a smaller piece of work. Just don't expect everyone to understand and be on the same page as you.

THE CHALLENGE OF SYSTEM THINKING

The challenge when it comes to system thinking, especially when it comes to work, culture, and employee experience is often that it can feel invisible. This is especially true if everyone is off working in their silo, it can be time-consuming and often not deliver something tangible in the instant results.

It can be made or broken depending on how well you can bring stakeholders together and enable them to see the value in letting go and working together on something bigger. In my experience, should you choose to ignore system thinking and not pay it even a slight bit of attention, the result often means you will only ever be fixing symptoms. Employee experience is a prime example of a system of sorts, it has its sub-system and elements at play whether that be attraction, onboarding, reward, performance, and so on. By not taking the time to look up in sense-making and asking how this plays into the biggest system, you put yourself in a silo.

Like the phrase system thinking states, it is first about 'thinking' the richness gained from applying this lens is real depth in looking at the problem, usually in the form of maps and tools to show things at play. These provide richer insights, connections, and narrative to share back with the business. With this narrative and insight, you can start to bring people together who as a collective can start to apply ownership of the sub-systems and elements. Over time, this will identify which stakeholders actually give a shit and want to truly create momentum and change.

Measuring system thinking is extremely hard, often because system thinking is about making a change before it becomes something that needs fixing later on or measuring something you maybe won't ever get to see the results of in your career. Use the story of Derek, the policeman, from earlier on. Measuring the impact of his street walking vs his colleagues who were finding people-boosting energy. Derek's role was one of proactiveness and preventative, while his colleagues' role was much more reactive.

Unfortunately, due to how many performance systems are set up, Derek's colleague will often be the one who gets rewarded because it's the amount of arrests for crimes committed that is the measurement, not the amount of crimes prevented.

For as long as a system rewards tactical solutions, we will always find ourselves in this cycle of addressing the symptoms and never the root cause. System thinking when stripped right back is simply looking bigger and wider and identifying where we can make a change for a bigger impact by simply saying, 'think bigger' (TB).

Look at oral care in children (an oversimplified example)

A dentist may identify that a child has a cavity. To stop the cavity from getting bigger, he will remove the decay and put in a filling – a reactive step to a problem. Now let's TB.

A dentist partners with local government or perhaps a children's TV show and creates a fun awareness campaign signalling the importance of brushing your teeth twice a day. Over time, this starts to reduce the risk of a cavity occurring (TB).

We could also use some form of scarcity or reward to help children do even more, maybe we add a unique twist to flossing, mouthwash (TB).

Perhaps we target the parents, we drive awareness around how much sugar is in the snacks they buy for their children and the impact it is having on their wellbeing. Maybe we could target schools and look at driving some form of school change around sugary snacks (TB). We could add an agent into water like fluoride. Start having a proactive approach to protecting our children's teeth.

As you can see the more proactive and bigger thinking you give to the problem, the tricker it becomes to measure. Measuring the reactive level of the dentist filling the cavity feels much easier, but that doesn't mean it's the right thing to measure.

I wanted to end this chapter on something maybe closer to home, one that am sure everyone can relate to and that is Covid-19

MAPPING PROBLEMS – COVID-19

Clever researchers at Carnegie Mellon have created two maps showing the problems that came up when Covid-19 showed its ugly head. One of the maps is 22-feet long and shows what they call a rough sketch of the problem. It identifies many of the challenges faced from policies, processes, and infrastructure using various tools discussed in this chapter such as stakeholder maps, exchange mapping, and feedback loops. The other is a respectful 18-feet long map showing a rich narrative around how Covid-19 came to spread so fast. While the topic isn't one I think anyone would want to relive, the map is a thing of beauty and one I recommend you check out.

Next stop the Incubate phase ...

INSIGHTFUL INGREDIENT

Buffer, the social media scheduling tool, is known for its transparency mainly because it's one of their ten values (default to transparency and trust) wanting everyone to be on the same page and removing doubt. Buffer shares all its employee salaries, not only internally but externally as well, it also shares its revenue, customer charging, and models. Signalling to new talent what to expect and living the values from day one.

#DANNYDISCUSSIONS

What comes to mind when reading about this?

....

....

....

....

....

....

....

....

....

....

....

....

....

....

SAID AND SEALED

- A system is a set of interconnected elements that function together as a whole.
- A system consists of sub-systems, elements, and sub-elements that are connected to each other.
- System thinking is a way of understanding how a system functions and how changes in one part of the system can affect the whole.
- It involves looking at the bigger picture and considering the relationships between different parts of the system.
- To apply system thinking in design, it is important to be curious and rebellious and to consider the long-term impact of changes.
- In the context of employee experience, system thinking can help to identify and address the root causes of problems and create more sustainable solutions.

← Scan me to be taken to resources

INCUBATE – DREAM & DISTIL

WHAT IS CREATIVITY?

What is it? Who is creative? What do creatives do differently to non-creatives? What about ideas, where do they come from? What makes a good idea vs a bad idea?

Is creativity a nature vs nurture problem and what does all this mean for employee experience?

As we move out of sense-making, we take our insight and move into phase two incubate. Here we are looking at how we can prime our thinking to really come up with radical ideas. Not only will you see that the black magic of creative thinking isn't for the chosen few but that it's also a myth and really anyone can do it.

Over the coming pages, it will start to become clear why nearly every part of the employee experience looks the same in the majority of organisations. What truly sets the exceptions apart comes down to thinking radically different and approaching the challenge in an innovative way. First, we need to know why thinking differently is important and how to get into this creative state and be open to it.

Brain states

There are thought to be five key brain states that give off a certain frequency and put us into a different state of being and thinking. Hans Berger first identified the Alpha (8–12hz) and Beta (12–35hz) brainwaves in 1920. As time went on and technology progressed, research began to identify more frequencies Theta (4–8Hz) Delta (0.1–3.5Hz) and the most recent is Gamma (30 and above) discovered in 1988.

Each brain frequency is fascinating, however, in the interest of keeping this book lean here is a simple breakdown:

Alpha (8–12Hz) is that meditative creative set where we are calm, allowing the free flow of ideas.

Theta (4–8hz) goes deeper than alpha, you move from the chilled present flow to being in a much more dreamlike state, you might find this when on a train, in a car, etc. random ideas start to come to mind.

Gamma (30 and above) is thought to be linked to when working in deep concentration and learning, it is often also mentioned in higher self-awareness. It is the peak performer.

Beta (12–35hz) is similar to Gamma in the fact it is about getting shit done. It is that moment when you just are feeling in the vibe, getting it done and hitting the beat on everything in meetings, and tasks. It tends to be your normal go to (or what your org would want you to be in).

Delta (01.–3.5) is the deepest state known to date. If you're in this state the chances are you're either a monk or a baby. It's hard to get to this state without falling asleep.

The reason I mentioned these states isn't to sound like some form of mastermind, far from it. It starts to help us understand why certain ideas come in the middle of the night, while others randomly pop up while daydreaming. We can't guarantee a certain brain state nor could we prove it without an ECG scan. We can, however, do our best to create the space to get into that state and allow creativity to flow and it often starts with the setting.

Set, Setting & Stim

The term set and setting is often used when people talk about their psychedelic journey. Instead, I am going to borrow the term and apply it in the following context:

- set = mindset
- setting = the space in which we work

When we want to move from really pushing the boundaries of ideas, or we want to really look under the hood of a challenge, then the thing we have, that beats all plays from a playbook or any tool from a toolbox, is our mindset. This mindset is something that needs to be present in every stage of design from sense-making, to incubate, to experiment and experience. That said, it's not that easy because what I am actually talking about isn't one mindset, it's two. Both are equally balanced, just as yin and yang.

Mindset to me is the frame in which we think, it is the fertilised ground on which our thoughts and ideas grow like little green shoots of new flowers. Our mindset, like many other things, is built on the experience and the stimulus (stim for short) we have given it.

Switching between these two mindsets is critical when it comes to coming up with new ideas and potential solutions. It can be a challenge, at first, to switch between these mindsets. Especially if, over time, we have been rewarded for being more in one mindset than the other. We start to value the output of the thinking that mindset produces over anything else. The good news is with a little bit of help and some applied friction we can switch between these mindsets.

The Dreamer mindset

This mindset does not see a ceiling, it looks past perceived barriers and asks what could be. This Dreamer mindset roams curiously asking why, what if, imagine if, why not. It's constantly learning, adapting, building new patterns of thinking. It can take something from nearly every interaction. You will know the type of people whose natural preference is to be a dreamer because often you will go to them asking for builds on your idea or to stretch it out. It is the person in the office that after you have spoken with them you come away buzzing with ideas and energy.

Often, in most companies, the people who love to be in this mindset can be found in (but not limited to) Marketing and PR. From an innovation point of view, these people tend to be found in R&D and often working in the initial ideation stage of the innovation funnel (often called stage gate 0) where one of their prime goals is to keep the funnel full with potential new ideas, solutions, etc.

In many aspects, they have the mindset of an apprentice and have over time managed to constantly keep it at a level where they don't allow past and current experiences to block their mind from new signals and patterns coming in.

Take a minute or so, read through the below, and then write the first five names that come to mind:

- Who is the person who gives you energy and you walk away from sparking with new ideas?
- Who is the person that wouldn't be out of place at an adlib show?
- Who is that person who shares random stories, challenges modern conventions?
- Who is the person who can somehow make a connection between a bat, a chair, and great leaders?
- Who is the person who is always trying new things? One week they are at poetry, next they are at a coffee conference, following week at a LARP (live action role play) show.

However, staying in this mindset consistently while allowing you to come up with great disruptive ideas can sometimes, if not controlled, take you too far from the art of the possible. That is why we need the distiller mindset.

The Distiller mindset

If the Dreamer mindset is looking out on a wide vista and asking what could be, the Distiller will narrow the focus and challenge the ideas with logic and grounded thinking. This mindset helps remove ideas that may not get off the ground and often help distil down a big idea if needed into smaller elements that we can try. This mindset is the mutual partner of the dreamer and it's needed.

Imagine if we were stuck on an island, and we can see there is a storm coming in so we need to come up with an idea of how to stay dry. The dreamer mindset may look at a box jellyfish in the sea and consider making it into a wonderful waterproof hat. While, of course, this is a crazy idea, nobody would want this on their head. But the dreamer is looking at the challenge thinking 'imagine if'. From the outside, it can feel idiotic (if you think that is a daft idea, right now then you're in a distiller mindset currently).

But look around in the world and you can see the dreamer's fingerprints everywhere – in the wetsuits we wear to go swimming and surfing, to the methods of transport like trains and planes, right through to helping children put their trainers on with the Velcro used. (The term of looking at nature for potential innovation is actually called biomimicry.)

The distiller mindset would apply a much more narrowed logic to the idea (maybe you did that in the paragraph above and thought it was a silly idiotic idea) and applied some form of reasoning to it, by clearly stating that it is one of most poisonous things in the world and to first scale it down and look at alternative things such as the leaves of that Giant Taro tree. This mindset helps play a critical friend to the dreamer mindset and can be found across the organisation.

You know who the people are with this mindset, they tend to be really good at spotting blind spots. They challenge the thinking by asking questions and sometimes telling you why it won't work. They have a realist and often restricted (in a good way) approach, 'have you thought about xyz?' and so on. They help the dreamer pause for a second which can stop them going into a board meeting suggesting you should bring all new hires in on unicorns and instead to offer up an alternative solution like a shuttle bus.

However, staying in this mindset consistently while it will allow you to create safe ideas, often these are not disruptive or innovative and can often be seen in many org or places already.

I am sure you can now start to see that both mindsets are a superpower, you are neither JUST a dreamer or just a distiller. You can be in either mindset at any given time. I am not saying you enjoy it but as a human you can go between the two (with a little help) and you will need to. Through the design process you will be called on and you will need colleagues to do the same in order to move forward.

Just remember this ...

A dreamer isn't the fun mindset and the distiller the anti-fun mindset as I've heard many times before, both are equally fun, trust me. These mindsets are of equal measure. Bringing them in at the right time is critical in the same way that bringing them in at the wrong time can have a terrible effect on the project. However, a rule to remember is that these mindsets (not people) don't mix well; they are like oil and water. I am sure you've been in a design lab, workshop, or even just an ideation jam where you need everyone to be primed with the dreamer's mindset only for Bob to pop up out of the blue saying, "That won't work here because of xyz".

This isn't a Bob problem, it's a mindset one. We haven't got Bob primed for the mindset we need. Over the session, the mindset will keep popping up, maybe through words, body language signs, tuts, etc. but by the end you might want to high-five Bob's face with a chair. Please don't do that. Instead, perhaps you need to spend a few more minutes getting Bob's mindset in line.

If not, this distiller mindset will start to spread around the group like a dose of chickenpox in a nursery, leaving you with a lot of level one ideas that are seen across 80% of other businesses. We will touch later on how to get round this in more detail but for now please note mindset mixing in a focused session is a no no for when we want to come up with innovation ideas.

- **Dreamer**
  Explorer, zoomed out, divergent expansively thinking

- **Distiller**
  zoomed-in, reduced, convergent logical thinking

The impact of getting the wrong mindset in the wrong session is too risky, that is why in my design flow you can see being a dreamer and a distiller are two very separate touch points.

A QUICK STORY

PAPER CLIP STORY (NO IT'S NOT CLIPPY FROM MICROSOFT)

In a 1968 experiment, George Land and Beth Jarman conducted a research study to test the creativity of 1,600 children ranging in ages from three to five years old. The researchers asked the children to come up with as many uses as they could for a simple paperclip.

The results of the study were shocking, with 98% of the 5-year-olds scoring at the 'genius level' on the test. George and Beth retested the children at ages 10 and 15 and found that the proportion of children who scored at the genius level decreased significantly, with 30% at age 10 and 12% at age 15.

They also tested a group of adults and found that only 2% scored at the genius level. The results of the study showed that young children have a natural ability for divergent thinking, or the ability to come up with many ideas. This ability tends to decrease as people get older, due to the influence of convergent thinking, or the tendency to filter and discard ideas that are deemed 'dumb' or 'stupid'.

The test is used by NASA as part of their selection process for hiring engineers and scientists, as the ability to come up with many ideas is essential for innovation in the field of space exploration. The test was also used by other organisations to evaluate the innovative thinking of potential employees.

THE SETTING FOR SUCCESS OR A SETTING FOR FAILURE

Funny isn't it how, when, and where we get our ideas from, often they come at really random times and weirdly so in random places. We can often overlook the importance of the setting at which these ideas come to us or worse still take it for granted. The interesting thing is the setting at which we allow new ideas to come to us is often done by our own design knowing or unknowingly, the setting often becomes the enabler to the mindset.

As we move into this incubate stage, we need to create the setting required to discover and dream up new thinking and ideas while also creating a setting in which these ideas can be challenged and maybe thrown in the bin.

Before we get into designing the space, it's important that you acknowledge what the setting is that gives you energy, maybe it's when you are surrounded by people or bright colours. Perhaps they come when you are out in nature or doing your hobby of choice, could it be that music helps or does it hinder.

Just pause reading this and make a mental note of the setting you are in right now.

How are you feeling?

- Do you feel sparked with energy, ideas, and connections?
- Are you dead as a dodo waiting for your next coffee fix?
- How about the lighting, are you surrounded by natural light or does it resemble the light found in a prison cell?

Now, think back to the last moment when a new idea just popped into your head that you couldn't let go of. The chances are one or all of these happened:

- You were relaxed
- You were smiling and laughing
- You were in what felt like a safe space

- You switched off from thinking about the weeds of the problem
- You had an expansive conversation with someone else
- Maybe you were surrounded by lots of different stimulus

We will discuss in detail later about designing a setting for the mindsets we need. Use the time from now until then to just be active in acknowledging what places give you energy, what takes it away, and be alert to the setting in which it happens and the mindset it enables.

DREAM

Touchpoint one in the incubate phase is dream, as I am sure you can see by the name, it's a clear signal of the mindset we need going into it. However, it is not just the mindset we need, we also need to expand the demographic of the people in the room as discussed in sense-making.

Bringing in a wide spectrum of people from different backgrounds means we are going to bring in different beliefs, systems, and expectations. The dream stage is a very collaborative stage built heavily on co-design. If you look around the room (metaphorically speaking) and it isn't full of white men you are already setting yourself up for success, however, everyone in that room still needs to bring their full self to the party.

THE FULL YOU

At the start of my career, I had a niggling in the back of my head that I wasn't good enough. I still think that now even though I know I am. I guess that's what's allowed me to move through different careers from Employee Experience, L&D, Consulting, Director, Innovation, Manager, Co-founder, Podcast Host, and so on. But it wasn't always like that, I would hide my dyslexia, dial down my Manchester accent and try to learn big words to impress, and show up as this version of myself that wasn't me.

I learned very quickly that I hated everything about that. So instead I started to see that actually the things I was trying to mask were my superpowers. My dyslexia and sharing it meant I didn't have to worry about it as everyone knew. This is without going into the true benefits of dyslexia i.e. the problem-solving aspects. My Manc tones and simple language was actually why people wanted to talk to me.

Mancs have a friendly disarming tone (especially when speaking to the USA folks, once they know what I am saying that is). Being able to break down and share learning in simple language, along with a few swear words, started to become a real strong point and over time it is what got me to create the Mindchimp podcast. These are just little elements of the full me. However, there is much more to it.

From being a child, I was notoriously known for picking up hobbies and going all in then dropping them a year on. These hobbies included scouts, karate, painting Warhammer models, and later on in adulthood, it moved on to photography, golf, video editing, CrossFit, football. I believe this is a simple example of collecting experiences and remixing them to create something new. In fact, the only thing to have really stuck is mixed martial arts, weightlifting, and problem-solving. However, a few other things have always stuck with me; a love of bright colours and a love of hoodies.

It is rare to catch me out of a hoodie from 9-5, in fact, if I am not wearing a hoodie the chances are I am doing a talk or going to a wedding. I am a firm believer in dressing how you work best and for me that is in hoodies. I have even been known to rock up to a meeting wearing an Oodie.

So why am I telling you all this? It's simple: all the elements, plus many more, make up the full version of who we are. In a design lab or whatever you want to call it... the full versions are needed, the version that comes armed with experiences, expression, quirks. You will be amazed by the difference in those who fully show up in a workshop vs those who only bring their work self.

THE DREAMER'S SECRET

It is important to note the dream touchpoint is limitless, there is no brick wall to stop our ideas from getting out, it's a safe space to allow ideas to grow. However, from the outside it might look like a group of crazy people doing crazy shit with sticky notes, play doh, and odd paper prototypes.

Sending people out for Search & Discover might look like a waste of time for the untrained eye but it's simply not true.

Consistent generation of ideas might look like overkill but you couldn't be more wrong. Trust the process.

However, every now and again, you might get challenged on these as being fluffy or a waste of time.

In my experience, walking the challenger through the principle behind what we are doing and how it has been used for many years often helps settle any nervousness. The principle good old compound interest.

Compound interest is a term used in banking. Simply put, it's where the interest you earn on your money earns interest over time leading to a larger amount of money.

Coming up with new innovative ideas is no different. We have an idea (funds), we put it into a savings account (incubator, design labs, etc.) and it gets fed stimulus (interest). This then creates bigger ideas which in turn increase the stim and so on. We will talk more later about building on ideas but be aware that a well-designed few weeks/months design labs is anything but random.

Over the next chapter, we will look at some solid principles on how to enable people to think bigger, we will look at some simple cues and rules that help to generate ideas and allow them to flow easier, we will look at how to use space to spark ideas.

Let's jump into cues and rules.

COOL CUES & RULES

Cues are everywhere, from the tech we use in our busy day, to the body language we give out, through to how animals communicate in mother nature. From attracting the opposite sex, through to showing we are a friend and not a foe. They help us make sense of the world, and we also use them to help others make sense of their world and what to expect.

The poisonous dart frog often found in Central and South America is small in size but mighty in colour. These bright colours are what is known in the animal kingdom as Aposematism. This is a form of cue to predators to stay away, it basically screams, 'I am super toxic and may be deadly, so do us both a favour and move on as there is nothing to eat here'. These signals don't necessarily need to be colours.

A simple signal seen every day is the handshake, historians believe the motion of joining hands and shaking them in an up and down motion was to send a cue to the other person to say, 'I am not carrying a weapon and this is a relationship built on trust and good faith'. The up and down motion, historians think, comes from trying to dislodge any secret weapons they may have hidden up their sleeves.

The space in which we operate and work in gives off a strong signal as well, think libraries, meeting rooms, dentists, playgrounds. The car we drive when moving across lanes on a motorway or going around a roundabout. All these things have cues about how to act and behave but also to tell others what we are going to do next.

Here is a situation:

Imagine you bump into Sue in the canteen, she is someone you like to impress, now's your opportunity to share an idea you've been working on. Brimming with excitement, you approach Sue.

"Hey Sue (insert pleasantries), so I've been working on this idea on how we could make flexible working better (followed by lots of details)."

Once you pause for breath, Sue says she loves the idea but it wouldn't work because of (insert various reasons).

You come away from the conversation feeling flat, maybe because the idea didn't go anywhere or Sue has given you a lot of information you didn't really need or want just yet. Now this isn't Sue's fault at all, it's actually yours. You hadn't set up any cues for how you want Sue to act and you also didn't really tell her what you wanted out of the interaction.

Let's tweak the interaction a little bit and try again:

> "Hey Sue, so I have this idea that I want to share with you about flexible working. Right now, it's a fledgling idea. I was wondering if I could share it with you and you might help me identify any blind spots it might have?"

Or:

> "Hey Sue, so I have this idea that I want to share with you. Right now, it's a fledgling of an idea. I was wondering if you could help me think bigger on it and level it up?"

These two interactions signal clearly to Sue what you need from her and what your expectations are on the interaction. Now it is a two-way street and a muscle that needs the repetition and practise from both sides of the interaction. You need to signal clearly what you want but Sue needs to also be actively listening and give you what you want.

Okay, let's look at the situation from the other side, this time you're Sue. Here's a bit more context to set the scene, you have just come out of a board meeting looking at stats and figures all day. It's not your favourite activity but needs must. You head over to the canteen to grab a quick lunch before the next meeting, feeling pretty low on energy, and you hear:

> "Hey Sue (insert pleasantries) so I've been working on this idea on how we could make flexible working better (followed by lots of details)."

Seeing the opportunity to get a word in and not knowing what's needed from the interaction, you share that you love the idea around making flexible work better. However, it won't work because (insert reasons). You apologise and explain that you're running late for the next meeting and rush off.

Sue could have done two very simple things here to make the interaction better:

She could have simply asked: how do you want me to show up here, what do you need from me to help your thinking, what role do you want me to play here?

A simple sentence I often use when someone wants to have an interaction but hasn't signalled what they want from it is: 'do you want me to play critical friend?' (a term I first came across from Jo Byrne), or 'do you want me to be your wing person and take the idea higher?'.

A simple sentence cues up both parties to know the rules and what they want out of the interactions, while removing the risk of the other person looking like a bit of a fool by giving the opposite of what was asked. It ultimately creates a safe interaction.

The other thing Sue could have applied if she didn't use the sentence above is the WTF approach.

Nope, not What the F**K but actually Wait, Think, Find.

Look at the same situation where Sue applies WTF:

Sue has just finished hearing about your wild idea to make flexible working better. Rather than going straight in with what is still her distil mindset from the board meeting she takes a moment, waits for a second, and lets the idea mature in her mind.

Next, she thinks about the idea as a whole: Where would this work? Why would it work? Why wouldn't it? The final idea is to break the whole idea down into various pieces. Instead of thinking the ideas won't work, she finds a piece of the idea that does and shares, "I love this bit of the idea, it could really work in x department as a test".

This Wait, Think, Find approach is crucial in the dream stage when we need to come up with big bold thinking.

While some of the team's ideas as a whole might not be great, every idea has a good element in it.

For example, pretend we are designing a great day one experience:

Idea – have a private limousine pick all new hires up, take them down to the harbour, and bring them all in on speedboats (boldish idea).

Wait: shut the idea down instantly
Think: What elements make up this idea? Travel to work, novelty, personalised

Find: I love that we are thinking about how people travel to work on day one and how we can own it. I love the feeling of the white glove service a limousine gives.

While the whole idea might not be doable, an element of the idea is, and that gives us something to work with – a white glove service feel.

With anything like this, getting repetition in matters. I have found that over time the more we set up simple cues and rules the better, you can have fun with them as well, they don't all have to be something like 'Hey Sue, I want you to be my critical friend here'.

Take, for example, a referee's yellow and red cards:

A referee's rights aka 'Ref rights'

Coming up with ideas in an incubator/design labs isn't a solo thing, often people think it's the facilitator, leader, or project lead who needs to come up with the ideas. Their first priority is to create a space where everyone can generate and come up with ideas and stop people showing up in the wrong mindset for what's needed. It's inevitable that some people can sneak in early with the opposite mindset to what we need – they come in with a distilled mindset when we want them in the dreamer mindset or vice versa.

Over time, I have come up with a little playful cue activity called the Ref's rights. Here, as someone leading the session, you print out a set of cards consisting of two yellow cards and a red card per person in the session. At the start of the session, you cue to the group that the rule is simple, if you hear/see/feel anyone in the team/group distilling down ideas when we should be dreaming and building off other ideas we can issue them a yellow, if they do it again issue another yellow, leading to a red card.

If someone gets a red card, they leave the session. Thankfully, this has never happened. However, giving everyone the power of the cards and setting them out on the desk is a simple yet powerful reminder of how to show up for the result we needed.

This cue also works when we are distilling down ideas, if someone keeps reverting back to the big dream mindset when we need to distil down on them.

Easy as ABC

How many of you pictured Jackson 5 singing this song right now?

When moving through the dream touchpoint, it is not uncommon to feel like things are moving fast, usually it is high energy, high stimulus, and lots of idea sparks are flying. Due to the nature of this touchpoint, the last thing we want is for any early fleeting thoughts, ideas, or builds to be lost in the madness of it all.

That is why we do ABC!

ABC = Always Be Capturing. It is a simple rule. At any point throughout the day, you should always have a Sharpie and sticky note in hand. I have had fun with this in the past where randomly I'll shout, 'Sticky Note' and see who gets caught out with no sticky notes or Sharpie in hand. Those who get caught out will often have a forfeit to complete on the spot such as 'name 10 random uses for a spoon'.

Throughout the dreamer and distiller touchpoints, it would benefit us to listen and capture with two lenses, what we are hearing, seeing, feeling externally but also what we are hearing, seeing, feeling internally. For example:

External – perhaps you are all sat around a table chatting about performance. And while one person is speaking, someone makes a passing statement about how mid-year and end-of-year review cycles are like a trip to the dentist. You wait six months to be told you need a cavity filling in and you must clean your teeth better.

However, before we can capture that simple thought connection of a dentist visit and performance reviews, someone else jumps in and takes the discussion in a different direction. The dentist statement gives us an opportunity to look at the performance challenge very differently. Later on, we have to capture it in the flow.

Now, imagine if when that statement was said you had a sticky note and Sharpie to hand. You could quickly capture it down and let the next idea flow without slowing down the conversation. This then gives you a point of reference to anchor back to later, while in the present it may seem there is no value from it.

I promise you there is value, just pause for a second and challenge your brain to come up with random links between a dentist and mid-year performance.

Internal – perhaps you are all sat around a table chatting about performance. While one person is speaking, someone makes a passing statement about how mid-year and end-of-year reviews are done very differently to how they were done at their last place.

Maybe they go on to share at their last place they did something called the 12P (every month is a mini performance review). This sparks something up in your mind, perhaps it's a question about 12P, a quote, it could be something as simple as, 12P makes me think about the months in a year which gets me thinking about the season cycles of a year.

It doesn't have to make complete sense and in fact we should try not to make sense of it in the moment. Our job later on is to make sense of it and see if then it inspires or provokes ideas.

Again, creating these cues and rules simply makes it easier for people to understand how we need them to show up, but in a fun way.

ELMO AND COOKIE MONSTER

How many of you know Elmo and the Cookie Monster from Sesame Street?

Both of these make a great physical and visual cue at any stage of the design process, they can also be used in meetings to pull the team out of any rabbit hole they are down and stop people hogging the spotlight in meetings.

It is funny, Elmo and the Cookie Monster are two of the most fluffy, cheesy tools I've ever come across. Yet, when I've used them internally or externally with clients, they love them ... let me tell you about these two prompts:

ELMO – is an acronym for Enough Let's Move On.

ELMO is a cue introduced at the start of any meeting or design lab by the design facilitator and is a tool we all have the power to use if needed. The sole focus is to keep the meeting/lab progressing forward. As can be the case for most things, it only takes one prompt or piece of insight to bring people down from their broad dreamer thinking into distilling the idea.

Conversations are often rich and valuable but are often taken off topic or go too deep in the weeds. What ELMO creates is a simple cue linked to a rule that everyone agrees on at the start. If, at any point, anyone throws a physical ELMO teddy in, shouts ELMO, or drops a GIF into a virtual session, we all must instantly stop and move forward with no hurt feelings.

I have had great fun bringing in another Sesame Street character:

Cookie Monster – this one is for the facilitator only. One of Cookie Monster's famous quotes is "nom nom nom" or "me want cookie" and it is a similar concept to ELMO. The facilitator chucks the cookie monster in and the team needs to be prepared to go searching for cookies. The facilitator only uses this if they can see the group are struggling to generate ideas. This isn't to be confused with a break.

Often when the cookie monster is thrown in, the facilitator will get the team up and give them a simple task, completely unrelated to the challenge they are working on. In the past, I have had teams make little things out of Play-Doh, fold napkins. By giving the brain something else to feed on, it allows the subconscious to start working on the problem in the background.

It is the gift of a good facilitator to know when the team needs to sweat the thinking vs overthinking and creating blocks... remember, even whales have to come up for air. Note: Elmo's origin is unknown, however, I came across it when working with Saqib and one of the best innovation firms in the world: ?What If! Innovation .

SETTING UP A SPACE

War rooms, design labs, incubators, huddles, regardless of what you call it, when you go into this dream touchpoint having dedicated space it makes life 100x easier.

The space that we set up is a living thing, I am not talking about just having a meeting room and that's it. No, space needs to be one that drives creative thinking, gives you energy. It is a space that the minute you walk in you know it is different, the cues around you signal, 'the work done here is very different'.

Think back to the last time you used a meeting room in the office for any form of design.

Did you move the furniture around to create more free space? Did you bring in tactical props to inspire? What about the lighting? Was it natural lighting? What about the seats? Did they all look different? The walls, did you decorate them? Was there lots of white space to write on? What about sound, did you have any music on or was it deadly silent?

I am going to say you answered most of the questions with a no. If you did, don't worry you're not alone. In my experience, most would also say no. Yet businesses across the world expect their employees to go into these spaces, feel creative, be inspired and innovative, and walk out with a new EX product that stretches the art of the possible and is radically different.

There is a reason why spaces used by innovation companies like IDEO, ?What If! Innovation, Bow & Arrow, Board Of Innovation look radically different to the spaces their clients work in. It's because they have identified the chance of something even slightly innovative coming out of a normal meeting room is very slim. Yet, it's something pretty easy to fix with a little effort, creative resources, and the right mindset.

It's a very simple equation that works and it all comes down to quality:

Mindset + Space + Stim x Approach = Better Ideas

If you put mindsets in a space with the same type or lack of stimulus, their ideas will be the same. A great example of how susceptible we are to the things and people around us, is from Derren Brown, someone who I've met and researched for far too long:

A QUICK STORY

DERREN BROWN

Derren, invites a creative PR agency to a meeting room in London, he arranges for a taxi and video crew to pick up the PR people and bring them down to the meeting room. Once they arrive, Derren tells them he's opening up a taxidermy store, he wants them to come up with a poster advertising that store. This poster needs to have a company name, logo, and strapline.

He gives the PR team 30 minutes to come up with the poster but before leaving the room he places a sealed envelope down with a few ideas he's drawn up (the PR Team cannot see the ideas as they are sealed). After half an hour, Derren returns to the PR team and asks them to present their poster idea. The team walks the mentalist through the ideas. He asks the PR team to open the sealed envelope of his idea, Derren places the designs side by side and both ideas are nearly identical.

Derren then walks them through the process of how he made this all happen, replaying the taxi journey which you see is a well-crafted journey, full of little cues and prompts and stimulus, slowly but surely putting the image in the PR head without them knowing.

This is a simple yet elegant example of how susceptible we are as humans and how little things can prime us into a state of doing and thinking.

Imagine you take a group of employees from across the business, all part of the same culture, using the same process, etc. and then put them in a typical, uninspiring meeting room. You ask them to dream up potential new ventures, products, or ideas – what do you think the outcome will be? I put my money on that it will be a lot of average ideas because the typical meeting room is a very dull space for any form of EX innovation.

So let's break down how to create a better space to inspire people to truly dream bigger and stretch the art of the possible.

Have a fixed space

I have seen over the years the upside and downside of not having a fixed space, often orgs are set up to be flexible with meeting spaces, yet not flexible to book a space out for weeks or months at a time.

If you are looking at designing a better employee experience, or perhaps a certain area of the employee journey and you're going to do it in the right way, then you and the team need a space that surrounds you with the data, insights, maps, thinking, and so on. The team ideally should be totally immersed in the challenge.

Now, before you say, 'Well, Danny that's not how we work now we have this thing called hybrid and tools like Miro'. I know we do and it's valuable but having a space you can work in as a team surrounded by the challenges, ideas, and stimulus helps to get the juices going and subconsciously allows your brain to connect patterns you don't even see yet.

Move furniture around

Close your eyes, picture a typical meeting room or training room, in the centre is either a U-shape table layout, or four tables or one big table bang in the centre. To one end of the room is a giant TV screen, coming from the floor up to the table is a load of cables allowing people to come in with their laptop and connect it up to the monitor. What does this meeting room signal to people coming in?

The space we work in is a playground for the mind. I empower you to be rebellious, disconnect the cables and separate the tables, move them to the outskirts of the room. Watch as your space instantly starts to feel freer, it has a lot of breathing space and starts to signal possibility. Don't worry about IT kicking off, tell them I told you to do it.

x3 times your white space

Cyril Parkinson was the creator of Parkinson's Law, he noted that any work or task that needs to be done will fill up the time given. For example, if you have 30 minutes to come up with an idea, it will take 30 minutes.

This law applies to white space, if you have only one whiteboard to capture ideas and thinking then once that board is full we will stop. A simple way to get round this is to have way more white space, the more the better. Have walls you can write on, tables you can write on, anything that will just create more white space.

In the past I've used chalk tables, walls that can be written on, I've used tablecloths that can be written on, I've used static giant flip charts, written on windows. Whatever it takes to create more white space. If you can't, then this room isn't right for the output needed.

Decorate the walls

This is a simple tool I picked up from my great friend Saqib Mohammed (to his friends, it's Saqib) back in my training days, over time I have developed it. Saqib, before every induction, would decorate the walls with visual stimuli. This would often be people such as Sir Richard Branson, Mother Teresa, and so on. It was ultimately people who have made a positive impact in the world.

Depending on the group, sometimes people would ignore the external stimulus, however, more often than not it would grab people's curiosity to ask why. This would then allow Saqib to use it to link a story or a value from the business. Over time, I have taken this technique and started to build it out when working with clients. Often my walls are full of different types of stimuli similar to Saqib's approach. I turn these walls into something that I have the team actively engage in or more from a passive approach. We will talk about stim in the next few pages. But for now, note that not making use of the wall space is a rookie error, decorate the walls how you see fit to give the room character but make it something that will inspire and enable the outcome needed.

Add music (optional)

This is optional, some love a bit of background music, some hate it and can't think with it on. My goal tends to be to use it like a tool, have it on at the start with some upbeat music and use it sparingly throughout. You will be amazed at the power of Send me on my Way, by Rusted Roots, can have on a room. Playing with audio is one of the most untapped tools yet can change a mood almost instantly. In my experience, music works better in dreams than it does in distil.

Add colour

Simple, just add it. A meeting room full of bright multi-coloured sticky notes on the wall instantly looks like a place where creativity can happen, but often that is the end result. Instead, inject colour in the room beforehand, simple things like adding multi-coloured seat covers, bright pink, orange, green, and so on.

We make the mistake of doing things in simple black and white. However, you will be amazed at the difference injecting a bit of colour can have ... find the opportunity to do it. Ask yourself, is this colourful enough? Would a child enjoy being in here?

Lighting

Another simple one, bend over backwards to try and get a room that has windows, the amount of times people have hit a bit of a wall trying to come up with potential ideas, only to look outside at nature and a new flurry of ideas come rushing. If you don't have natural lighting, then you need to add more breaks to get out into nature.

Speaking of nature:

Take the space out the office

We will talk more about getting outside later in Search & Discover, however, you could challenge your thinking before even finding a room. Ask yourself, is this space right? What if I took the room to an outside space? What if I rented an Airbnb for a week and turned that into a space.

Now, I am not saying we should be like these big bands that go to live in LA for a year to create their next album, but there is something to just upping your room space to somewhere very different. Imagine if you could work at another client's space for a month or if you worked in a wooden hut in the woods for a month. Challenge the thinking and see what's possible. Even booking a WeWork might just be what you need.

Take the door off but be mindful

Okay, perhaps don't take the door fully off, but at the bare minimum have it fully open. The reason behind this is twofold. It allows people outside to be nosey, it creates curiosity and envy, and people will naturally gravitate to see what's going on. At that point, you can invite them in to help with things such as coming up with ideas, adding fresh eyes to the challenge (all depending on the challenge), or testing the thinking. Sometimes you're too in the weeds and start to look at things based on Goldie Locks that everything is just right.

Once I was leading the team on designing a new product for a large FS. We had designed this experience that blended physical and virtual and I noticed we started to map out things based on our bias and assumed everything was going to work as planned. Wanting to test my assumption, I reached out to the receptionist who had shown a little interest in what we were doing.

I invited her in and asked her to navigate through the paper prototype we had created, while the rest of the team took notes on the interactions. Guess what, the paper prototype we created was all wrong. It did not match the basic shortcuts and expectations the receptionist had become so accustomed to through using other apps. Never underestimate or devalue the beginner's eyes, they bring a unique perspective to the challenge.

Remember the space which we operate in is also the space others do too, we have to be careful where the room is in relation to the other spaces. We don't want to limit the output and we don't want to annoy the neighbours.

A QUICK STORY

BAD SPACE DESIGN CREATIVITY

A few weeks back, I was getting shown around a newly renovated floor of a current employee workplace. I was new to the business so with fresh eyes and the inner XD geek in me, I took it all in.

As I was being shown around, my guide (let's call her Lisa), was showing me the comparison of this floor to the older floor layout still waiting to be upgraded and conveying how far they had come. It was leaps and bounds ahead of the older floors. Lisa was showing me round, as I was taking in all the natural light, plants, whiteboard, and new tech Lisa then said something to me that shocked me like an ice cube on a sensitive tooth. She mentioned that even though the spaces are beautiful, many of the collaboration spaces weren't being used at all.

Taking this in, as we continued to walk round it was easy to see why, but only due to the fresh eyes. Of course people weren't using this open collab space because it was right next door to the quiet space and a pool of desks used for deep work with a sign saying, 'quiet zone'.

The result was that people who wanted to collab didn't use it for risk of being too nosey, people who wanted to focus didn't use it in case next door was trying to collab ... in the end, this beautiful natural lit space was something of a no man's land.

Two questions to ask yourself when looking at the space are: Would someone from Disney feel creative here? How about Nike, Apple, Innocent? Does this space capture curiosity, wonderment, and does it feel somewhat wholesome? Having a good starter space for creativity makes everything easier, it also makes your stim pop out. I guess now is a good time to talk about stim.

Setting up your creativity system

Stimulus is a nudge, provoke, or reminder that lights up our brains and helps connect new thinking. It often adds value in two ways, slowly but surely or it can come fast like a bullet train. Either way, it's a critical part of innovation design, a means of connecting new thinking and ideas, and stops us from just coming up with the same ideas.

Edward Debono, the originator of the term 'lateral thinking' and the six thinking hats approach, also came up with the term 'rivers of thinking'. Edward says our brains are good at finding a problem but are often flawed in assumption.

He says that every experience, routine, habit is like a raindrop hitting a mountain (our brains) and over time these raindrops turn into rivers (our thinking) going downhill. When our brains identify a problem they quickly identify a solution based on these rivers of thinking. While this might be great for quick decision-making, it does restrict us and we often get stuck in this river, unable to dream bigger, more expansive when we want to be innovative.

This simple analogy of a river of thinking, teaches us to pause, and remind ourselves to challenge our own perspective and perception. To see the same thing from many different angles.

When I think about perception it is like my hard rules of real life. My perception is my reality. Yet perspective is trying to see the challenge or world from a different point of view, hence walking in somebody else's shoes. If this is a shock to you please stop and read back over sense-making. A great video that captures this is from Joyner Lucas called *I am not racist*. Be mindful when checking this out as it's created to be provocative, it includes words that some may find triggering.

Here's a simple experiment to show how our so-called river of thinking works. You have forty-five seconds to draw:

- A flower
- A house
- A car

The chances are your images look something like this:

In order to get out of our so-called rivers, we need a Kisbee (life ring) or a helping hand and that is where we introduce the power of stimulus.

Stimulus isn't just stuff you stick on a wall, it's much more than that. If you strip it right back, it is anything that can provoke new thinking into a situation. So while it can be things you stick on a wall, it can also be experiences or props. The goal is to help us inspire or connect unseen patterns. The more we can get people thinking with their hands the better.

These props could be a list of provoking thoughts, such as:

- How would Nike approach this challenge?
- How would Zippy approach this challenge?

Bringing the outside world in is so important to stretching the thinking here, bringing in a simple snapshot of an example of how other businesses tackled simple challenges really help as well as some simple triggers.

Imagine if your solution used a freemium model or imagine if your solution was a subscription service. These props should also stretch out much more than work so look at nature, wildlife, tribes, etc. The props you bring in don't have to have a direct link either.

In the past, I have flooded rooms with all kinds of props from Play-doh, puzzle games, everyday manual items. The goal isn't to create a direct link but a nudge to the brain to connect any unseen patterns. Bringing in guest speakers close to the challenge or addressing it in another industry can really get people thinking differently.

I was once looking at redesigning the onboarding for an innovation company and brought in guest speakers from Monzo and Butternut Box. One is in financial services and the other is approaching dog food in a fresh and unique way. It can be daunting at first finding these props, experiences, and stimulus for the dream touchpoint but once you have a few early ideas the rest start to flood. Before getting the project team together, have a think about the challenge and write the answers to these questions:

- What non-digital things do you use every day & why
- What subscription services do you pay for & why do you pay for them
- What elements make up this challenge
- What, who, how, and where do these elements exist
- How do others overcome these challenges
- What can you learn from wildlife, a playground, pampering services

Here is an example:

Perhaps you're looking at creating better leaders.

Stim Set 1:

Stim and props might be a bit of competitor analysis e.g. This is how Red Bull do it, this is how another telecoms company does their leadership solution, and so on. Aim for around thirty examples. Remember, this can be big companies but also small start-ups

Stim Set 2:
Might look at how Scouts and Girl Guides approach leadership, what about the army? Which animals demonstrate a form of leadership? How would Apple approach leadership? How would Ikea approach it? What about Disney? Props here could be Mickey Mouse ears, Scout badges, and so on. I once took some Butternut Box and Tiny Rebel packaging into a workshop to demonstrate the difference between a basic service vs a service that's focused on the experience.

It is important to flag once more that we are not looking for answers here, just simply something to take us out of our own rivers of thinking for now.

On previous projects, I have played with stim in various ways. I've made it clear as day for people to find, but I've also hidden it and waited for people to come across it. Another little tip I picked up from my friend Saqib is to hide things under chairs. Over time, some will find it, some won't. When someone does, the air of curiosity and wonderment instantly increases. If you want to get super cheeky with it, drop little hints such as 'you're probably sitting on the answer, you need to look hard'.

SEARCH, DISCOVER, COLLECT

This shouldn't come as a shock to you that I am going to tell you to get out of the office and get moving. There is a big wide world outside your office with so much stimulus for you to tap into yet rarely do we do this. I am constantly collecting stim, even when I am not working with a client or on a project. It's turned into this little obsession. The two simple ways to do this is by getting out in the wild and also collecting the fleeting thoughts by Search & Discover.

Search & Discover

A QUICK STORY

CHANGE IN PERSPECTIVE

As I write this, I have just come off the back of taking the team out for their first Search & Discover. The project team is working in a Hollywood model (basically, it's where the manager directs their focus on one project, then cherry picks the skills and employees needed to make it work in a short time).

So this could be the first time everyone is working with each other. Having had many conversations with each of them before we all got together, it quickly became clear they all had their own bias or fixed ideas of a solution for this project. It's here where I have two options, I can either tell them it is too soon to know the right solution, or I could allow them to stretch their thinking and have their own aha moments. I decided Search & Discover was the way to go.

On the day, we kicked off the project with some thinking about the scale of the challenge and what we wanted to do with it. After being in the weeds for a while, I threw in the Cookie Monster and asked them to put their coats on. I told them the ABC still applies and to bring sticky notes and Sharpies. We headed out the office and in the direction of the tube. The team, not knowing where they were going, were capturing moments of fleeting thoughts, ideas, stim even before we got to the tube (this is the power of Search & Discover, it makes you look at things very differently if you focus the mind).

The team was curious, and dare I say excited, to see where they were to end up. I mentioned to them the themes and challenges coming up about perspective and perception, priming them to look and challenge their own internal dialogue.

As we got to the final destination, the team had already captured lots of fleeting thoughts and stimuli just from getting out the office and on the tube. We hadn't even got to the experience yet.

We arrived at our destination, an immersive multi-sensory experience museum in London. Before we all went in, I reminded them of capturing any thoughts, ideas, feelings, even if they didn't make sense.

Throughout the experience, we looked at how things aren't what they seem. When we look at the same piece of art, we all see something different. We were able to play and experiment with light, scale, colour. The team and myself were constantly capturing. As we came out, the team was in a much more creative and open mindset.

As we got on we made our way back to the tube, I challenged the team to capture as many things that caught their eye. This could be people, billboards, tech. I asked them if you were to redesign the tube experience how would you experiment with it. How do you think PR experimented with the billboards? What about the ticket self-serve machine? What can we take from that to apply to our challenge?

Once we got back to the office we had over sixty new pieces of stim we could use to bounce off, these then became part of the wider dream workshop later on when we moved into codesign.

While Search & Discover can be a lot more focused or more abstract, its goal is simply to challenge the thinking, see the world with a new lens, and allow creativity to flow. You will be amazed what you can achieve once you step outside the office.

Collect

I mentioned earlier that I have a strong addiction to capturing stimulus, it's not only in the work scene either. Throughout my life I have always had the curiosity and been able to find wonder in the simple things. As I have become older, I have started to identify the value in what these things make me think but never captured these thoughts down. At best, I would capture down these thoughts in Notes on my phone or on a Word document if I remembered. A few years back (while looking for stim), I came across a German sociologist named Niklas Luhman who would radically change how I collect ideas and make sense of them.

Niklas Luhmann is an author of over seventy books and hundreds of scholar articles. These books and articles had a broad discussion of things from love, right the way through to law. Two topics I would never put together (unless I was a lawyer hired to defend a criminal in a crime of passion case, or an author working on a dark romance novel where a lawyer falls in love with the criminal they are helping... maybe that's another book to write).

Anyway, in order to capture so much richness and broad subject matters he came up with a system that helped him capture knowledge and insight called the Zettelkasten method.

The approach is simple: Niklas would capture anything he found insightful on a card slip. These could be simple fleeting thoughts (a thought that would normally be gone in an instant), or they could be more thorough ideas, such as his understanding on various topics, or books he read. Each card slip would hold one piece of information, he would then tag the slip with a number for reference, then place the card in a box next to other cards that matched the tag. This card slip is called a Zettle.

Over time, the categories grew tremendously with broad topics and themes. However, these slip notes would allow Niklas to develop new thinking around topics that any normal person wouldn't connect. This divergent approach to connecting thinking and ideas allowed Niklas to generate a lot more innovative ideas, developing richer articles and books at record pace.

Similar to how our brain works, by stretching thinking and challenging initial ideas with new ideas Niklas just came up with a way to relieve our brains of information, overload in essence, he created a second brain to hold the thinking and patterns over time. Fast forward to 2023, this method has moved from a card box approach to a digital approach with tools such as Obsidian, Roam Research, and Notion, all allowing people to carry a second brain around with them in their phone.

My current second brain that captures random pieces of wonderment and fleeting thoughts looks like this. The bigger the node, the more my brain is connected on it.

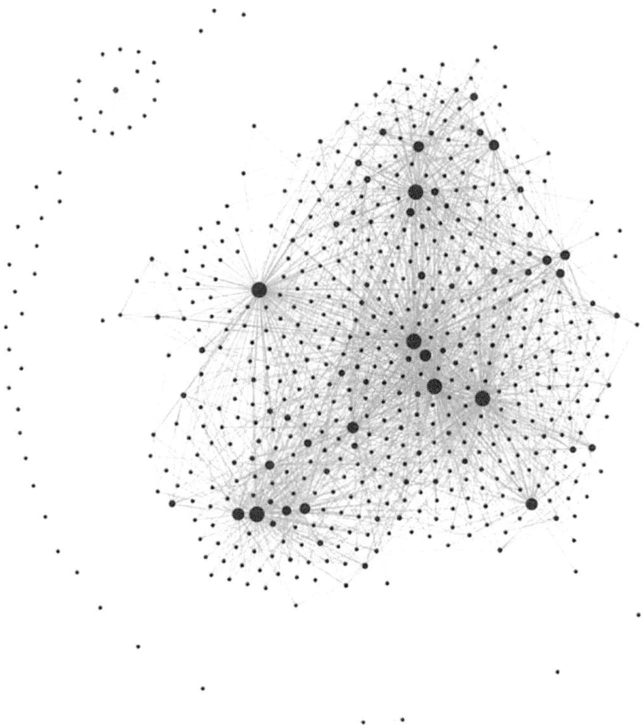

While my second brain has depth in hundreds of different topics, from problem-solving, to employee experience right through to cults, it also has randomness captured in fleeting moments.

Some random ones that I have captured over time but are linked to my thinking:

- Bee colonies
- A venture capitalist's approach to making bets
- Innovation
- Wildfire
- Fungus that grows on ants

Throughout this book, you have been reading snippets of Stimuli I have created and collected over time.

INSIGHTFUL INGREDIENT

On the first day of joining Radio Flyer, every new employee is presented with a unique miniature welcome wagon, accompanied by a personalised handwritten note from the CEO expressing gratitude for choosing to be a part of the Radio Flyer team. Additionally, a book on the family history of the company is also given to the new employee.

Even if you just printed the Insightful Ingredients from this book and stuck them up, you would be on your way to a good collection. When to introduce this fresh stimulus is a tricky question and I have personally done it many different ways. The reason it's tricky is because laziness and the brain wanting life to be easy can creep in.

#DANNYDISCUSSIONS

What comes to mind when reading about this?

....

....

....

....

....

....

....

....

....

....

IDEAS ON TAP

Our brains are great at creating short paths from A to B often leaving us in this river of thinking. Nearly all sessions, where the goal is to dream and create fresh ideas and thinking, fail in my experience. There are still outcomes but they fail because they settle for low-level Tier 3 ideas. Very rarely do they hit Tier 2 and nearly never hit Tier 1.

The reason for this is because sitting in Tier 3 is easy and fun, we all walk away feeling great but rarely is it ground-breaking to the business or industry you're in. Tier 3, no matter what the challenge, often you will find certain ideas such as:

- Could we create an app that ...
- Maybe if it had a Tinder-like mechanism ...

These ideas are all valid and we may come back to them, but they are easy and they don't make our brains work all that much. Similar to changing gears in your car, you have to go through gears 1, 2, and 3 but you wouldn't stay in them for too long. Unfortunately many organisations value Tier 3 – the shot in the arm, 60-minute blast – then later we find ourselves questioning where the innovation is. Why is everything the same?

Tier 2 ideas are where we start to go beyond the Tier 3, we start to push the thinking a little wider, we start to positively challenge assumptions and structures and elements around the challenge, our brains start to light up differently. It is here where we truly start to lean on to that child-like dreamer state. Tier 2 ideas start to naturally feel a little bit more out there.

- The team interviews the new hire, not the manager
- The new hire decides their own job title

It is between Tier 2 and Tier 1 where you will hear excuses but for now understand we can go way bigger with the idea which leads us to Tier 1.

Tier 1 is weird and wonderful, this is where we really stretch far and wide to the edges of possibility. While the ideas in this space rarely come to full fruition, many of the elements of the ideas are what provoke true innovation.

- Let's give everyone in the team the Alan Sugar, 'You're fired' power
- The team has a new manager every week
- The team vote for how many holidays they take this year
- The teams each decide the other team's bonus

It is at Tier 1 where we are really breaking down the constructs and looking deeper and wider at, not just challenges but, the white space around it. This tier, while rewarding, is hard. It challenges the people in the room to think much wider, which they will, but you need to be ready for the excuses. The top three tend to be:

Excuse 1: I am out of ideas

At this point, put your hand up to their face and tell them to stop talking, the more sass the better. Of course, I am joking. However, it is not uncommon to hear this excuse. Hearing this when you are running the labs should be a yes moment. What you are really hearing is that people have started to move out of Tier 3 ideas.

Their brains now need to start working a little harder, this often means they are open to having some stimulus given to them to help spring off another load of ideas. As someone running the lab, you could perhaps send them on a break and then quickly spread stimulus all around the room ready for when they come back.

Excuse 2: I like my first idea

Bloody bias, well it's a little more than that, it's actually called The Einstellung Effect which in a nutshell is a mental barrier. It's like your mind has captured you and your idea and built a wall around you to stop you from seeing other solutions. My friend Melis Senova, author of *This Human*, has a nicer way of putting it, she calls it Solution Seduction which I love.

You can also be hit with a double whammy here if the person stuck with this solution seduction is the loudest powerful person in the room. The trick here is acknowledgement. Address their idea, backlog it, and challenge them for more. You also want to stop them manipulating the room and swaying the people to like the idea because it's theirs.

I recommend having people send in initial ideas ahead of everyone getting together for the lab and de-identifying them. You as a facilitator play them back as Tier 3 ideas and ask people to take elements they like from the ideas. This allows the loud person to see their idea has been acknowledged but also be open to new ideas and challenges.

Excuse 3: I am tired

Okay, this isn't really an excuse heard that often, however, it's something you can see start to happen in the room. At this point, I will often throw in the Cookie Monster and get up and out. This can often be on a Search & Discover, a walk in the park, a walk on a roof terrace. When people are tired, it can be easy to call it a day. I recommend holding your line for a little longer and the reason is that tiredness can be used as a great tool to get us stretching that little bit further.

It has been long thought that actually when you're tired your logic brain starts to switch off, more decision-making becomes harder, and the ability to push back any illogical ideas becomes harder i.e. you become more open to allowing Tier 2 and Tier 1 ideas to come in.

A study done by Professor Mareike Wieth at Albion University set out to test this, Wieth gave a list of analytical and insight problems to over 400 students, the team identified two core groups; night owls and morning larks. What the study found amongst other things is when both groups hit mental fatigue they became much more open to identifying unexpected insights. Another story I loved hearing was shared by comedian Joe Rogan on his show with Matthew Walker, author of *Why We Sleep* (which is a great book), he shared how some comedians and writers use tiredness and sleep deprivation as a strategy to come up with new ideas and scripts.

Joe shared how a group of writers on News Radio would get together at night, chill together, play video games, and just hang out, then at 2/3 in the morning they would start to write till around seven in the morning. Using this silliness and overtired approach, they would stumble on set looking worse for wear and hand over some hilarious scripts. Matthew states that the prefrontal cortex of the brain is the first thing to switch off when you become tired so you start to become more childlike.

I am not saying we should follow the News Radio approach at all, however, what I am saying is there is value in sitting with tiredness a little longer and using it as a tool to get to Tier 1 ideas.

Episode 1109 – Joe Rogan podcast – 89:00 min mark

FRANKENSTEIN REMIX

Over the coming chapters, before we move on to distil, I will share some simple methods and approaches on how to get us thinking and approach challenges differently, and how we move from Tier 3 to Tier 1.

Ideally, you have used all the insight collected from sense-making, you have identified a few MOO (moments of opportunity) and a few Burning Platforms (MOO that we identified as areas for radical change and innovation), you have selected the right mix of people to be in the room and ahead of coming into the dream lab, you've asked all of them to suggest some potential ideas ahead of the session.

You have de-identified the ideas and put them into what I like to call the Insightful Ingredients section. All the ideas should follow the T-Bar template (we will cover this later, for now just know all the ideas follow the same structured layout). In this Insightful Ingredients section, you may want to have some stimulus from other areas i.e. how other people, companies, bodies are approaching similar challenges to your MOO and Burning Platform again following the T-Bar template.

The first action we want to do to stimulate the thinking is to get everyone comfortable with identifying and connecting unseen patterns. The first thing we are going to do is create two lists.

List A – random items:

- Apple
- Spoon
- Bike
- Lightbulb
- Phone
- Watch

And so on, try to get at least 25 items.

List B – all the things we love and use in our lives. This can be tools, subscriptions, services, apps, events:

- TikTok
- Spotify
- My dog
- Coffee subscription
- My car
- Costa app

Again, try and get at least 25 (if people struggle, ask them to look at the apps on their phone, the ones they use the most, then ask why). Next, we are going to write why and what we like most about the things on List B.

- **TikTok** – allows me to switch off, gives me a laugh, I learn something new
- **Spotify** – music for certain situations to prime my mood i.e. gym, feel good, etc. It's music on tap
- **My dog** – makes me to go out for a walk, makes me see when I work too hard by needing attention
- **Coffee subscription** – personalised to my taste, gives me new coffee to try, removes effort
- **My car** – allows me to get from A to B, removes travel limitations, gives independence
- **Costa app** – rewards me for buying coffee with free cake and coffee as regular treats

Next, we connect the two lists together with what I like to call the Frankenstein remix, (taking a cue from the Frankenstein's monster aka the monster of different pieces). The goal here isn't to come up with anything ground-breaking as such, but more priming them to find unidentified connections.

This will make sense in a moment, trust the process!

- **Apple** – **TikTok** – allows me to switch off, gives me a laugh, I learn something new
- **Spoon** – **Spotify** – music for certain situations to prime my mood i.e. gym, feel good, etc. It's music on tap
- **Bike** – **Pets** – makes me to go out for a walk, makes me see when I work too hard by needing attention
- **Lightbulb** – **coffee subscription** – personalised to my taste, gives me new coffee to try, removes effort
- **Phone** – **car** – allows me to get to A to B, removes travel limitations, gives independence
- **Watch** – **Costa app** – rewards me for buying coffee, get free cake and coffee

Task the team to now come up with some random ideas, thoughts, or a potential product, service, experience then put them together:

> **Bike** – **Pets** – makes me go out for a walk, makes me see when I work too hard by needing attention: The bike had an alert set to it so each day an alarm would go off telling me to get out on it, the only way to shut the alarm off was do a minimum of 5 miles.

> **Lightbulb** – **coffee subscription** – personalised to my taste, gives me new coffee to try, removes effort. We create a recycling model where we replace all the lightbulbs in your house with energy efficient ones, we recycle the old lightbulbs and for an extra cost per month they could subscribe to a hue colour lightbulb programme.

We want to get the team thinking and connecting in non-traditional ways. Once the team has generated a handful of ideas for each Frankenstein remix, ask them how they found it. Would you have naturally connected bikes and pets, lightbulbs and coffee? Take the opportunity to remind them about WTF (wait, think, find).

We are now going to follow a similar approach only more focused on the MOOs and Burning Platforms. Ask the team again to create a list of the MOOs and Burning Platforms as well as the elements that make them up. For example, maybe the Burning Platform is around recognition: people are leaving because they feel it doesn't exist or is flawed and they don't feel valued.

- Element: Trust
- Element: Incentive
- Element: Promotion
- Element: Social kudos

Again, the bigger the list the better, try to capture 8-10 elements that make up each MOO or Burning Platform.

Once the list is built out, ask the team to now have a look at the T-Bars that are up. What do you like? Maybe it is not the full idea but more an element of an idea. Give the team twenty minutes to take in all the T-Bars that are stuck up.

Then ask them to create a list of the things they love from the T-Bar and also the stuff they use and have seen outside of work but still specific to the platform and elements for example. Again, aim for as many as possible.

Therapist – allows me to talk openly without judgement, code of conduct
Microsoft – KPI incentives only when you develop others
Army – collect badges on experience to show promotion
Ben & Jerry's – social activism, they make a stand and shout out on socials

Now you guessed it, it's time to put these together:

- Element: Trust – **therapist** – allows me to talk without judgement, code of conduct
- Element: Incentive – **Microsoft** – rewards me for helping others
- Element: Promotion – **Army** – immerses me in real life scenarios to gain experience fast for promotion
- Element: Social kudos – **Ben & Jerry's** – we should shout about our people externally

Now it is time to remix and see what service, experience, product we have dreamed up.

> **Trust** – **therapist** – allows me to talk without judgement, code of conduct: it would be great if all teams were given a team therapist who had to sign a code of conduct not to share specifics with HR but team members could really share how they are feeling and what they are dealing with. This could help to support employee experience and wellbeing and identify true human trends.

> **Social kudos** – **Ben and Jerry's** – we should shout about our people externally, imagine if we create an open to all, external top ten. Where our competition can go in and see who our top ten employees are and why. If an employee is poached this could trigger a more thoughtful conversation around promotion incentives rather than waiting till mid or end of year. This would also give the external shout-out and validation.

Running a simple activity like this allows us to nearly move out of Tier 3 thinking, the group gets to apply random connections and reframes, as someone running the dream lab you get to identify people who have come in with the distilled mindset and nip it in the bud quickly.

As someone running the innovation lab you can use this activity to generate more ideas by simply moving the elements around.

So for example: **Trust – the Army** – collects badges on experiences. Simply replacing 'therapists' with 'the Army' will generate a whole wealth of ideas. After a simple exercise like this, we could have easily generated 100+ ideas that are instantly better than the typical Tier 3 "let's add a Tinder mechanism" type ideas.

The next thing to do is to turn these ideas into more T-Bars and add them to the Insightful Ingredients wall in order for us to spring off them again and take us deeper into Tier 2 thinking and dare I say Tier 1.

T-BAR

The T-Bar is a simple template that allows you to build out your idea a little bit more, it also makes it easier for people not in the room to understand the idea later on. This simple template allows you to add more context and depth to an idea and articulate it much better.

Often, depending on the activities used to move through different tiers of ideas (and there are many), it can get a bit messy, especially if we are using various sketching methods. I have seen in many design/innovation labs, which I have run and also been part of, where the ideas that progressed aren't the best ideas but rather the better drawn ideas (hello aesthetic usability effect). The T-Bar allows you to add an element of fairness by de-identifying who came up with the idea and ultimately allowing all ideas a fair chance.

Hand each member of the lab a piece of A4, ask them to turn the paper landscape and draw the letter T (uppercase) down the centre of the page, it has to go across the height and the width of the paper. Once done, your piece of A4 should have three sections. We need to give each idea a unique name, the cooler the better, this will cover the top of the page above the T.

There is much debate about whether we should name ideas at this stage or just give them simple names like Idea A, Idea B, and so on. The reason behind this is that people love to buy into slogans, sayings, stuff that sounds cool. However, to go down the idea A, B approach your facilitator would need to know each idea generated and then present it back. Which becomes a bit of a task if you have to do that for 50–100 ideas.

On the right side of the T, you want to describe the core elements of your idea. We aren't looking for War and Peace at this point. What we want is a core and concise description of what the idea is. Feel free to write it in the format you like. I have had the most success with the following, a simple bullet-point format.

- Imagine if ...
- How it works
- Why it needs to exist and why it's important to the challenge

To the left of the T, you now need to draw a visual representation of the idea that allows people to read what you've said and then get more depth and understanding of the idea by seeing a visual drawing of what it is or how it can work. Don't worry, you don't need to be some slick artist to draw the idea up. Stick people, arrows, and basic shapes are fine.

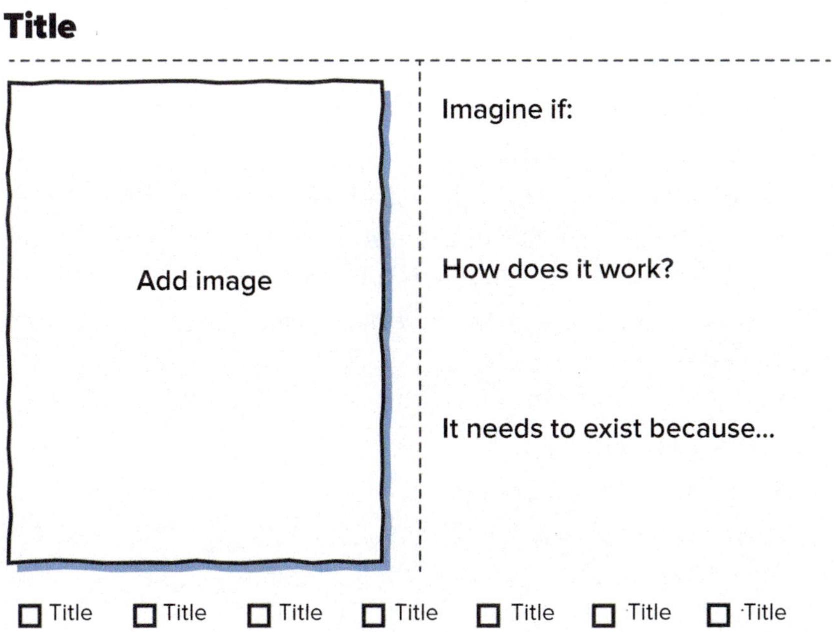

Once done, in stepping away from the A4 you should be able to read the idea name, understand in the description what the idea is, and see a visual drawing to bring it to life.

I tend to add below a couple of checkboxes. Depending on what we are designing, for example, let's say we went into the innovation lab looking at the experience and HR products from how we attract people through to passing probation.

The tick boxes might be: Attraction, Talent acquisition, Onboarding, Induction, and so on.

Once the T-Bar is complete, you would tick which box your ideas fall under. This helps later down the line when we want to group ideas.

Once all your ideas are converted into respectable T-Bars, you now want to stick these ideas up in the Insightful Ingredients area. You might be having an aha moment now where you have realised you're starting to create your own stim. If so, kudos to you! If you haven't, come on people, where is your head at?

Once the ideas are up on the wall, allow the team to take in each idea. The only questions people can ask at this point are clarifying ones i.e. what does this word say? After the team has taken in all the questions, ask them if there are any ideas they don't understand and address those.

CREATIVE CONSTRAINTS

Ask each person, or group to grab a piece of A4, in portrait. Ask them to draw out a simple table like the one shown. In the top left box, write the name of the MOO or Burning Platform. Then down the left column, write all the rules, norms, and conventions that surround this platform. Along the top row, to the right of the name, label the cells with build, bend, burn.

Build = add more of rule
Bend = remix the rule, tweak it
Burn = remove the rule altogether

By adding these constraints, you start to look at the idea very differently. Rather than seeing a whole, you break it down into elements and pull on threads that hold this idea together.

Name of idea	Build	Bend	Burn
Rule 1			
Rule 2			
Rule 3			

Here is a non-exhaustive example of what a creative constraint may look like for dining out at a luxury restaurant. Yours could be around wellbeing, career mapping, and so on. The options are endless, here is an example:

By the end of this activity, you should have a list of perceived rules, norms that currently surround the MOO and Burning Platform then to the right you have a list of cues to what the rule could look like if we amplified it and built it out more. After that, you should have a list of cues which apply a unique bend on the rules, the quirkier the better. And finally, to the far right, you have a list of cues on what could be if you removed that rule altogether. These creative constraints are to send a simple signal to get you out of the BAU thinking and get you dreaming about what could be from three unique lenses – Build, Bend, Burn.

As you can see, instantly I am starting to challenge the elements of what make up a typical restaurant and self-provoke. This simple activity will get you to stretch the thinking and ask why it needs to be that. With these new found cues we are going to move on to another constraint; good old time boxing.

Dining at a restaurant	Build
You can book a restaurant three days ahead of the date	Imagine if you can only book in more than three days in advance
Restaurants have 1 waiter per table	Imagine if each table had many waiters
Restaurants have menus	Imagine if the restaurant has 12 different menus
Dress respectably for the restaurant	Imagine if you can only dress in a certain colour
Restaurants have adequate lighting	Imagine we added a lot of light
Restaurant staff are respectful	Imagine if staff had to become your best friend
Restaurants serve food	... ...

Bend	Burn
Imagine if the restaurant was invite only	Imagine if there was no pre-booking
Imagine if the waiter was tech, apps, and robots	Imagine if you had no waiter other than you
Imagine if the menu wasn't written in a book	Imagine if the restaurant had no menus
Imagine if you could only dress in a theme or fancy dress	Imagine if we remove clothing altogether
Imagine if customers could alter their lighting	Imagine if we remove all lighting
Imagine if staff treated you with no respect	Imagine if staff couldn't hear or speak

TIMEBOXING

Timeboxing is a tool applied from across a wide spectrum of areas, it is mostly known as the agile principle. However, it's a technique that's been applied by various well known CEOs such as Elon Musk. It's also a fantastic tool to use for coming up with radical ideas by simply adding a fixed time constraint to a task and signalling to the brain 'it's time'. It is also a tool if you find yourself looking down at a blank page not knowing where to start.

Remember Parkinson's Law from earlier? The time we give to a task is the time it will take to do the task, well here we apply it. It could be really easy to have three months to come up with ten ideas. Our brains will sit back, chill, put their feet up, and sip pina coladas until we get near the deadline and then lo and behold by the end of the three months we have the ideas. But that also works the other way, if we have only thirty minutes to come up with 100 ideas, our brains will adjust accordingly.

We signal to our brains that we have x amount of minutes to come up with x amount of ideas, no ifs or buts. Google Sprint was the first to make this timebox approach famous for coming up with some rapid ideas, famously named Crazy 8, which I will go over shortly.

An important note before we get into Crazy 8; performing at the wrong time in the lab will generate Tier 3 ideas. The trick to the technique is to do it when people have moved out of that and into Tier 2 and 1 thinking. By helping guide the team through Tier 3 earlier, doing the Frankenstein remixing, and creating some cues that help stretch the thinking around the challenge, performing Crazy 8 would now become much more valuable. Running Crazy 8 is something I do or don't do depending on the group and where their energy is and how fatigued they feel.

CRAZY 8/FAB 4

When it comes to Crazy 8, everything is pretty simple to do and understand. As long as we are all clear it's going to feel crazy. The goal is to individually create 8 ideas in 8 minutes, however, the ideas need to be sketched out. So no paragraphs of writing, always use shapes, arrows, and matchstick people, and if you're an artist type person feel free to go full art mode.

Highlight to the team, 'Nobody will see these drawings but yourself, as long as you understand them'. For now, that's all that matters and the ideas don't need to be ground-breaking as such, in fact each idea could be a unique twist on your last idea or they could all be completely different ideas.

Hand each team member a piece of A4 paper and ask them to fold their piece of paper into eight sections or four (Crazy 8 and Fab 4 are the same thing, the only difference is the number of ideas and the time spent on each idea. Fab 4 is 4 ideas and each idea has 2 minutes, Crazy 8 is 8 ideas and each idea has 1 minute). Explain each of the sections on your paper as a frame for you to draw an idea, e.g. you have 8 minutes to get 8 ideas down.

Every minute you move to the next square, not a minute too soon or a minute too late. Check for agreement with head nods around the room. Get the 8-minute timer ready, count down from 5,4,3,2,1 and hit go on the timer. Every minute, nudge the team to move on to the next square and so forth for the remainder of the 8 minutes. Once the time is complete, tell everyone to put down their pens and ask them how they feel. Now's a good time to let them go grab a drink and fresh air.

Upon return, the team now has to select which one of their ideas they love the most, prompting the team to try and look beyond the first idea. Advise that the goal is to look beyond a fully formed idea, we aren't looking for a complete solution, we are looking for the idea that has the most room for opportunity, differences, and that ground-breaking feel.

Once the team has each selected an idea, we now need to add more meat to it. Here we could simply ask them to create another T-Bar or we can go a little more creative and ask them to create a product breakdown and customer review. Make the team aware that everyone will be seeing this and they will be presenting it back to the audience.

A typical product/experience overview and review structure done on A4 tends to look like this:

- In the drawing section: this displays a neat version of the HR product, experience, or service. This could be a front cover image or a flow of how it might work.
- Description and hook: this is a simple description of the problem being solved and how. It also needs a catchy hook line.
- Features: this should be a list of all the features this programme, solution, tool has to offer.
- Benefit: what does each feature offer the person who uses it or is in it.
- Reviews: create a few made up reviews. If you project into the future, what might be said?

Once the team has finished writing up their product breakdown, pin them up in the Insightful Ingredients area. Before we ask each person to present back their idea, hand out a sticky notepad to everyone with a Sharpie and advise that while the person is presenting back, each person in the audience needs to capture two positive 'Yes' notes and build on those ideas.

For example, pretend I am presenting a new idea for a dog massage parlour that tailors to our cute furry friends. As I am presenting the idea to the audience they are adding a 'Yes' and an idea to a sticky note, these could look like:

- Yes and you could offer a tooth brushing service to get rid of their bad breath
- Yes and this could be mobile for owners who may struggle to get to the parlour

If the audience is around ten people, by the time I have finished presenting my ideas back to them, I should collect another 20 potential tweaks or cues to the idea I presented. The final step will be to look at the future builds and apply them to your idea or if possible spark off another idea and capture that down in its own product.

By the time this activity has finished, the Insightful Ingredients wall should consist of initial ideas from the Frankenstein remix, ideas then developed into T-Bar, larger cues developed from the creative constraints and these have then sparked significantly more ideas from the Crazy 8. These ideas have then been turned into product overviews, these product overviews have then had some stretching done with 'Yes' notes and potentially shaping more ideas. All this is based on one MOO/Burning Platform and the assumption that you're doing this approach on just one idea.

If you want to take 4 of your ideas and apply the above approach you can, but for now I am sure you can picture a wall covered in broad ideas stretching the imagination.

At this point, it is worth giving the team some time to go through the idea in a simple fashion, following the ABC. The team take it all in and capture any elements they love about the idea, any fleeting thoughts, or any future 'Yes' notes and builds.

A typical next approach would be to inject some fresh thinking into the mix, this could be bringing in a guest speaker, creating an immersion room or doing a bit of meddling. Either way, it's often a good idea at this point to throw in the Cookie Monster.

When in the dream state you can always dream bigger and bigger but at some point there will be a time limit and often time is tight. I would pull on the meddling matrix to help inject some fresh thinking and stretch the ideas from a different point of view. This has a two-edge approach.

1. It gets people out the office and talking about the challenge from a unique point of view
2. The chances are someone/something has a similar problem to what you are facing and often has a solution

EXTERNAL MAP

In my whole career, I've constantly mentioned on podcasts, articles, and so on that the answer to your problem 90% of the time is not in your business or your industry. Alternative World Map allows us to start looking at the challenge from a distance, to stop looking at it in isolation and solely in the context of your business. Meddling matrix allows us to look wider at the problem, look at who else may have a similar problem and take cues from how they have overcome it.

I often use a template similar to the one overleaf. What this allows you to do is to refresh yourself on the problem and the traits, but also start to think wider and identify who we could chat to in order to stretch our thinking.

Moving from the centre outwards, put the challenge, MOO, or Burning Platform in the centre square. Moving out to the next square we want to add 'The What', this is the DNA or the traits that make up the centre square. Often this could be simple things like trust, time management, communication, empathy, compassion.

Moving out again to the next 'The Who' section, here you put all the areas outside of your initial world that have these challenges. Perhaps if we were to look at trust here you could put solicitors, teachers, priests,

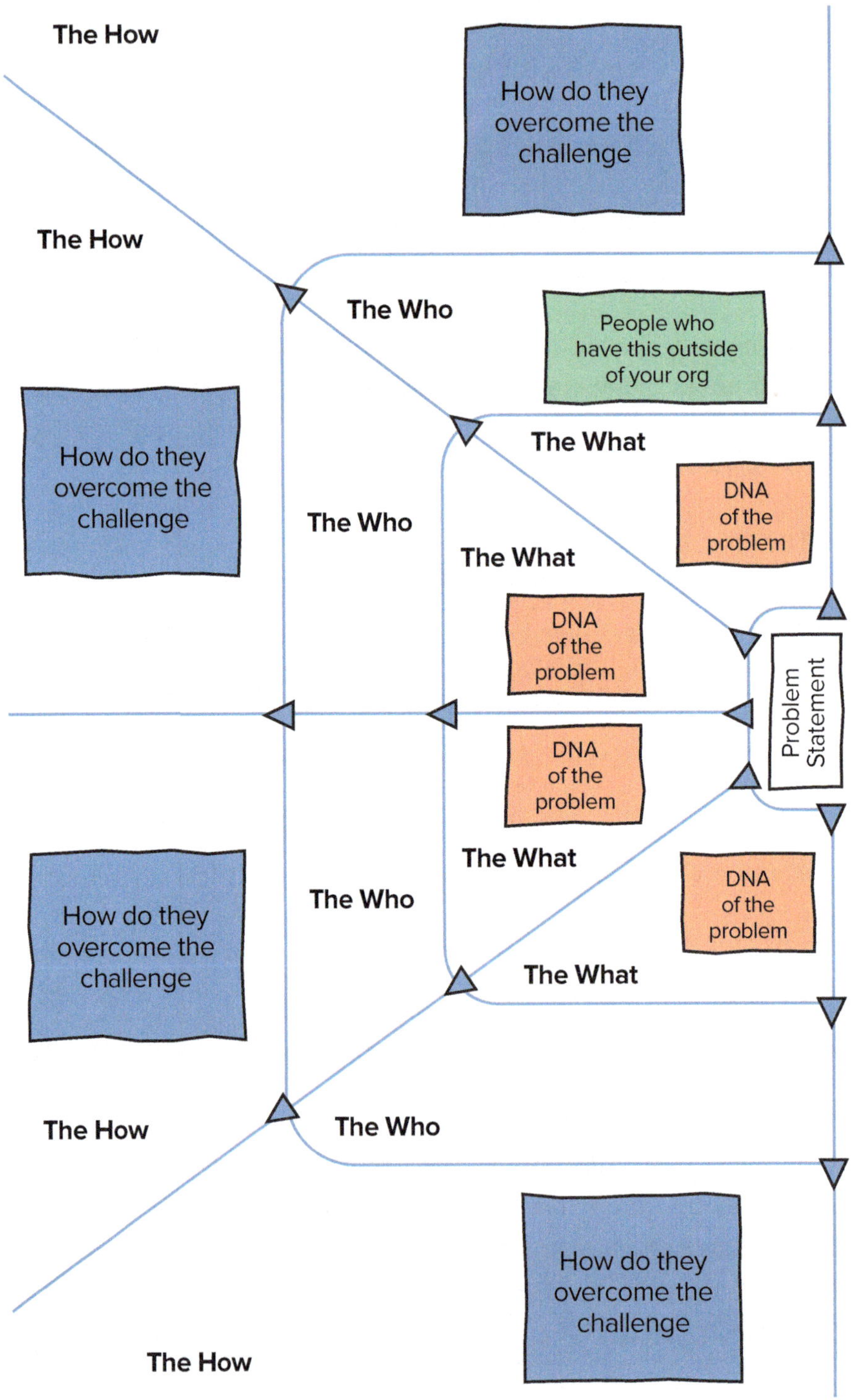
The How
How do they overcome the challenge
The How
The Who
People who have this outside of your org
The What
DNA of the problem
How do they overcome the challenge
The Who
The What
DNA of the problem
Problem Statement
DNA of the problem
The What
DNA of the problem
How do they overcome the challenge
The Who
The What
The How
The Who
How do they overcome the challenge
The How

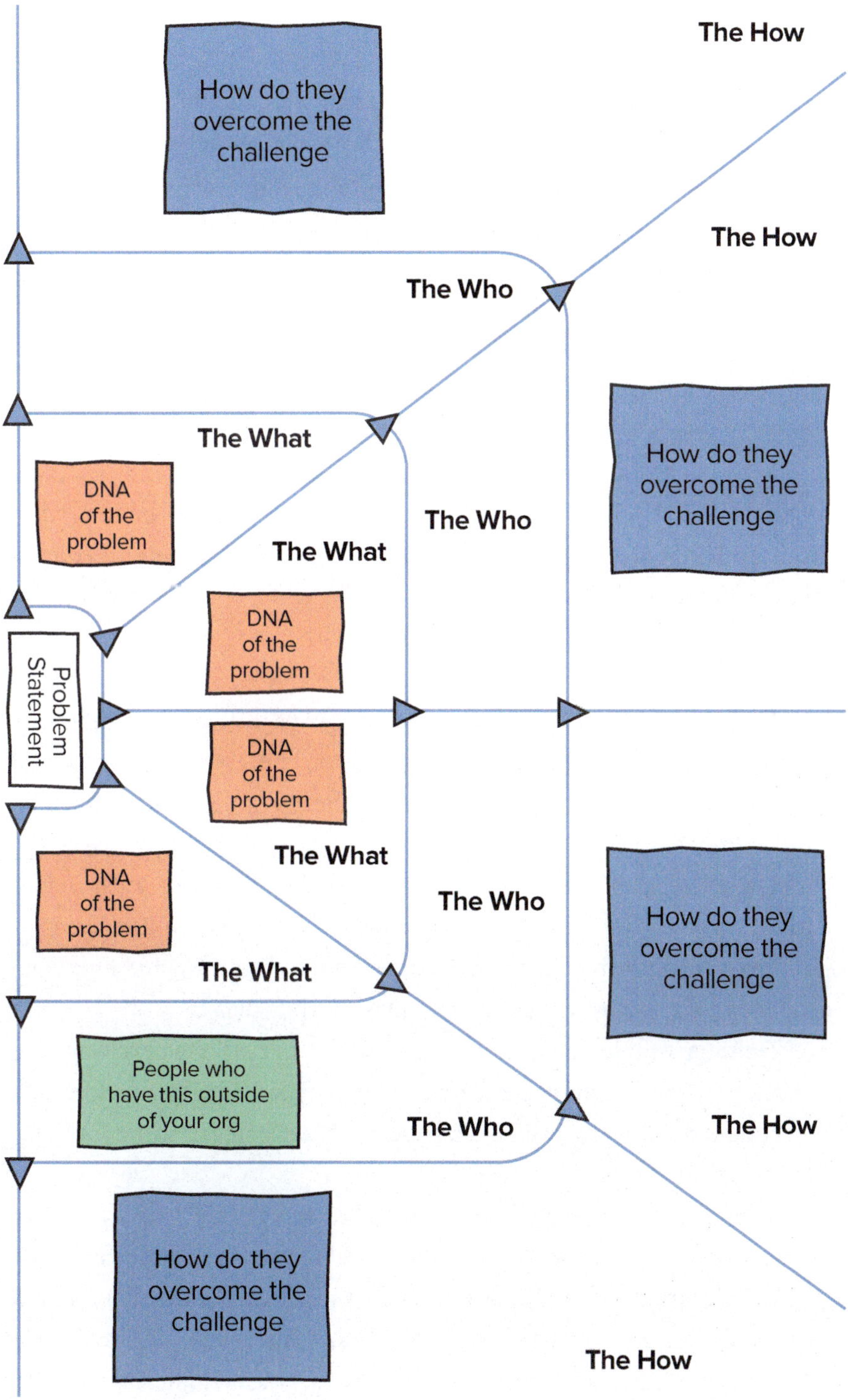
The How
How do they overcome the challenge
The How
The Who
The What
DNA of the problem
The Who
How do they overcome the challenge
The What
DNA of the problem
Problem Statement
DNA of the problem
The What
DNA of the problem
The Who
How do they overcome the challenge
The What
People who have this outside of your org
The Who
The How
How do they overcome the challenge
The How

adult private party organisers. For communication, you may put PR, copywriter, frontline call workers. Perhaps one of the elements is community, here you could look at Scouts, Army, etc. You can also use some of the people identified in the Insightful Ingredients activity.

The goal is to think bigger, noting down people who you wouldn't naturally link to the core challenge but who you would link to the DNA. Do not play it safe.

The next step in the final box is speaking to these people. Of course, you might now know someone who set up adult parties but perhaps you may know a Scout leader. Either way, the goal is to get in touch with some of these people and have a chat with them.

You will be amazed how awesome people in all walks of life will be open to having a chat with you by simply putting a call out on LinkedIn, Twitter. The goal is to get in touch with some of these people and have a chat with them.

The main output from having chats with these people is to understand their How.

How do they build trust? How do they have difficult conversations and what tricks and tools do they use? We don't necessarily want to steal their solution as it may not fit, however, there is an element which we could apply to the challenge.

Once the map is filled out, you should be presented with a map full of some new thinking that generates some sparks of new ideas. It is important that the Hows are localised with the group and everyone knows what the How captures are and what they mean.

Doing a simple playback here to the group is the fastest way, I've found, to not only bring people up to speed but to also allow them to ask questions or share any initial thoughts that may come to mind for them ... (remember ABC).

Wild card note: when doing the map, it is worth injecting a wildcard element to the map. Personally, I like to add nature as the wildcard, this could be animals, plants, seasons and so forth such as gorillas, blood bats, and ants. Now, of course, often we can't interview these wildcard elements but there is enough content and observation material to go off.

One of my favourite stories I have read is about vampire blood bats, often the things of nightmares. These little bats are a great example of community, sharing, and building strong bonds. The bats are known for creeping, often crawling, not flying up on their prey and biting into the rich blooded vein of its prey. However, what wasn't known until recently is that these bats regurgitate the blood with other bats to keep the community healthy. It has also been noted that these bats will also share blood with other bats outside of their community in an attempt to build bonds of trust.

I am sure many of you would never instantly go to blood bats or ants to look at a community but by simply adding these to your map, you are forcing yourself to stretch your thinking and identify something from them that could be valuable.

I believe that instantly looking at how bats share blood gets me thinking about how we create communities digitally and non-digitally, how many are built on great relationships vs being forced? What might a community look like if, in order to get access, they had to give and share first? This simple approach allows us to reframe the challenge and look at it very differently, similar to the next approach: Inversion.

INVERSION

This simple approach doesn't have to be a long drawn-out process. Over the years, I have found it useful in a few situations, when either the team starts to fall into the distilled mindset too soon or if they start to slow down on idea generation. Inversion is an approach used by many CEOs, however, it can be tracked right back to the ancient stoics such as Seneca. I don't have the time, or the word count, to get into stoicism so inversion, in a nutshell, is a way of thinking and reframing the challenge to look at the opposite of what you want.

For example, if we wanted to redesign 121 sessions between managers and employees, rather than asking how a leader would create a rich conversation between employees and managers, we would ask what a leader does to create a terrible conversation between them. This approach allows us to then focus more on the traits that make something bad. It is a simple reframe tool that can be used to switch up the thinking. I use it sparingly mainly because if it is not facilitated well or the concept isn't made simple it can force people to become super reductive and overthink the whole thing.

However, there is value in looking at the bad or negative sides of things for innovation. At this point, the room should be covered in ideas, stimulus, posters, T-Bars. Some ideas may naturally feel better than other ideas, what we really want to do here is zoom in on the 'not so good' ideas.

The 'bad' ideas (no such thing) still have a lot of untapped potential. Hand out three sticky dots to each person in the group and ask them to individually go through the ideas and place a sticky dot on the ideas they really don't like. Perhaps it's dull, or uninspiring, or doesn't get you excited. Just because you don't vote on an idea or perhaps you believe it can't be achieved. Once the dots are all used up, take the three ideas with the most dots and move them over a clear white space. Ask the team to score these ideas out of ten, then get a general consensus of the score as a group, perhaps they land on 4. After this, hand each member of the team two pieces of A4 paper and fold each piece into 9 blocks. In the centre of the first piece of paper, ask the team to take one of the bad ideas and draw it up.

Next, you should have eight remaining blocks. In each of the squares, they need to draw a better version of that idea. Each drawing needs to take the original idea from a 4 to a 7 out of 10 idea. Give the team 10 minutes to work their way through the blocks. Once done, have the team playback each of their squares to the group. Now, on the second piece of paper, tell each of the team members to take one block/idea from sheet 1 and place it into the middle of sheet 2.

They now have ten minutes to come up with 8 alternative versions of that idea. Once the time is up, go around the team and ask them to present their ideas to the group. The group will then vote which of the ideas is their favourite, the most voted idea is then converted into a tomorrow narrative.

Tomorrow narrative

A tomorrow narrative is a tool to help the team overcome present blockers and instead look into the future. Assuming the solution, product, or experience is a ground-breaking success, so much so that it has been recognized by the Harvard Business Review.

Hand out a blank Harvard Business review template like the one shown:

Give the team 30 minutes to mock up what the front page would look like, what the headline and the description would say. What image would you use to demonstrate the experience/product or service? What would the date and impactful quote say in the top right? Once done, have the team present their front page and stick it up in the Insightful Ingredients area.

If time permits, allow the team to find pictures on the Internet and cut them out. Turning this into something that they feel and not just another drawing can really add value to the activity. Most of the tools used in dream touchpoint are by design, tactically they force us to tap into the creative side of us by asking us to draw things, fold things, use colours, stretch our thinking outside of our normal world, and collect breadcrumbs of fleeting ideas and thoughts in the hope they can be used later.

However, we live in a digital world. Not making use of the digital tools around us would be a real shame, so where possible using things such as Butter, Miro, Figma, AR and VR for immersion would all add a layer of extra creativity to the thinking. AI for instance, while it's ultimately a tool based on data going in, can simply be used to produce some stimulus for us to spring off later down the line.

With the likes of things such as ChatGPT, Lensa, and random innovation generators, these tools allow us to outsource thinking, ask for help with writing, or ask for a picture to be converted into digital art. It makes sense we have them as tools to turn to, however, there is a big catch here. We must not rely on them, these ideas are often built on many data points that already exist. To create something really new is a skill we humans must not lose. So use AI but only for stimulus and only when our own ideas are completely dried up.

The art of letting go

I often see typical sessions like this; people get locked in a room for an hour or two, they do a typical brainstorm activity and all walk out feeling great, only to have not achieved anything of real value. This is what makes my dream approach different, you don't just have one dream and that's it forever.

It isn't a standard shot in the arm hour session. In fact, it's anything but, it gets you out of the meeting room, it gets you looking at the problem from different walks of life, it brings the outside in. It stretches your thinking and your questioning. It is done over days and weeks, not minutes and hours, but more importantly it is reflective, it gives these fleeting thoughts the time to mature and grow a little. These chapters are not an exhaustive set of activities nor must you do them in a set order.

It's a bit like cooking, the pages you've just read are a list of ingredients but with them you can do what you like, you can try them in different orders. You can add more ingredients, you can take some away. While the activities I have covered here are what I would call core activities i.e. they give you the most bang for the buck, each has their limitations and it is up to you to find them in your group as they are unique.

I may have a very structured way of running my dream sessions. Maybe they are like yours, maybe they are not, it doesn't really matter too much as long as the principles and mindsets are taken on board.

There are only two things left to cover before we move on to the distil mindset.

TIME OUT

In a typical ideation session, reflection time is nearly non-existent. If it does exist, usually it is a few minutes here or there. Unfortunately, what can happen is we don't let ideas incubate and grow in our minds, we rarely ask our minds to stop thinking about it and allow our subconscious to take over which is bonkers. It can mean the people who first like to reflect or need more time to come up with ideas don't get the opportunity to add value.

Often the most crazy or simple ideas come when we aren't thinking about them, they come in the shower, in the gym, and in a lot of cases come after a dream session is done. I like to think the reason this happens is similar to what I used to do when babysitting my nephews. I would load them up with sugary treats and get them bouncing off the walls then hand them back over to their parents. Similar to the dream touchpoint, we load the brain with lots of sugary treats (stimulus), next we get you bouncing off the walls with new thinking. Then we leave you to it for a little bit to crash and allow the subconscious to kick in because we are all drained from thinking and it's this moment when ideas come.

Sara Blakely, the CEO of body sculpting underwear brand Spanx, talks about her approach to switching off and letting the subconscious kick in. In various interviews, you can hear Sara talk about an activity she calls the faux commute. Over time, Sara has identified that often her best thinking and ideas come when she's in the car. However, because she lives so close to the Spanx HQ it's not really a long drive. So instead, Sara gets up a few hours early before she is supposed to be in the office, she will drive around Atlanta aimlessly taking everything in and observing day-to-day life. Interestingly, Sara said the name Spanx actually came to her in the car.

Listening to Sara's story, it doesn't come as a surprise to me that her best ideas come to her while driving. Many of my best ideas came to me in the bath or when I used to do Brazilian Jiu Jitsu. Maybe it's the moment before being choked out that my brain turns off the non-important stuff. Perhaps it is the introduction of doing something that gets you fired up naturally like a hobby.

There have been studies that have shown that the brain needs new novel experiences the older it gets to fend off illness such as Alzheimer's. So if doing something different in the name of coming up with new ideas doesn't do it for you ... do it for your brain health.

I have actually played with something similar to what Sara mentions. As someone who reads a lot, often overthinks, and can fairly happily sit with my own thoughts I wanted to see if doing something completely different helped or hindered ideas and thoughts. I decided that for a few hours I would do a task based activity. I chose gardening, well basically turning soil over, filling a wheelbarrow, and putting it in a skip. Around the two-hour mark, I found that my inner voice came up with random ideas and answers to questions I had forgotten all about.

When in the dream touchpoint, it is vital that you go big and bold with the ideas, however, fitting in reflection time between the activities and sessions is critical and often overlooked. What is the sweet spot for this I hear you ask, well I don't know. I have played with hours, days, weeks and not come to a conclusion but what I have come to understand is the value of adding it in far outweighs the value of missing it out... so go and take more hot showers, lie longer in that hot bubble bath, or go try out the geek hobbies you fancy trying but don't want to tell anyone about. If challenged, tell them I told you to do it in the name of coming up with new game-changing ideas.

Getting it ready for distil

So my rough calculations are that by the time you reach this stage, you will have a few hundred ideas, some focused on the Burning Platform or Moo, or some based more around the DNA of the challenge. You have remixed ideas, you have challenged the structures that are often linked to a Burning Platform, you've created various pieces of stim to create even more ideas.

The next aspect is to make these ideas a little palatable for when we present them and move into the distilled mindset. We are not yet talking about measurements but more just a snapshot per idea. Covering what the idea is, why we think this idea is important and highlighting a few scales of appetite.

If we get this right, when we move to distilling down, it makes a lot less friction and makes for some nice shorter chapters. First, let's talk Radars and filtering.

Radars

What a Radar chart allows us to do is put together a visual representation of potential per idea, they allow us to quickly see any striking difference and outliers in the idea and where each idea may fall short but may also overachieve.

In some instances, we will be able to back it up with data, while in other situations we may not be able to, especially if it is truly innovative in its approach. This is why in the following books we will dig deep into experimentation and look at validating or disproving ideas at pace.

For now though, we need to get together a criteria for each arm of the Radar and an internal measurement. Before we get into setting these Radars up, ethically you need to share with the stakeholders and decision-makers that the Radars are built on a group discussion only and are used, at best, to help steer a conversation on where ideas could go based on some secondary research or gut feeling. They are all assumptions for now.

Getting early thoughts on your potential solution is vital throughout this whole design flow. Ideally, you should be constantly going back out to employees and users to get early feedback.

Assuming time is on your side, you could get some initial insight to build your Radar out via:

Quantitative evaluation: this involves using numerical data or metrics to evaluate ideas. For example, you might use surveys.

Qualitative evaluation: such as interviews, focus groups, or observations to evaluate ideas. This can provide insights into people's experiences, perceptions, and emotions, which can be useful for understanding how an idea is received and how it could be improved.

Expert review: this involves gathering feedback from experts in a particular field to evaluate an idea. This can be useful for assessing the feasibility, potential impact, or novelty of an idea, and can provide valuable insights and advice for improving it.

Peer review: this involves gathering feedback from a group of peers who are familiar with the problem or challenge that the idea is intended to solve. This can provide a diverse range of perspectives and can help identify strengths and weaknesses of the idea.

Identifying these early insights can be helpful for the Radars but we have to always be mindful of the bias this early insight from people around us can give us, and that it doesn't become a blocker to taking an idea into full experimentation in the wild.

Whenever I create a Radar, my first three arms are Desirability, Viability, Feasibility. These three are the core structure that I build the other arms around. The other arms could be Innovative, Impact, Ease of use, External competition, Shareability, Uniqueness, Business goals, and so on as seen on the next image. The arrow with the word 'kudos' could be replaced with a measurement here.

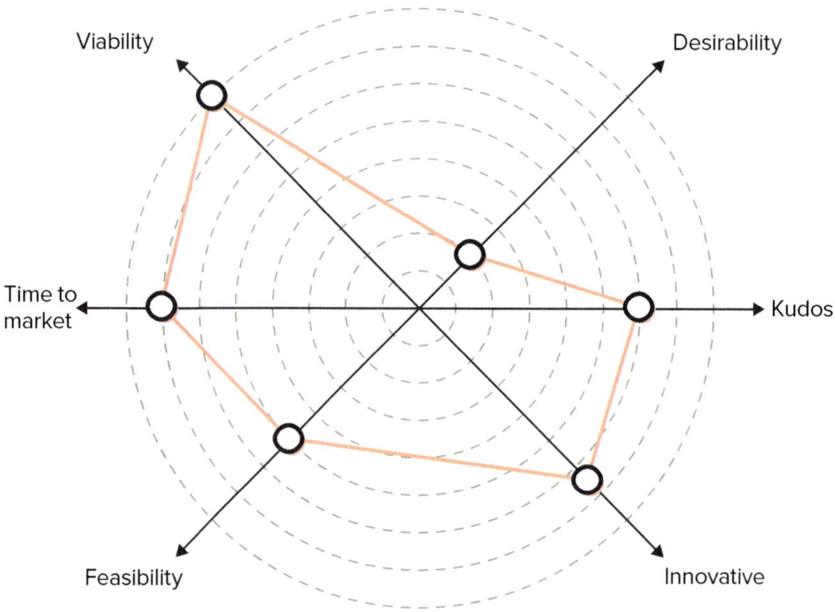

Whatever arms you suggest for the Radar, make sure you have designed a group scoring metric before mapping out. The more the marker is in the centre, the lower the score. For example, in the image above we can see this suggested solution scores really low on Desirability, however, Viability is coming out pretty high.

There are many other tools we can use to measure simple things such as a basic decision matrix but I always find myself going back to the Radar especially when lots of data does not exist to disprove or validate the idea.

Once an agreed scoring process is created and each idea has been scored, we now need to do our own filtering process before we build out the final ideas into SOAP (story on a page) ready for distilling down.

The Jam problem – Level 1 filtering

We need to make the distil touchpoint easier and remove an element of choice. I know I know you're probably screaming 'why, isn't choice good?'.

Well, yeah, but too much choice is not good, this is due to a phenomenon known as 'the paradox of choice'. This phenomenon suggests that offering people too much choice can actually decrease their likelihood of making a choice altogether.

A study conducted by psychologists Sheena Iyengar and Mark Lepper, found that a display table with 24 different types of jam generated more interest than a smaller display around 6, but resulted in much lower sales.

In fact, having a small selection resulted in 10x more sales. It seems with choice, similar to many things, too much of it can be a bad thing.

Due to the potential of choice fatigue, it's usually at this point we stop people from freaking out thinking they need to write a SOAP (story on a page) for 300 ideas and instead explain that we need to reduce down a bit. The nature of being in the dream touchpoint is to come up with new innovative products, often none of them have been tested.

The goal is to present back to stakeholders all the ideas and let them decide which they want to progress. Then each idea should get a fair share of the limelight and its own SOAP. However, let's say the business wants to see the top 20 ideas (which often, wrongfully tends to be the case) then your first goal is to filter the ideas down to the core 20. It's pointless doing a full soap for 200 when only 20 are to be seen.

At this point, I would go back to the criteria of why we are here and start to filter out ideas to that criteria using the Radar. For example, pretend the business has asked for white space innovation and 60 of our ideas are scoring low on innovation, then I wouldn't present them and instead move them into a form of backlog. This might not instantly take your ideas from 200 to 20, but applying some simple criteria filtering will help to take a fair amount of the ideas out early.

Remember, we are not throwing these ideas in the bin. For now, they are falling into a backlog of ideas. Which means, at any point, if we hear something from the stakeholder that they want something more, we have a whole load of ideas to start to show and spring off. We can also use these ideas in other sessions as potential stim starters.

SOAPS

The final step is creating the remaining ideas that are aligned to the original criteria of the challenge and create a SOAP per idea. A SOAP is basically a story on a page, it consists of four key elements:

- Visual
- Description
- Insight
- Radar

Once a SOAP is completed, it should be simple enough to put in front of anyone, and the readers understand the story of why this SOAP was created. It should tell the story from MOO with some insight and describe the idea. The good news here is that while from the outside this may feel like a big lift, it really isn't. You have everything you need around you to create it. This is what a typical structure of a SOAP looks like:

Cool name – so this can be debated. Some people love giving their product a cool catchy name, while others think we can apply bias to a

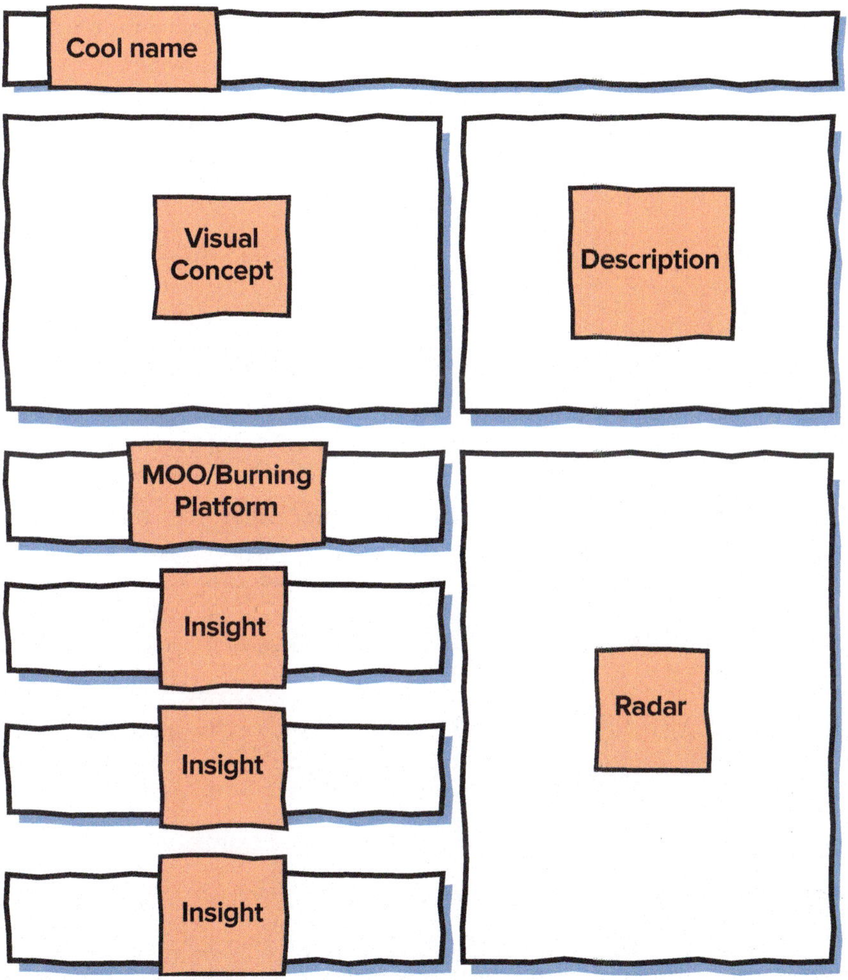

name and instantly love or hate it. I, personally, am somewhere in the middle. It can be cool but also I need to understand what it is. If the name is too abstract then try again. Remember, you should be able to blind test these with people. We need to give each idea a fair shot and it starts with a clear name.

Visual concept – in the top left section is where you want to put a higher fidelity version of the concept. It might not be a digital product, it might be suggesting a new day 1 experience. For example, in this section is where you capture the existence of that idea (you should have a low-fi version of this from the T-Bar).

Description – to the right is where you write out the description of the product, service, or experience. Be concise with your words, it's about selling the art of the possible. It helps to think of it as a sales pitch (this should exist on your product poster, and T-Bar)

MOO – this is the MOO or Burning Platform statement you used to spring off for ideas, it is what you created in sense-making.

Insight – these are the insights gained from sense-making word for word. This section, while it may feel small, is super important and it allows people in the distil touchpoint to see why your idea may actually work and how people are feeling.

Radar map – here is where you drop the visual Radar map, on how you as a collective score the potential of the idea.

I try to do the SOAP building at the end of the day and pin them up on the walls. Then, as we leave the lab, on the walls the final ideas are built out into a SOAP ready for the fresh eyes and mind of the distillers.

DISTILLER

As we move out of the dreamer touchpoint and into the distiller, we have some core tasks we need to do:

1. Check if the team are right for this next touchpoint – Distil
2. Challenge the ideas
3. Distil down the ideas to 20 and identify which we want to take over to experimentation

Hopefully, we have made this easier for ourselves, as we either have a large selection of SOAPS to look at, or we have a huge wall of ideas and insight that we set up from the night before. Although, with all this, it can still become tricky to filter down. Before all that, we need to ask, do we have the right people in the room at this stage?

Our bias toward our ideas – let go of Lego bricks

Remember, earlier in the book, I mentioned that we need to have the right mindset in the room and how having someone come into the dream touchpoint with a distil down mindset is the very thing we don't want? Well, the same applies here, only this time we don't want people who are stuck in their dreamer mindset. There are a few things we need to acknowledge from the get-go.

- Many of the ideas we have come up with often are not instantly doable
- Many of our ideas especially at the Tier 1 level are average at best
- We may have to break down ideas into elements
- The idea may not be worth doing
- You are not your idea

There are many more things but use the above as a simple primer. We need to ask if we have the right people in the room. Just like American football coaches play offence and defence, we may need to rotate the team for the output.

The types of people we want in the room at this point are the people who are close to the business. They are close to the project but not necessarily close to the potential solutions and concepts that have been generated. These people often (not always) tend to be shot callers in one way or another or have a good finger on the pulse of the business, often project managers are great for this.

Project managers have great awareness of the business, they know what things have been tried in the past but often are not so fixed in their way of thinking that they don't want to try anything new. Ideally, what we don't want in here just yet is our stakeholder group, mainly because the ideas are not in any presentable and fair format.

Once you have rotated your team (if needed) and injected some fresh distil thinkers, it is worth going over the scene setting around what we need and don't need from people i.e. big dream thinking.

In these instances, I tend to follow a structure similar to the one below:

1. Identify the 10th person
2. Playback and consume the ideas
3. Filter through potential impact

Often, if I am working with a client who is more adventurous and has deeper pockets the distil touchpoint would be much bigger and also allow us to collect and use data as a primer. However, the assumption here is our customer/stakeholder doesn't have bags of resources, so we are going to filter down the ideas to some core selected ideas and then take them into experimentation. In order to move through this stage and stop us going round in circles we have ELMO, but we also need a little more called the 10th person.

10th Person

This is a term taken from one of my favourite books called World War Z. The idea of the 10th person is to stop the group thinking, their role throughout the distil touchpoint is to wear many hats, such as critical friend, devil's advocate, rebel without a cause. Whoever has this gets to have a whole load of fun but equally has a lot of importance.

Their role, simply put, is to stop groupthink, so if 9 out of 10 people agree on something, it's up to the 10th person (aka the chosen one) to disagree, to assume that the other 9 people are wrong and challenge the thinking.

While the 10th person will at some point have to accept that maybe the other 9 people were right, it allows the group to pause for a minute and check their thinking. Now the chances are the 10th person won't be needed all the time, as rarely does everybody agree in the room from the start. However, when the group feels like they are getting to a general consensus that is when the 10th person steps in and challenges.

The 10th person isn't actually one person, it's a role that can be spread across the group as and when needed. The facilitator can also play the 10th person if needed, or they hand out the roles to someone on each exercise once it's completed. This simple rule only works if at the start of the session we get a team agreement that it's a role, not a person, and it is built on good intentions.

For example, if we filter out the ideas which could have the biggest impact in the business. We as a group all agree. The facilitator would call out someone in the group and give them a few minutes to put together a case as to why the other 9 in the group might be wrong. The 10th person will need to then challenge the thinking group assumptions.

The 10th person is a time box exercise at around 5 minutes. Don't let it go on longer than that, as it can zap the energy out of the room. The goal is to simply spark a deeper conversation around the end result.

Once we, as a team, all agree on the 10th person approach, it is time to share the ideas and concepts to the group.

Playing back

At this point, the ideas have already gone through some basic filtering based on how well they match the early criteria. They have then been mapped out into a SOAP and pinned up on a wall. We have potentially drafted in a whole different team to help us distil down these ideas and we need them to understand each idea at a level where they can make a decision.

There are many methods in how to playback these ideas. What is important is that we remove all bias and group thinking first. The task is simple: get an individual feeling of the ideas while giving the ideas the time to be explained. I have tried a few different, but simple, ways to do playback and filtering.

It is important to mention that as this may be a fresh group of shot callers who are super busy, you will need to set the scene and give them a reminder of why we are here, sharing the challenges, Moo, and Burning Platforms we identified.

The ones I find myself always going back to are below:

Silo scoring

This setup is simple. First, number each idea, let's assume we have 50 ideas. Then hand out a basic scoring card to each person in the room. Their job is to listen to each idea that gets presented back to them and score it. Each idea gets a set time to be presented back and questioned.

In the past, I have given each idea around 4 minutes – 2 minutes to present back and 2 minutes for questioning and scoring. Play around with the timing here, again if free time is on your side then give each idea a few more minutes. The group can't discuss the idea or scoring with each other, but they can ask a few questions about the idea to help get a better understanding of it. I recommend having the facilitator present back the ideas for various reasons:

1. Usually the audience hasn't got prior experience with them, so they are unlikely to apply any bias based on the presenter. Early in my career, I was once out having post-drinks with the team after we had been through distil touchpoint. I had let each individual who came up with the idea present it back to the audience. My thinking was that their passion for the idea would come through and help with storytelling and it did to be fair. However, while in the pub I sat down talking with one of the distillers and asked how they found the session.

   While explaining they were sceptical at first, they also shared how they did not like two of the people who came up with the idea so they marked them down. From that point onwards, I changed how I did the playback. This simple bias creeps in knowingly and unknowingly. Ideas can be made and broken in how we tell stories. So the more we can standardise it the better. A simple way to do that is have one consistent presenter who hasn't got past work experience with the group.

2. The facilitator has no skin in the game, they don't have a preference for an idea. One of their only driving factors, at this point, is to keep the group moving forward. Due to this, the facilitator is more likely to be strict on giving each idea the same amount of time. They are also less likely to go off on a tangent and instead will follow the same formula of the playback:

- Here is idea number 1
- The idea is (reads word for word the description) and shows the visual
- This idea we have linked to (insert Moo or Burning Platform)
- The DNA of this idea has come from various pieces of user insight (read insight word for word)
- We have early scoring estimates of the idea but again this is a guess (show Radar)

Once the idea playback is done, the team can't discuss the idea between them, however, they can ask the facilitator a few questions about the idea before scoring. Once the questions are answered, ask the team to score the idea.

A typical scorecard could look like the one overleaf.

Once all the ideas are presented and scored, ask the audience to hand in their scorecards. Next, we need to get the average score of the idea. To do this, simply add up the scores of the ideas, then divide by the number of people scoring. Do this for each idea to get a feel of where the energy and appetite is for each idea then map them out on a scale of one to ten and present back the visual.

I will let you decide your points metric as the card could change depending on the business objective. However, going right back to chapter one – desirability is key, that question should be weighted more than the others.

Do this for each idea to get a feel of where the energy and appetite is for each idea then place them out in order of lowest scorer to the left, highest to the right, and let the group see where they landed.

Score card

Idea ______________	Hell no	Hmm	Interesting	Hell yeah	Add weighting
Desirability Our employees would have the want or desire to have, use, or experience this idea. It aligns with the needs, wants, and preferences of the target audience identified.	☐	☐	☐	☐	☐
Feasibility As a business, we could implement this idea based on current resources, skills, partners, and constraints. We could implement and sustain this idea over time.	☐	☐	☐	☐	☐
Viability This idea has potential for long-term financial and commercial success for the business. It could generate enough revenue to justify the resources invested in it.	☐	☐	☐	☐	☐
Business Uniqueness This idea has unique characteristics, that differ from anything seen currently in the business and from our competitors. Will people remember it in 10 years time?	☐	☐	☐	☐	☐
Alignment to Business Strategy This idea fits well with an org's mission and long-term vision and is linked directly to its overall goals and objectives.	☐	☐	☐	☐	☐
Speed This idea has the potential to be spun up quickly in the context of the business and adapt at pace to changing market conditions and opportunities.	☐	☐	☐	☐	☐
Identity This idea could build enthusiasm, interest, and energy in the context of the business and its audience and the challenge at hand enabling easier adoption.	☐	☐	☐	☐	☐
Total Add up the total for each of the columns.	☐	☐	☐	☐	☐

Blind voting & Live voting

Perhaps a quicker, more interactive and fun way to do this is start with the facilitator presenting back the ideas.

But this time, the facilitator has three groups:

- Hell no
- Maybe baby
- Hell yeah

After each idea has been presented, the facilitator will ask the group to close their eyes tight and keep them closed. He will then ask the group, after the count of three, to vote. If they think the idea is a 'hell no', they vote thumbs down. If they think it's a 'maybe baby', they vote with a sideway thumb. And if they think it's a 'hell yeah', they vote with a thumb up. The audience can't change their mind and must keep their eyes closed. The facilitator will say reset at which point the group can put their hand/vote down and open their eyes. By the end of this simple activity, your ideas will have fallen into three categories.

Hell no, Maybe baby, Hell yeah

To take this a little further, once you've identified the groups, follow the 10th man process on the maybe baby ideas to move them into either the hell yeah bucket or hell no bucket. The final variation of voting is similar to blind voting, only this time we use an app like Mentimeter or a live poll tool. After each idea is presented and the team has voted on the idea via a mobile app, we move on to the next idea and so on. Only once all the ideas have been consumed and voted on, does the group get to see which ideas came out more favourably than others.

You may be asking 'why are you not doing a typical dot vote approach?', which is a great question. I do use dot voting in various parts of my design process, however, when it comes to filtering out the ideas, I try to avoid it.

Many times I have seen dot voting go sour, not because it ended in a mass brawl, but because the team has identified who in the room they need to please, usually the person of highest power. Once this happens, group think becomes unstoppable as everyone tends to upvote their idea even though it may not be the best choice. Also, dot voting makes it easy for people not to think, as it is easy to go with the majority and just vote on what others have voted for because it's a safe bet... we want active thinking not group think.

As simple as 2x2

At this point, hopefully you should have filtered down ideas either by the highest score, thumbs up, or hell yeah... so scientific. It's easy to make the assumption that we need lots and lots of data to prove a success when it comes to creating a new innovative HR product. Actually, it's not that simple, often we have data and insight on the tension and pain points which guide us a little but we don't know what will or won't work.

The goal in this stage isn't to pick a winner, instead, it is to find which ideas align with the criteria. We will get all the data we need later in experimentation but first, we are trying to present back to the business some innovative concepts that we would like to take forward to validate; however, these concepts have to capture the hearts of the stakeholders in order to get some form of resource or budget to move forward.

The prioritisation grid is one of the simplest filtering tools and one I pull out of the box regularly. First, you will need to decide your labels for the X and Y axis – maybe it is innovation vs time, impact vs time, cost vs impact, and so on. Whatever your labels, make sure you pull them from the initial criteria or scope.

Next, gather together around the remaining ideas and go through each idea discussing where the ideas would sit in a 2x2, like the one seen in the next illustration. Discussing the ideas as a team is important, mainly because as a collective we all have to be comfortable and confident that the mapped ideas are in the right place. We all completely buy into them and at any point can explain why the idea is placed where it is. A large selection of these ideas will be getting presented back, so it's worth taking the time now to air out any concerns or booby traps.

Imagine the criteria for 2x2 was impact vs effort, your 2x2 would look a little like this:

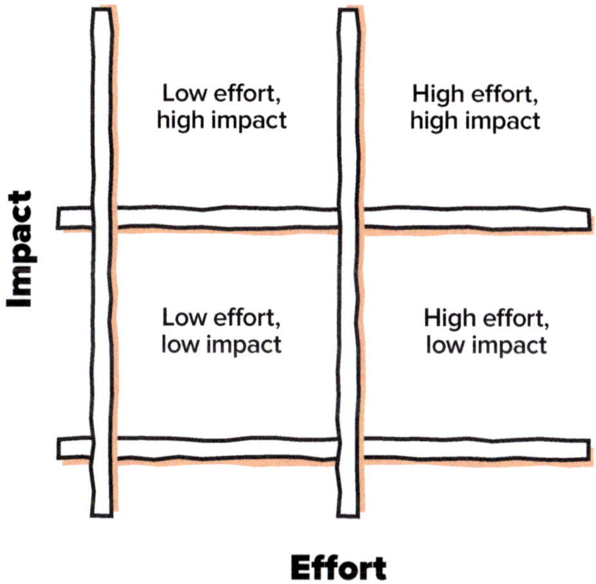

After the ideas discussion and all ideas are mapped, it should become easier to see which ideas we want to look at first, second, third, and forth. At the simplest level, this tool is used to help prioritise. Often the ideas in the top left quadrant are done first, followed closely by the ideas in the top right quadrant.

The ideas that fall in the bottom two quadrants I won't throw away but they would fall into my idea backlog which I might look at later. But they don't provide me with anything that will be useful or valuable.

At this point, the ideas should have been through various filters, and challenges, and had rich conversations. Often here you are left with a handful of ideas, let's say ten. It's these ten ideas that you are going to present back to the stakeholders and hope they feel energised and excited enough by them that they will allow you to go create some basic prototypes and run some experiments to test desirability and prove/disprove that these ideas have something to them ... so tell me, are you feeling lucky?

Show me what you've got

Okay, so we have chosen ten ideas, as a collective we feel comfortable where we have got to, the next stage is presenting back the ideas in a compelling way. Now, you might be thinking 'erm where is prototyping?'. Which is a valid question. The main reason prototyping isn't here yet is right now we don't know what we are prototyping on.

The last thing we want to do is prototype something that may never get the green light because, as a concept, your stakeholders don't like it. When moving through my process, I try to only spend time on the stuff that matters to get us to the next gate or phase. Sometimes it's about first building trust and a good relationship with your stakeholders, rather than pushing them too much ... (that can come on other projects).

Prototyping is valuable for sure, however, I would only start to do that when moving into experimentation. Reminds me of the saying by Abraham Lincoln, "Give me six hours to chop down a tree and I will spend the first four sharpening the axe". That applies here, I would rather use the hours earlier for better sense-making and getting to the root of the problem than creating a paper prototype for something that may never see the light of day. However, once the stakeholders love it, then we move on to experiments and prototypes because they become much more valuable. Okay, back to presenting.

While we are not prototyping, that doesn't mean we shouldn't bring the concepts to life. Now I am sure that around here I should talk to you about the power of storytelling, but the reality is you have everything you need to tell the story. It's in your SOAP, it follows a simple storytelling structure.

Sense-making – Bad times – Problem and data and insight

Dream – Potential concept ideas based on the problem, data, and insight

Distil – Ideas reduced down based on problem, insight, and criteria

Next step – Experiment and validate on the idea to get to better times (see next books)

Often there is nothing more powerful than using the word-for-word statements we got from interviews. In the past, I have had statements such as 'I wanted to kill myself', 'the onboarding put me in a dark place, I couldn't sleep, I was constantly crying and lost a lot of weight'. Now, tell me that isn't impactful. This is why the insight needs to always thread to the ideas to really drive home the human problem being faced. So feel free to add an element of storytelling when presenting back the ideas just make sure you add that same amount of magic to each idea.

The four tried and tested approaches I use at such an early stage in the process are:

Art exhibition

You will have seen these at any conference around the world, it is a 6 to 10 ft poster that is free-standing and often displays an advert. You can basically print whatever you like on these and the quality is really good. Simply print one idea out per pull-up, use your cool title, the description, as well as more statements from sense-making to really bring the tension to life. Use an open space and place all of your idea out.

Invite your stakeholders to the space and greet them with cake and tea/coffee. Set the scene that around the room are ten exhibition pieces and today we are looking for them to commission some of the work. Advise the stakeholders to look around and take in each piece in 30 minutes. We will then present each piece in finer details and answer any questions they may have.

Okay Danny, why the cake and the theme? This is something I have learned over the years, your stakeholders want an experience as much as the employee and customers, they are no different. Also, giving the stakeholders tea and cake does two things. One, it instantly disarms them and slows them. Often stakeholders are moving from one meeting to another, so by giving them tea and cake it stops them bringing their last meeting in here. The second one is simple, giving people something for free often makes it easier down the line when you ask them for something ... that's without getting into the fact that when you have chocolate or sugar you instantly become a little bit happier.

This mini experience sends a clear cue, this isn't just another meeting but something to be experienced and savoured, dare I say understood. The chances are it will also be the highlight of their day, so lean into the quirkiness of it.

Soaps

Simple one here, you have the SOAPs that you have developed, you could hand these over to an illustrator and web designer who could make them much more visually appealing. This simple site would allow all the stakeholders to dig deeper into any insights or spec should they wish. You can make a simple Wix or web flow site look amazing with a decent template. While it might lack the glitz and glam of the art exhibition, what it does give is simplicity and allows stakeholders to look at the ideas when they may have a bit of downtime.

Storyboard

Another alternative is to create a storyboard. A basic storyboard is a visual representation of the steps or moments that matter as the employee/user goes from pain point, to solution, to overcoming the challenge or task. I have seen this done many different ways. Often the typical approach tends to be a collection of frames (a frame is a drawing of a moment or step) that shows the steps the person will take. Usually, the frames are drawn up by an artist or illustrator to help add an element of polish to the story.

Underneath each frame is some text to help bring to life the story and communicate the tensions and aha moments. The typical approach I tend to take with presenting a storyboard is to map the frame across the room, then invite the stakeholders to the room. Then I or someone in the team will walk the group through each frame, while the others collect the feedback that is shared from the stakeholders. If you wanted to make this a little different, you could easily create a visual comic book for each idea and send them out to the group... remember, while it's about bringing to life each and every idea, it is also about being fresh in how you approach it and having some fun with it too.

Videos/audios

The final approach I suggest testing out is the use of videos and soundbites, often there is nothing more powerful than hearing the words being said by a real person. As mentioned at the start of the chapter, in the past I have taken some of the data statements and then brought in actors to record a cold, hard hitting clip to bring to life the impact.

You don't even need actors, ask some of your friends if you can record them saying these statements. Usually, I will use the same person to record the statement i.e. 'I was in a dark place constantly crying' then I will ask them to record a message assuming we overcame the challenge and how happy they are now ...

When presenting these back, often I will open up with a sad audio or video message from the actor, followed by a 3-minute video explaining the solution followed by a happy audio/video message from the actor. All of which ultimately will convey the journey/story and the impact the potential ideas can have.

Whichever approach you want to use to get across the story, just make it consistent across all the ideas to ensure no extra bias can slip into a preferred style of presenting over another.

You might be thinking, wow all this sounds expensive and while yes, I would always advise that if you have any budget or resources left to invest in a good visual designer, videographer, or copywriter, but it doesn't have to stop if you don't have the budget. You will be amazed what an iPhone and £10 subscription to Canva, Figma, Zencaster can get you.

Coming to the end – a quick note on broken dreams

Have you ever had a dream about a random person, then suddenly woke up feeling loved up, yeah me neither (insert the eyes emoji). However, we can often feel like that with the concepts we have built out. The reality, when moving through the dream and distil touchpoints, is that a large percentage of the ideas are not all that great, however, they have to be the sacrificial goat in order for us to get where we are right now.

Over time, I've tried various different ways to validate harder and in some situations you can, by going through various audience testing between idea cycles, but often it ends up expensive and a lot of the time you end up with the boiled rice of ideas. The only thing that has allowed me to get over this is to keep a backlog of ideas in the hope that one day they may become useful, maybe not in the current form but in the form of a trigger, a prompt, or to be converted into a piece of stim when designing elsewhere.

Often when doing a handover with a stakeholder/client on where we have got to, before experimentation and experience design, I will present a large Miro board which shows them all the ideas we went through to get to the top ten.

Eventually, you will need to get comfortable with letting go of these ideas because everyone has them and they can often come thick and fast. All these ideas are not the next Instagram that you think they may be and that's fine. Whatever concepts get dropped or chosen to move forward, remember it's an idea, it's not a piece of you and it is not a reflection on you either. Over time, you simply have to just let go of your Lego bricks.

SAID AND SEALED

- There are five brain states (gamma, beta, alpha, theta, delta) that can affect creativity and idea generation.
- Set, setting, and stim refer to mindset, environment, and stimulation as factors that can impact creativity.
- The dreamer mindset is open, curious, and imaginative. While the distiller mindset is critical, analytical, and decisive.
- Creative tools and techniques include brainstorming, visual thinking, lateral thinking, and idea synthesis.
- Creative thinking can be nurtured and developed through practice, learning, and exposure to diverse perspectives.

← **Scan me to be taken to resources**

WHAT NEXT?

So that's it, we have come to the end of book 1. If you made it here, well done you. The chances are you're an open minded thinker and see beyond typical old ways of thinking. The goal with all these books is not to give you a set recipe to follow, it's to give you an understanding of the ingredients.

Most books focused on human-centred design are just a whole lot of activities without any depth. That's fine if we are trying to create lots of cook and microwave assistants, but that is not what we are trying to do. We are trying to create chefs who have depth and a rich understanding of the ingredients to know what will work and won't work.

Design is never a recipe to follow, it's full of twists, turns, dead ends, and boobytraps. It's also full of joy, impact, and aha moments. The dream for me is that by the end of all the books you don't follow my design process at all ... but instead, you create one that is unique to the/your challenge.

Design isn't a cookie cutter, nor is it easy. With the knowledge I'm sharing, you will come away asking more questions but more importantly, you will know what to do and why.

For me, I wanted *The Insightful Innovator* to be more of a why than a how.

I do share more of the hows and some chapters that didn't make the cut for this book in my bi-weekly newsletter. Head over to:

https://www.weareknot.co.uk/subscribe

What's next at the time of writing this book?

First a holiday, then I have a start-up to sell, and a season of the Mindchimp podcast to record. Of course, I also have book 2 to complete, the good news is the second book shouldn't take half as long as the first one as the structure is already done.

The Experience Engineer (Book 2) will be focusing on experimentation and experience design. We will also look deeper into what innovation is and isn't and how not to blow your resources on hunches and instead blow it on educated gambles. We will deconstruct some of the best examples of experience design and look at how we can add some of the elements into how we design for a richer, more visceral experience.

Thank you and good night.

Alrighty then, let's give this a shot!

First off, let me just say a big thank you to the many people who made this book possible. Without your support, encouragement, and occasional kicks up the arse, I'd probably still be staring at a blank page wondering where to start. You folks help in ways I can't even explain but I'll try anyway at the end of this page.

Now, let's talk about this book baby. Writing a book I imagine is like being a parent to a child. You start off with a tiny seed of an idea, and then you spend months (or years in my case) nurturing it, feeding it, and watching it grow into a fully formed manuscript. Then you decide it's going to be a collection of books and before you know it you have way too many kids.

Along the way, there are moments of joy, moments of frustration, and moments of sheer terror when you realise you've made a terrible mistake or it's going to grow up and be a little shit. It is at this point you start to think you should have gone into a more lucrative career like a professional bottle top maker. But you stick with it, because, well, it's your book(s) and you need to see it through.

And just like with a real child, you want your book baby to grow up to be the best thing it can be. You want it to be funny, informative, and maybe even a little bit cheeky. You want it to be something that people will read and say, 'Wow, this is awesome! I never knew Employee Experience could be so interesting', or 'Wow I haven't ever seen the Employee Experience from the point of view of design and innovation', or maybe it's 'Wow, Danny is the new Messiah!' (Okay, maybe they won't say that last one, but you get the idea).

So, that's what I've tried to do with this book. I've poured my heart and soul and a shit load of money into it. I've tried to make it as fun and engaging as possible and remove as much of my dyslexic writing as possible. I have also learned so much about the publishing industry and about myself ... every cloud eh.

I hope that by the end of it, you'll be laughing, learning, and maybe even want to reach out to know a little bit more.

If you do find yourself enjoying this book, then please do me a favour and spread the word. Tell your friends, your family, your co-workers, and that guy who always sits in the corner of the coffee shop muttering to himself while staring directly at you. Let them know that there's a new book in town, and it's got even more personality than a Kardashian at a red carpet event.

I'd love to hear what your reason was for buying this book! I've no doubt what you've read has started the sparks flying but if you want to chat more on this then reach out on LinkedIn (details below).

Thanks for coming on this journey with me. Let's go make some magic and I will see you in book 2 – *The Experience Engineer.*

Danny x

MENTIONS

- My Dog Rufus: whose timing was perfect, he had the unique skill of knowing when I needed to take a break from writing to give him a tickle.
- Helen: Your love and faith in me to keep pushing myself is something I needed throughout this book. Without it, I promise I would have jacked it in after day two and would never of written it. P.S. Thank you for being my human spell check.
- My mam and dad, and my brothers (Lee and Bradley) for helping me throughout life with my crazy spelling and helping me learn to lean into it. Thank you for never dampening my curiosity but instead fuelling it and allowing me to turn it into a superpower.
- The Rebel Alliance and Mindchimp Community: having a safe space to share thoughts and ideas has been so powerful in helping me shape my thinking.

Individuals:

- Mohammad Saqib (who wrote the foreword) – thank you for being the person who lit the fire in me to want to design better experiences but also by helping me see how I can be a better all-around person. And for all the great stories you share, you make the world a better place my friend.
- David James – always being a good set of ears and creating space for me to share ideas.

- Gemma Paterson – for everything from helping with Venndorly, being a beta reader, and just being the best cheerleader anyone could ask for. You always have my back.
- Melis Senova – for being the best unofficial mentor ever, thank you for creating a book that changed how I see the world. Also, after every conversation with you, I came away knowing a bit more about my design character. Go buy her book *This Human – Design Character.*
- Nick Shackleton-Jones – for putting me in contact with the initial publisher and suggesting I could write a book in the first place. I value every one of our chats.
- Sam Netherwood – I value every one of our conversations, I like to think we both walk away feeling provoked in the best way possible.
- Perry Timms – for always being supportive, be it in ideas, podcasts, or design approaches, thank you for the coaching when dealing with tricky folks.
- Sahid Umarji and Greig Wilding – for being part of the experience that got me here, I always take value from our conversations and also many laughs.
- Helen Marshall – for being an awesome beta reader, but also for busting my arse to write the book. Your nudges matter more to me than you know.
- Kate Graham – for constantly having my back, listening to me go on and on about the same stuff, and more importantly pushing me to turn a snowflake of an idea into an avalanche of books (this is all your fault).
- Patrick Mullarkey – for providing awesome beta reader feedback while you were on your holiday ... Legend.
- Tim Roberts – for being ever encouraging, helping with all things Mindchimp in the early days, and writing a book that is unapologetically you ... big fan!
- Natalie Ann Holborow – thank you for quality-checking the first initial chapters of this book when they were a complete mess.

- Nick Petch – for being a beta reader, but also being an unbiased set of eyes and ears. I value our DMs, every time I look back I either learn something or remember something I forgot.
- Jo Byrne – who would have thought that one time we met when I was judging an award that you would go on to be my go-to for nearly everything like help setting up the Mindchimp event, helping with the community, beta reader, the list goes on. You are awesome and everyone needs a Jo Byrne in their life.
- Dave Officer – for making sense of my shocking scribbled drawings and turning them into the lovely illustrations you see in this book.
- Kirsten Rees – thank you for not only being an editor to the book and making it way more readable but providing ongoing support along the way (especially in the moments when the thought of writing a book was killing me).
- Catherine Williams – thank you for turning the Word document into something that is pleasing to the eye in digital and print.

Okay, if you made it here you can have a bonus page. I asked a few friends to roast me. Here's what I got ...

TOP SECRET PAGES NOBODY READS

"Oh goody, a book. Another thing that Danny won't stop talking about for the next few years. At least some of it is vaguely useful."

—Jo Byrne

"Whenever people ask me about Danny, my answer is always the same: it isn't appropriate for me to comment on ongoing investigations. We will just have to wait for the full report."

—Nick Shackleton-Jones

How People Learn by Nick Shackleton-Jones

"Danny once borrowed money from me. He then changed his number and stopped responding to all my messages on social media. Danny, if you're reading this, I want my £1.46 back."

—Brij Palicha

"Danny once walked up to me with a T-shirt saying, 'What's your problem?' on it. Rumour has it that he reveals in this book where he's got that tattooed."

—Gemma Paterson

"If he writes like he speaks, you'll only understand about 50% of what is in the book, but I guarantee it's insightful"

—Charlie Kneen

"What Danny doesn't know about Human-Centred Design ChatGPT can tell you anyway so it doesn't matter."

—Sam Netherwood

"Is it Method Man? Ghostface Designah, The GZA,
No it's the Wu-Tang Dan.
Seals rips it, raps it, reveals it."

—Perry Timms

Transformational HR by Perry Timms

"If dressing up as a unicorn at a conference represented a career high for Danny then this book represents his career low. I only scanned this to write an early review and thank my lucky stars I didn't pay good money for it – let alone read it in depth. If you've bought this book after reading these reviews then more fool you."

—David James

"As an Australian, I can't really make out what Danny is saying half the time. I'm happy he finally started writing it down."

—Nick Petch

"Dipping into this book will be like stepping into Danny's mind: intensely creative, alarmingly organised, and full of useless facts. And you'll (almost) certainly leave better off for reading it, but also thinking, 'What the fuck just happened?'"

—Helen Marshall

"The best thing Danny ever said to me was, 'Take your own advice mate'. If he's taken his own advice to write this book then do yourself a favour; close it now & donate it to your local charity shop."

—Tim Roberts

Break the Mould by Tim Roberts

"Danny has a nice choice in hoodies, I also have some nice things to say. But I'll keep them quiet for now."

—Adam Kara

"When Danny first came across me, I know for a fact he was irritated by my vocal social media posts and wondered who the hell I thought I was. After many years of friendship, I can now reveal I am still thinking the same about him. Maybe this book will help us all find out."

—Kate Graham

"What's lovely about Danny is that he never changes, he never lets fame go to his head. Always makes time for you if he can. I'm certain that now he's finished this book he'll start returning my calls."

—Alice Thompson

"I once worked with Danny, that was enough."

—Joe Hildebrand

"Danny, in fine form constantly challenges the norm, even with this. "Give me a roast for the back of the book," he says. Here you go ..."

—Melis Senova

ABOUT THE AUTHOR

Daniel Seals has over ten years in Leadership, Learning and Development Design, and Innovation. Having turned around many employee experiences to get the most out of teams and individuals, he's spent that time honing his knowledge on the various approaches to design and putting those into practice.

A podcast host, Founder and Head of Employee Innovation, Danny wears many hats working in and guiding HR, Talent, and Learning teams to move from paper to prototype to innovative products, services, and experiences ... It's safe to say he gets it. This Manchester man knows culture, Innovation and Design, and has tried and tested each aspect of design before it hits the pages of his first books.

Connecting with Danny:

LinkedIn – https://www.linkedin.com/in/dannyseals/
Website – https://www.weareknot.co.uk/
Newsletter – https://www.weareknot.co.uk/subscribe
Podcast – Search Mindchimp wherever you get your podcast

Printed in Great Britain
by Amazon

29313392R00159